I
Sharing t

Inigo Texts Series: 6

Ignatius: Sharing the Pilgrim Story

A Reading of the Autobiography of St Ignatius of Loyola

Peter Du Brul, S.J.

GRACEWING

First published in 2003

Gracewing
2 Southern Avenue
Leominster
Herefordshire HR6 0QF

and

Inigo Enterprises
Links View, Traps Lane
New Malden
Surrey KT3 4RY

ISBN 0 85244 536 9

Typesetting by
Action Publishing Technology Ltd, Gloucester GL1 5SR

Printed and bound by
Antony Rowe Ltd, Eastbourne BN23 6QT

CONTENTS

*REFERENCES TO THE AUTOBIOGRAPHY ARE BY PARAGRAPH NUMBERS; ALL EDITIONS HAVE THESE SAME NUMBERS.

Cover illustration:
Las Meniñas
by Diego Velázquez

PREFACE

There are still many people who do not know that St Ignatius Loyola produced an autobiography. Perhaps this is not surprising: its mode of production was somewhat tortuous – he spoke it rather than wrote it to an admiring secretary who took no notes but from memory dictated it partly in Spanish, partly in Italian. It lay forgotten for nearly two centuries in the Jesuit archives in Rome. It was not translated into any vernacular language until the beginning of the twentieth century. How unnecessarily secretive and excessively tortuous these Jesuits can be!

But there really is nothing to hide and nothing particularly complicated about Inigo's testament. On the contrary, Inigo emerges from his own story as a remarkably straightforward storyteller with an eye for colourful detail, a marked sense of humour, and always the desire to describe how God was working in the process of his life. Perhaps its very simplicity is what irks some of his more sophisticated successors: this at times singing and dancing clown steeped in the myths and prejudices of his own times, some mistakenly think needs radical deconstruction before respectable reconstruction.

Fortunately other contemporary Jesuits have taken their lead from the example of Jerome Nadal who did so much to persuade Inigo to tell his own story in the first place and thereafter to use this narrative as a basic tool for Ignatian formation. It is this tradition that Peter Du Brul continues. He invites us to let Inigo's life in all its particularity evoke our lives in their contemporary particularity. It is amazing what a liberating model he is.

Du Brul's specific contribution is to bring the sensitivity of a literary critic to bear on a text normally outside his more immediate professional terms of reference. Perhaps it is this incidental experise that enables him to perceive what he calls a 'shy pattern' in the narrative. He also brings a wide cultural background including a strong artistic and visual sense which he shares with Inigo himself, to his labour of love.

As if this were not enough his position as a long standing teacher in bomb-battered Bethlehem challenges him to see in the founder's testament, which also included a famous pilgrimage to the same Holy Land similarly shattered and battered by religious and political strife, a still all too contemporary relevance. The inter-cultural and interfaith context is as sharp, if no sharper, than ever, and still cries out for something like Ignatian commitment to face up to, however little the immediate hope of resolution.

What particularly persuaded me to publish this work was the very fact that it was a scholar's labour of love working outside his immediate area of expertise with no particular hope of publication. This sense of detached personal commitment and enthusiastic, idiosyncratic interest shines through every paragraph.

Add to this the enthusiastic backing of Fr Michael Ivens SJ, and an opportunity to publish for the first time Michael's own revised version of William Yeomans's translation of the autobiography/testament and you have reasons, full measure pressed down and flowing over to justify this latest Inigo Enterprise.

Billy Hewett, S.J.
Director, Inigo Enterprises

INTRODUCTION

In the early sixteenth century, printed books were new. They brought about profound changes. The new information that the books made available – at least for those who could read – had an effect comparable to that of the internet today. It not only widened people's horizons, but also transformed the way they experienced themselves. This is one of the reasons why there were such far-reaching religious changes in the sixteenth century. We tend to think of these changes as a parting of the ways: Western Christianity split into two rival camps, Catholic and Protestant. But the changes involved more than an institutional split: cultural factors, too, made the Christianity of early modernity – both Catholic and Protestant – profoundly different from its medieval counterpart. It is well known that the Protestant Reformation began from Luther's careful, passionate study of the Scriptures. It is less well known that books also had their effect on the Catholic side. Ignatius Loyola was led to found the Jesuits and to initiate a whole range of reforms within Catholicism through reflecting on what he read: in his case, a book of Gospel stories, and some biographies of the saints.

Ignatius's *Autobiography* or *Reminiscences*, presented in this volume by Peter du Brul, does not by any means tell us the whole story of his life. But it does testify to a central aspect of that story: a man gradually learning to find the voice of God amid the new human possibilities opened up by early modern culture. This is a story that we all can share, to quote the very title of this volume. As we read the story of Ignatius's pilgrimage, we can be led to think of our own life story and perhaps begin to reassess it. And perhaps too some clarity will come; perhaps we too can come to 'recognise the diversity of the spirits' at work within us; perhaps we too can come to discover the true life for which God has created us in Christ, from the foundation of the world.

Philip Endean, SJ

PROLOGUE
of Fr. Jerome Nadal

I and other Fathers had heard from our Father Ignatius that he had asked God to grant him three benefits before he died. The first was that the Institute of the Society be confirmed by the Apostolic See. The second likewise for the Spiritual Exercises. The third that he might write the Constitutions.

When I remembered this and saw that he had obtained everything, I was afraid lest he be called away from us to a better life. Since I knew also that the holy Fathers and founders of some monastic institutes had been accustomed to leave to their successors by way of a testament, such advice as they were confident would be helpful towards their perfection. I therefore waited for a suitable time to ask this from Fr. Ignatius.

It came in 1551 when we were together and Fr. Ignatius said: "Now I was higher than the sky;" having experienced (such is my conjecture) some ecstasy of mind or rapture as he frequently did. Full of respect I ask: "What was it, Father?" He changed the conversation. Judging this to be a favourable opportunity, I ask and beg the Father to tell how God guided him from the beginning of his conversion, in such a way that his story would be for us in place of a testament and fatherly instruction. I say: "For now you have obtained those three things, Father, which you desired to see before your death, we are afraid you may be called away to heaven." The Father excused himself on account of his work: he could give neither time nor attention to it. However, he said: "Say three masses about this matter: you, Polanco and Ponce, and tell me what you think about the matter after your prayer." "We shall think exactly what we think now," I said. He added very gently: "Do as I say." We said the masses; gave him the same reply and he made a promise. The following year when I again came back from Sicily on my way to Spain I asked the Father if he had done anything. "Nothing," he replied. On my return from Spain in 1554 I again asked. He still had not touched the matter. Thereupon, moved by I know not what inner impulse I said with great insistency to the Father: "It is almost four years, Father, since I asked you, not only on my own account, but in the name of the other Fathers, to explain to us the way in which God instructed you from the beginning of your conversion. We are convinced that this would be of the greatest use to us and the Society. Now that I see you have not granted our wish, I am emboldened to say this to you; if you do what we so desire we shall use such a benefit most carefully, if you do not do it we shall not on that account be dispirited, but we shall have the same confidence in God as if you had written everything."

The Father made no reply, but called Fr. Luis Gonçalves (the very same day, I believe,) and began to relate to him these things, which Father Gonçalves since he had an excellent memory, later wrote down. These are the *Acta Patris Ignati(ius)* which are being circulated. Fr. Luis was an elector in the first general Congregation, and was elected Assistant to Fr. General Lainez. Later he was tutor and spiritual director to King Sebastian of Portugal, and is a Father of outstanding piety and virtue. Fr. Gonçalves wrote partly in Spanish, partly in Italian according to the secretaries at his disposal. Fr. Anibal du Coudray, a learned and pious Father, translated it into Latin. Both the author and the translator are still living.

PROLOGUE
of Fr. Luis Gonçalves da Camara

1* One Friday morning in the year 1553, it was the 4th of August the vigil of the feast of Our Lady of the Snows, the Father was in the garden adjoining the house, the apartment known as the Duke's. I began to give him an account of certain matters concerning my soul and amongst other things I spoke of vainglory. The remedy the Father gave me against this was that I should refer all that I did frequently to God, striving to offer Him all the good I found in myself, recognising it as His and thanking Him for it. All this he told me in such a way that I was greatly comforted and so quite unable to keep back my tears. The Father then told me how he had been harassed by this fault for two years to such an extent that when he embarked at Barcelona for Jerusalem, he did not dare tell anyone that he was going to Jerusalem, and likewise in other similar situations. He further added that since then he had experienced great peace of soul, as regards this point.

An hour or two later we went into dinner. Whilst Master Polanco and I were at table with him, the Father said that there was something that Master Nadal and others of the Society had often asked him to do, but that he had never made up his mind about it. However, whilst thinking the matter over in his room after his conversation with me, he had experienced such devotion and such a strong inclination to do what they wanted that he was quite determined to do it. He spoke too in such a way that it was plain that God had shown him very clearly that such was his duty. The thing was this; to give an account of all that had passed in his soul up to the present time. He had also decided that it was to be myself to whom he would reveal all this.

2* At the time our Father was in a very poor state of health. But, although it had never been his way to promise himself another day of life – rather, when someone said, "I shall do that in a fortnight's time or in a week", the Father invariably replied, as though surprised, "Really! And you expect to live that long?" – nevertheless on this occasion he said that he expected to live for three or four months in order to be able to finish this task. The next day I asked him when he wanted to begin. He replied by telling me to remind him of it every day. I cannot remember for how many days it was, until he found a suitable time for it. Since however he did not find such a time because of his other business, he eventually told me that I was to remind him every Sunday. At last in September, I do not remember the exact date, the Father summoned me and began to tell the story of his whole life including the follies of his earlier years, clearly and precisely and in great detail. Afterwards he sent for me two or three times in the same month and carried on with the story up to the first days of Manresa, as can be seen by the change in handwriting.[1]

3* Our Father told the story in his usual way, that is to say, with such clarity of style that he seemed to make the past live again for his hearer. Hence there was no need to ask any questions since the Father remembered and recounted everything necessary for the understanding of his narrative. Immediately afterwards, without saying a word to the Father I used to go at once to put it down on paper, first of all in note form which I then expanded into the present text. I took great pains to write down nothing but the actual words I had heard from the Father. If, as I fear, I have failed in anything, it is that in my desire not to deviate from the Father's words, I have not been able to render the full force of some of his expressions. As I have said above, I wrote in this way until September 1553. From that date however, until the arrival of Fr. Nadal on the 18th of October 1554, our Father was always giving some excuse on account of his bouts of ill-health and the various affairs of the moment. He would say to me, "Remind me of it when this business is

1. The handwriting referred to is that of the successive scribes to whom da Camara dictated the narrative in its final form. In the original text, which does not survive, the change of handwriting (and hence of scribe) would have indicated an interval in the narration.

finished". When it was finished, I would remind him and he would say, "Now we are busy with this. When it is over, remind me."

4* When Fr. Nadal arrived he was very pleased to see that we had made a start and told me to pester the Father. He often remarked that there was no way in which our Father could do more good to the Society than by this, "In all truth," he said, "it was a founding of the Society". He, too, often spoke to the Father about the matter. Our Father told me to remind him again when the business about the endowment of the College was over; but when that was ended it was when the affair of Prester John was arranged and the letters had been sent off. We did begin the continuation on the 9th of March, but then the Pope, Julius III, became seriously ill and died on the 23rd of March. The Father put the matter off until there was a Pope. This was Marcellus II, who immediately took ill and died. Our Father then delayed the work until the election of Pope Paul IV. After that, on account of the very hot weather and his many occupations he was forever being prevented. This went on until the 21st of September when there began to be talk about sending me to Spain. At this I urged the Father very strongly to make good his promise.

He told me to meet him at the Red Tower on the morning of September 22nd. When I had finished saying Mass I went to him and asked if that were a suitable time.

5* He told me to go and wait for him at the Red Tower so that I should be there when he came. I gathered that I should have to wait for him there for quite some time. When I was in the gallery speaking to a Brother who had asked me about something, the Father happened to pass by and reprimanded me for failing in obedience by not waiting for him in the appointed place. Nor would he do anything that day. Then we redoubled our requests to him. So it was that he came back to the Red Tower and dictated as he had done on previous occasions, walking backwards and forwards. I was anxious to observe the expression on his face so, little by little, I drew closer to him, and then the Father said to me, "Observe the Rule." Later on, unmindful of his admonition, when I again drew close to him, (it happened on two or three occasions), he repeated the rebuke and walked away. Finally, he came back to the Red Tower later on to complete the dictation of what is written down here. However, since I had for some time been preparing for my journey, (the last time the Father spoke to me on this subject was the very eve of my departure), I was not able to write down everything in full in Rome. Since I did not have a Spanish secretary in Genoa, I dictated in Italian from the notes I had made in Rome, and finished the work in Genoa in December 1555.

End of the Prologue of Gonçalves da Camara.

INIGO: ORIGINAL TESTAMENT
THE AUTOBIOGRAPHY OF ST. IGNATIUS LOYOLA

CHAPTER I

1. Up to the age of twenty-six he was a man given over to the pleasures of the world. Out of a vain, vehement desire to win renown, he took special delight in the career of a soldier.

So it came about that he was in a fortress which the French were attacking. Seeing clearly that they could not defend themselves, those in the fortress were for surrendering on condition that their lives should be spared. He, however, argued so forcibly with the Commandant that he persuaded him to attempt a defence, even though it was against the advice of all the officers. These, however, also took heart at his courage and spirit. When the day came on which they were expecting an artillery bombardment, he made his confession to one of his companions-in-arms. The bombardment had been going on for some time when a cannonball struck him on one leg, completely shattering it, and since the shot passed between his legs the other was also seriously wounded.

2. When he fell, those in the fortress immediately surrendered to the French, who, after taking possession, treated the wounded man very well with every mark of courtesy and friendliness. After he had been in Pamplona for some ten or fifteen days he was taken on a litter to his own part of the country. There his condition became much worse, and doctors and surgeons were called in from everywhere around. They decided that the leg would have to be broken again and the bones re-set; since, in their opinion, these had become displaced because either they had been badly set in the first instance or because they had moved during the journey, and as it was they would never mend. So the torture began all over again. During it, as during all the other operations he suffered both before and afterwards, he spoke not a word and gave no other sign of pain than to clench his fists tightly.

3. But his condition still grew worse. He was unable to eat and there were other symptoms which are usually signs that death is approaching. Since the doctors held out little hope of his recovery, on the feast of St. John he was advised to make his confession. He then received the last sacraments on the Vigil of Saints Peter and Paul, and the doctors said that if by midnight there was no sign of improvement, he could give himself up for dead. The sick man had a devotion to St. Peter, and Our Lord willed that at midnight on that very same night he should begin to recover. So rapid was the improvement that a few days later he was pronounced to be out of danger of death.

4. The bones had now begun to grow together, but below the knee he was left with one bone growing out on top of another. As a result, the leg was shortened and the bone so protruded that it was an ugly sight. He could not bear such a thing since he was determined to follow a wordly career and judged that it would deform him. Hence he asked the surgeons if the bone could be cut off. They replied that it could be done, but that the pain would be greater than any he had hitherto suffered, since the bones had healed and it would take some time to cut one. Nevertheless he was determined of his own will to undergo this martyrdom, though his elder brother was horrified and said that he himself would not dare face such agony. The wounded man endured it with his usual fortitude.

5. After the leg had been cut open and the projecting bone removed, they set to work to apply remedies to correct the shortness of the leg, using many ointments, and stretching the leg continually by means of appliances which caused him many days of torture. But Our Lord restored him to health. His condition so improved that he was better except that he could not stand on the leg and so was obliged to stay in bed. He was addicted to reading worldly and fictitious books, known as tales of chivalry, so now that he was feeling well he asked for some of these to while away the time. However, in that house there were no books of the sort he was accustomed to read, so they gave him a *Vita Christi* (LIFE OF CHRIST), and a book of the lives of the saints, in Spanish.

6. He read these books a great deal, and was rather taken with what he found in them Moreover, when he left off reading, he used sometimes to think about what he had read; and at other times he thought about the things of the world which had previously been the invariable subject of his thoughts. Of all the vain thoughts which came into his mind there was one which so gripped his fancy that he would become completely absorbed in it for three or four hours without noticing the time. He used to imagine what he would do in the service of a certain lady: the means he would take in order to reach the country where she was, the mottos and the words he would speak, the feats of arms he would perform in her service. He was so carried away by all this that he did not see how impossible it was for him to bring it about in reality, for the lady was not of the ordinary nobility, not a countess nor a duchess either, but her rank was higher still than any of these.

7. However, Our Lord helped him, making other thoughts, born of his reading, follow these other imaginings. For, whilst reading the life of Our Lord and the Saints, he would stop to think, reflecting within himself; "What if I were to do what St. Francis did, or what St. Dominic did?" So in his mind he turned over many such things which seemed good to him, always proposing to himself hard and strenuous tasks; and when he proposed such things to himself, it seemed to him that he could easily put them into practice. But his whole way of thinking was to say to himself – "St. Dominic did this, therefore I ought to do it. St. Francis did that; therefore I ought to do it." These thoughts too lasted for quite a time, and then after some interruption the worldly thoughts mentioned above came back again, and he dwelt on them for a long time. This succession of thoughts, so different in their nature, went on for a long time, and he always dwelt on the thoughts, which came to him, whether they were about the worldly deeds he wanted to accomplish, or others concerning God which took hold of his imagination, until, tiring of them, he turned to something else.

8. There was however this difference. When he was taken up with worldly thoughts he took great delight in them; but when he put them aside through tiredness he felt arid and dissatisfied. But when he thought about going barefoot to Jerusalem, eating nothing but herbs, and practising all the other austerities he saw that the Saints had performed, not only did he find great comfort in such thoughts but even after putting them aside he still remained content and joyful. However he did not pay attention to this fact, nor did he stop to ponder the difference, until one day his eyes were opened a little so that he began to wonder at this difference and to think about it. Experience showed that certain thoughts left him sad, others joyful, and so gradually he came to recognise the diversity of the spirits which were at work on him, the one from the devil and the other from God.

9. Since he obtained no small light from his reading he began to think more earnestly about his past life and what need he had of doing penance for it. There came upon him also a desire to imitate the Saints. He did not take into account the particular circumstances of each, but simply promised to do with the grace of God what they had done. What he wanted to do above all, as soon as he was cured, was to go to Jerusalem, as has been said above, enduring such great disciplines and austerities as a soul inflamed by God is wont to long for.

10. His former daydreams gradually faded away before the holy desires he now had, which desires were confirmed by a vision, in this way: Lying awake one night he saw clearly the figure of Our Lady with the Holy Child Jesus. At this sight he was filled with an exceedingly great consolation which lasted for a good time. It left him too, with such a loathing for his entire past life, and especially for what concerned the sins of the flesh, that it seemed to him that his soul was rid of all the images that had up to then been imprinted on it. Indeed, from that day until August 1553, when this was written, he never again gave the slightest consent in such matters of the flesh. From this effect it can be judged that the vision came from God, although he himself did not venture to say so with certainty, nor to say more than what has been affirmed above. But his brother, and the rest of the household soon became aware, from his external behaviour, of the change which had taken place in the depths of his soul.

11. He however did not trouble himself about anything, but persevered with his reading and his good intentions. The time spent with those of the household was devoted to speaking of the things of God, thus doing good to their souls. Finding great relish in the books, he got the idea of making brief extracts of the more essential events of the life of Christ and of the Saints. He then set to work with great diligence to write a book, since he had now begun to get up and go about the house a little. He wrote the words of Christ in red ink and those of Our Lady in blue ink. The paper was glazed and lined, and the lettering well done since he was a very good penman. He spent part of his time in writing and the rest in prayer. His greatest consolation came from looking at the sky and the stars, which he did very often and for long periods, since at such times he felt in himself a very great enthusiasm for the service of Christ Our Lord. He often thought about his plan and longed to be completely cured so that he could be on his way.

12. When he took stock of what he would do after he got back from Jerusalem, so as to spend his whole life doing penance, the idea came to him of entering the Carthusians at Seville, without saying who he was so that less account would be made of him, and there eating nothing but herbs. But on another occasion when his thoughts turned to the penances he wanted to perform whilst going about the world, his desire for the Carthusians cooled, since he was afraid that there he would not be able to exercise the hate he had conceived against himself. Nevertheless, he told one of the servants of the house who was going to Burgos to make inquiries about the Rule of the Carthusians; and the information brought back seemed good to him. But, for the reason mentioned above, and because he was completely taken up with the journey he hoped to make soon; and since, too, the matter would not have to be settled until after his return, he did not pay much attention to it. Instead, feeling that he had recovered his strength to some extent, he decided it was time for him to set out, so he said to his brother, "As you know, the Duke of Najéra is already aware that I am well. It would be a good thing for me to go to Navarrete" (the Duke was there at the time). At this his brother led him from one room to another, and with much persuasion began to beg him not to throw away his life, to consider what great hopes people had in him, to think what he could make of himself, and similar words all with the intention of turning him away from his good desires. But his reply was such that, without departing from the truth about which he was always exceedingly scrupulous, he avoided a direct issue with his brother.

CHAPTER II

13. So he set out riding a mule. Another of his brothers wanted to go with him as far as Onate, and on the way he persuaded this brother to keep vigil with him before Our Lady of Aranzazu, to whom he prayed that night for renewed strength for his journey. He left his brother in Onate at the house of one of their sisters whom he was going to visit and went on himself to Navarrete. It then came back to him that he had some ducats owing him at the Duke's house and it seemed to him right to claim them so he wrote a note to this effect to the treasurer. The treasurer said that they had no money. However when the Duke learnt about this, he said that even though he lacked money for all else, he would never be short of money for a Loyola, and wanted to give him a good lieutenancy in consideration for his past services, if he would accept it. He recovered the money and gave instructions that part of it was to be given to certain persons to whom he felt under an obligation, and part for the restoration and adornment of a picture of Our Lady which was in a sorry state. Then, dismissing the two servants who had accompanied him, he set out alone on his mule from Navarrete for Monserrat.

14. On the road, there occurred an incident which is worth relating for the better understanding of how Our Lord dealt with this soul as yet blind, despite the great desires he had of serving God in every way he knew how. He had determined to perform great penances, not so much now with a view to making up for his sins, but rather to make himself agreeable to God and to please Him. Hence when he resolved to do some penance the

Saints had done, he would decide to do exactly the same and even more. These thoughts were his entire source of consolation. He did not pay any attention to the interior virtues; nor did he even know what humility was, nor charity, nor patience, nor discretion which regulates and moderates these virtues. Instead his one idea was to perform great exterior works, without bothering about any more precise considerations, simply because that was what the Saints had done for the glory of God.

15. As he was going on his way then, a Moor riding on a mule overtook him. They fell into conversation and began to talk about Our Lady. The Moor said that he quite admitted that Our Lady had conceived without knowing man, but that he could not believe that she remained a Virgin whilst giving birth; and in support of this he gave such natural reasons as occurred to him. Despite the many arguments which the Pilgrim put before him, he was not to be moved from this opinion. Then the Moor went on ahead so rapdily that he lost him from sight, and remained thinking about what had passed with the Moor. At this there came upon him feelings which aroused discontent in his soul since it seemed to him that he had not done his duty. They also roused indignation against the Moor since he felt that he had done wrong in allowing a Moor to say such things about Our Lady, and was consequently now obliged to vindicate her honour. There came upon him desires to catch up with the Moor and stab him a few times with his dagger for what he had said. He struggled for a long time with these thoughts, but in the end he was still in doubt, not knowing what he ought to do. The Moor who had gone ahead had told him that he was going to a place a little farther along the same road, very close to the high road which however did not go through this place.

16. So, tired of examining what it would be best to do and unable to find anything certain upon which he could make up his mind, he decided on the following course of action: he would let his mule go on with a loose rein to the place where the roads divided, then if the mule followed the road to the village he would seek out the Moor and stab him with his dagger; if, however, the mule did not take the road to the village, but continued along the highroad, he would leave the Moor alone. He did as he had decided. Now although the village was only thirty or forty paces away and the road leading to it very broad and in excellent condition, Our Lord willed that the mule take the highroad and not the one leading to the village. Before arriving at Monserrat he came to a large town where he wanted to buy the clothes he had decided to wear when he went to Jerusalem. Accordingly, he bought some cloth of the type used for making sacks, coarsely woven and very prickly stuff, and had it made into a long tunic reaching to his feet. He also bought a pilgrim's staff and a small gourd, all of which he tied to the mule's saddle-bow.

17. He then went on his way to Monserrat, thinking as he always did, about the great deeds he would accomplish for the love of God. Since his head was full of the exploits of Amadis de Gaul and similar romances, some of his inspirations were in much the same style. Hence he decided to make a vigil of arms neither sitting nor lying down, but now standing, now on his knees for a whole night before the Altar of Our Lady of Monserrat, where he had decided to leave his clothes and put on the armour of Christ. Having left that town then and as usual thinking about his plans, he went his way. Arriving at Monserrat after praying and coming to an arrangement with the confessor, he made a general confession in writing. The confession lasted three days. He also arranged with the confessor about the disposal of his mule and had his sword and dagger hung before the altar of Our Lady. This was the first man to whom he revealed his plans, since up to that time he had revealed them to no other confessor.

18. On the vigil of the feast of Our Lady in March 1522, at night, he sought out a poor man as unobtrusively as he possibly could, and stripping himself of all his clothes, he gave them to the poor man and put on the garment he desired. Then he went and threw himself on his knees before the altar of Our Lady. There he spent the whole night sometimes on his knees, sometimes standing with his staff in his hand. He left as the dawn was appearing, to avoid being recognized, and went to a village called Manresa, but not by the direct road to Barcelona where there were many people who knew him and who would have treated him with honour, but by a side road. He had decided to spend a few days in a hospice, and to note down some things in his book which he kept very carefully and in which he found great consolation. He was about a league away from Monserrat when he was overtaken by a man who came in great haste after him, and asked if it was he who had given his clothes to a certain poor man as the latter claimed. He replied "Yes", and his eyes filled with tears of compassion for the poor man to whom he had given his clothes. He was overcome with pity because he understood that the poor man had got into trouble since they had presumed that he had stolen the clothes. So, for all that he tried to flee from the good opinion of people, he had not been long in Manresa before they were telling extraordinary tales about him, on the strength of what had occurred at Monserrat; and the gossip soon went far beyond the facts; he had given up such a great fortune, etc.

CHAPTER III

19. He begged for alms every day at Manresa, and he did not eat meat nor drink wine although it was given to him. On Sundays he did not fast and if he were given a little wine, he drank it. Since he had been very particular in looking after his hair, as was the custom of the time, and he had a fine head of hair, he decided to let it grow as it would, neither combing nor cutting it and not wearing anything on his head day or night. For the same reason that he had taken excessive care of them, he also let his finger and toe-nails grow. Whilst he was in that hospice, it very often happened that he saw, in broad daylight, something in the air close to him, and it gave him great consolation since it was very beautiful in a wonderful way. He could not make out exactly what sort of a thing it was, but it seemed to him to have in some way the form of a serpent, and had many things which shone like eyes, though they were not eyes. He took great delight and consolation in this sight, and the more often he saw it the greater was his consolation; but when it disappeared, he was upset about it.

20. Up to this time he had gone on in more or less the same interior state of greatly consistent joyfulness without knowing anything about interior spiritual matters. Whilst the vision lasted, or perhaps a little before it began, for it lasted for many days, he was fiercely assailed by an idea which upset him. The difficulty of the life he proposed was set out before him, as if someone were saying to him in the depths of his soul – "How are you going to stand this life for the 70 years that are left to you?" But feeling that this was from the enemy he replied inwardly with great vigour – "You wretch! Can you promise me one hour of life?" So he overcame the temptation and remained at peace. This was the first temptation he suffered after the one mentioned above. It came as he was going into a Church where he heard High Mass and Vespers and Compline every day. All this was sung and he felt very great consolation in it. He usually read the Passion during Mass, continuing always in his equanamity.

21. But soon after the above-mentioned temptation he began to experience great variations in his soul. Sometimes he felt so stale that he found no relish in the recitation of the Office, nor in attending Mass, nor in any other prayer which he made. At other times the complete opposite to this happened to him and so suddenly that he seemed to be relieved of the sadness and desolation as one takes a cloak off someone's shoulders. He now began to wonder at these variations which he had never experienced before and to say to himself, "What sort of a new life is this we are beginning now?" At this time he still spoke on occasion with spiritual persons who held him in esteem and wanted to talk with him. For although he had no knowledge of spiritual matters, nevertheless in his conversation he showed great fervour and great determination to go forward in the serivce of God. There was in Manresa at that time a woman old in years and in the service of God, and known for His servant in many parts of Spain so that the Catholic King had sent for her once in order to talk over some matters with her. This woman then, speaking with the new soldier of Christ one day, said to him, "May it please my Lord Jesus Christ to appear to you one day." He was quite amazed at this since he took the words literally, "How can Jesus Christ appear to me?" He kept up his usual practice of confession and communion every Sunday.

22. But in this matter he now began to have great labour with scruples. For although the general confession at Monserrat had been made with sufficient care and entirely in writing, as has been said, still it sometimes seemed to him that there were some things he had not confessed, and this tormented him greatly, since even though he used to confess them again he was not at ease. So he began to seek out spiritual men who might be able to cure him of these scruples, but nothing helped him. Finally, a Doctor of the Cathedral, a very spiritual man, who used to preach there, told him one day in confession to put down in writing everything he could remember. This he did, but after making his confession the scruples still came back, each time more subtly than the last, so that he was sorely troubled. Although he knew well that the scruples were doing him great harm and that it would be good to rid himself of them, he could not put an end to them. He sometimes thought that he would be cured if his confessor were to order him in the name of Jesus Christ, not to confess anything from his past life; and he wished the confessor would so order him but he did not dare to tell him that.

23. Then without his saying anything, his confessor at last told him not to confess anything out of his past unless it were something about which he was quite certain. But since all these things seemed quite certain to him, he derived no benefit from this order and was left in the same perplexed condition. At this time he lived in a little room that the Dominicans had given him in their monastery. He kept up his practices of spending seven hours in prayer on his knees, and of getting up at midnight, and all the other exercises already mentioned. But in all this he found no remedy for his scruples which continued to torment him for many months. On one occasion, being greatly afflicted by them, be began to pray and in the fervour of his prayer, he started to cry out aloud to God saying, "Help me Lord! Since I can find no remedy in man nor in any creature. If I thought I could find a cure, no labour would be too great to me. Lord, you yourself show me where to find it, and even if I have to run after a little dog to obtain the remedy from it I shall do so."

24. In this state of mind he was often assailed by a violent temptation to throw himself through a great aperture which was in his room near the spot where he prayed. But knowing that it was a sin to kill himself he began to cry out again, "Lord! I will not do anything to offend you," repeating these words and the former ones over and over again. Then there came back to him the story of a Saint who, in order to obtain something he greatly desired from God, had gone without food for many days until he obtained it. After thinking this over for some time he at last decided to do likewise, telling himelf that he would neither eat or drink until God had granted what he desired or until he felt that he was on the point of death. Because if he were to find himself so near death that unless he ate something he would presently die, he decided that then he would beg for bread and eat; (as if he would have ever been able to beg for bread or even eat it in such an extremity).

25. This idea came to him one Sunday after he had been to communion and he went for the whole week without letting a bite of food pass his lips. Nor did he give up his other exercises, also going to divine Office, praying on his knees, rising at midnight etc. On the following Sunday when it was time for his confession, since it was his custom to tell his confessor in very great detail all that he did, he told him now that he had eaten nothing all that week. The confessor ordered him to break his fast. Even though he still felt quite strong he obeyed his confessor, and on that day and the following he was free of scruples. But on the third day, a Tuesday, during his prayer he began to recall his sins to mind, and as if he were unrolling a ball of thread he went on thinking of sin after sin from his past life, and it seemed to him that he must confess them all again. Then at the end of these thoughts there came upon him a great disgust for the life he was leading and a great urge to abandon it. Thereupon it was Our Lord's will that he should awake as if from sleep. Since he had some experience of the diversity of spirits, thanks to the lessons God had given him, he began to examine by what means this spirit had come upon him, and so with complete clarity of mind he resolved never more to confess anything out of his past. From that day on he was freed from those scruples, being quite convinced that Our Lord in his mercy had been pleased to deliver him.

26. In addition to his seven hours of prayer, he occupied himself in giving help in spiritual matters to some souls who sought him out, and the time which was left over to him during the day he spent in thinking about the things of God that he had meditated or read on that particular day. But when he went to bed he often had great inspirations and great spiritual consolations which caused him to lose much of the time he had allotted to sleep, which was little enough. Thinking this over for some time he reflected that he had a certain fixed time for his dealings with God and in addition to that the rest of the day as well. In view of this he began to doubt whether these inspirations came from the good spirit and he eventually resolved that it would be better to put them aside and to sleep at the time appointed; and this he did.

27. He continued to abstain from eating meat and was quite decided on the point and had not the slightest intention of making any change in this matter. Then one morning after rising he saw before him meat all ready to be eaten. It was as if he were seeing it with his bodily eyes, but no desire for the meat had preceded the sight. And with this there also came upon him a strong assent of his will to eat meat from then on; and although he remembered his former resolution he was unable to doubt about his decision that he should eat meat. When he told his confessor about it later the confessor told him to examine the matter carefully and see if it were not perhaps a temptation. But after careful examination he had not the slightest doubt on the matter.

In these days God dealt with him in the same way as a schoolmaster deals with a child – teaching him. Whether it was because of his ignorance and lack of refinement of mind, or because he had no one to teach him, or again because of the firm will God had given him to be used in his service, he was quite convinced then and has always believed that God dealt with him in this way. Indeed he believed that it would be an offence against the divine Majesty to have any doubts on the point. Something of this can be seen from the following five points:

28. Firstly: He had a great devotion towards the Most Holy Trinity, and accordingly prayed daily to each of the three Divine Persons distinctly. Now since he also prayed to the Trinity a thought came to him: how could he make four prayers to the Trinity? But this thought gave him little or no trouble as being a thing of little importance. One day whilst reciting the Office of Our Lady on the steps of the same monastery his understanding began to be raised up as if he saw the most Holy Trinity under the figure of three (organ) keys. This was accompanied by such tears and sobs that he could not master himself. That same morning he took part in a procession which came out of the monastery and could not restrain his tears the whole time until dinner-time, and after dinner he could not talk about anything but the Holy Trinity, making many different comparisons and with great joy and consolation. It was such that for the rest of his life there remained with him this impression of feeling great devotion whenever he prayed to the most Holy Trinity.

29. Secondly: Once he was given a representation in his understanding, accompanied by great spiritual gladness, of the way in which God had created the world. He seemed to see something white with rays streaming from it and from which God made light. But he did not know how to explain such things nor did he well remember every spiritual inspiration that God imprinted in his soul during this period.

Thirdly: Whilst still at Manresa, where he stayed for about a year, after God had begun to send him consolation, when he saw the fruit he obtained in his dealings with souls he renounced some of the extreme practices he had hitherto cultivated, and he now trimmed his nails and hair. One day whilst hearing mass in the monastery Church of the same village, at the moment of the elevation of the Body of the Lord, he saw with his interior eyes as it were rays coming from on high. Even though it was such a long time ago that he could not now explain it very well, nevertheless what he perceived clearly with his understanding was to see the way in which Jesus Christ our Lord was in the Most Holy Sacrament.

Fourthly: On many occasions and for a long time too, when he was praying, he saw the humanity of Christ with his interior eyes, and the figure which appeared to him seemed to be like a white body neither very big nor very small, but he could not distinguish any of its members. He saw this often at Manresa: if he were to say twenty or forty times he would have no scruples about having told a lie. He saw it again at Jerusalem and again on the road near Padua. He also saw Our Lady in a similar form witout being able to distinguish any members. These things which he saw confirmed him at the time and gave him such a confirmation in the faith for all time, that he often thought to himself: If there were no Scripture to teach us about these things of the Faith he would be ready to die for them solely on the strength of what he had seen.

30. Fifthly: One day he was on his way out of devotion to a Church, named I think after St. Paul, just a little more than a mile from Manresa. The road to it runs along beside the river. On the way, occupied with his devotions, he sat down for a little while with his face turned towards the river, which flowed down there below him. As he sat there the eyes of his understanding began to opened. It was not that he saw a vision but he came to understand and know many things, as well about spiritual things as about matters of Faith and secular learning, and that with so strong an enlightenment that all things seemed quite new to him. He could not ennumerate the particular points he understood at that moment even though they were numerous, but he could say that he received a great enlightening of his understanding. It was such that if he were to put together all the helps God had given him, and all the many things he had learnt in the whole of his sixty two years, all these taken together would not, he thought, amount to what he had received on that single occasion.

31. After this had lasted a good length of time he went and fell on his knees before a cross nearby to give thanks to God. At that moment there appeared to him the vision he had often seen before but which he had never understood, namely the thing he mentioned before which seemed very beautiful with many eyes. But now there in front of the cross he saw clearly that the thing had not such a beautiful colour as usual, he then understood quite distinctly with complete assent of his will that it was the demon. For a long time afterwards it frequently appeared but to show his contempt for it he would chase it away with the staff he carried in his hand.

32. Once he was ill at Manresa with a violent fever which brought him to the point of death, so that he was quite sure that he would soon have to render up his soul. Thereupon a thought came into his mind telling him that he was a holy man. This gave him so much trouble that it was all he could do to keep putting away the thought and recalling his sins to himself. Indeed this thought gave him a harder time of it than the fever itself, and no matter how hard he worked to conquer the thought, he could not overcome it. When however the fever abated a little and he was no longer in such danger of death, he began to shout out in a loud voice to some ladies who had come to visit him, crying – that for the love of God the next time he was dying they must shout to him as loud as they could telling him he was a sinner and should remember the sins he had committed against God.

33. Another time going by sea from Valencia to Italy, there was a great storm and the rudder of the ship broke. Things came to such a pass that in his own judgment and that of many on board, no natural means could save them from death. On this occasion when he examined his conscience and prepared to die, he could not feel any fear on account of his sins or at the thought of being damned. But he experienced great confusion and sorrow because he had not put to good use the gifts and graces God, Our Lord, had given him.

On yet another occasion in 1550 he was very sick with a severe illness which he and many others judged would be his last. This time, at the thought of death, he felt such gladness and spiritual consolation because he was going to die that he burst into tears, and this became so continuous that he often stopped thinking about death so as not to have so much of that particular consolation.

34. During the winter he fell sick of a very serious illness and in order to care for him the municipality lodged him in the house of the father of a certain Ferrara, who was later the servant of Balthasar de Faria. There he was looked after with great care and many of the ladies of the leading families came to watch beside his bed at night out of veneration for him. After he recovered from this illness he still remained very weak and frequently suffered from pains in his stomach. For these reasons and also because the winter was cold they prevailed upon him to clothe himself adequately and to wear shoes and cover his head. So they made him accept two grey cloaks of very coarse material and a bonnet something like a beret of the same stuff. At this period there were often days when he had a great desire to speak about spiritual matters and to find people capable of such conversations. The time he had fixed for his departure for Jerusalem was approaching.

35. In the beginning of the year 1523 he left for Barcelona where he was to embark. Although several people offered themselves as companions he wanted to go quite alone, since his whole idea was to have God alone for his refuge. Hence one day to certain persons who were urging him to take a companion since he knew neither Italian nor Latin, saying what a great help he would be and praising him very much, he replied that though the man they had chosen were the son or brother of the Duke of Cardona he still would not go with him. For he wanted to have three virtues: charity and faith and hope, and if he were to take a companion he would look to him for help when he was hungry; and if he were to have a fall it would be the companion who would help him to get up; and because of that he would also give his trust and affection to him, but it was precisely this trust and affection and hope which he wanted to have in God alone. What he said in this way was what he felt in his heart. It was in this frame of mind that he desired to embark not merely alone, but without provisions. He began negotiating for a passage and succeeded in getting the captain of a ship to take him for nothing since he had no money, on condition that he was to bring some biscuit on board with him as provisions. Nor would they take him in any other way – not for anything in the world.

36. When he went about obtaining the biscuit he was overcome with scruples – This is the sort of faith and hope you have that God will not fail you? – etc. This thought was so successful that he was sorely troubled with it. In the end not knowing what to do, since he could see good reasons on both sides, he decided to put the matter in the hands of his confessor. So he told him how desirous he was of doing what was perfect and more for the glory of God, and explained the reasons for his doubts about taking provisions with him. The confessor decided that he should beg what was necessary and take it with him. When he asked a certain lady for help she enquired what his destination was. He hesitated a little about telling her, and finally did not venture to say more than that he was going to Italy and Rome. At that she replied in alarm, "You want to go to Rome! But the people who go there come back in I don't know what sort of state." By that she meant that they drew very little spiritual profit from being in Rome. The reason he did not dare say that he was going to Jerusalem was through fear of vain glory. That fear so tormented him that he never dared say from what part of the country he came or who his family were. Having at last obtained the biscuit he embarked. However, whilst still on shore, he found that he had five or six blancas left over from what he had obtained by begging from door to door, (for that was how he lived); so he left them on a beach there near the shore.

37. When he took ship he had been in Barcelona for a little more than twenty days. Whilst still in Barcelona, before he sailed, following his usual practice, he sought out all spiritual persons, even though they lived in hermitages far from the city, in order to speak with them. But neither in Barcelona nor in Manresa, during the whole time he was there, could he find anyone to give him the sort of help he wanted, with the exception of that woman at Manresa, already mentioned above, who said to him that she asked God that Jesus Christ might appear to him. She alone, it seemed to him, had penetrated to some depth in spiritual things. Hence after his departure from Barcelona he completely lost this anxious desire to seek out spiritual persons.

CHAPTER IV

38. They had such a strong following wind that they went from Barcelona to Gaete in five days and nights though all were terrified by the great tempest. Fear of the plague was everywhere in that country, but he took the road to Rome as soon as ever they disembarked. He was joined by some of the others from the ship, a mother and her daughter who was dressed in boy's clothes, and a young fellow besides. These went along with him because they too were begging. Coming to a farmstead they found a big fire with a large number of soldiers around it. These gave them food and a great deal of wine, pressing it on them in order to make them drunk. Afterwards they separated them, putting the mother and daughter in a room upstairs and the pilgrim with the youth in a stable. But about midnight he heard loud screams from the room upstairs. He got up to see what was going on and found the mother and daughter below in the courtyard, weeping bitterly and lamenting that the soldiers were trying to violate them. At this he was aroused to such anger that he began to shout – "Have we got to put up with this sort of thing!" and similar protests which he spoke with such good effect that all in the house remained dumbfounded, and no one did him the slightest injury. The youth had already fled so the three of them set off walking whilst it was still night.

39. Arriving at a nearby city they found the gates locked, and since they were unable to obtain an entry, all three spent the night in a nearby church which was open to the rain. In the morning they were refused entrance to the city, nor could they obtain alms outside the walls, even though they went to a castle in the neighbourhood. The Pilgrim felt very weak as a result of the crossing and all the rest. Unable then to walk any farther he stayed there whilst the mother and daughter went on towards Rome. That day many people came out from the city and learning the lady of the land was coming there he went to meet her and explained that his illness was merely the result of weakness, and asked her to allow him to enter the city in order to seek for some remedy. She readily gave him the permission. He then set to begging in the city and collectd many quatrini. After resting up there for two days he went on his way once again and arrived in Rome on Palm Sunday.

40. There everyone who spoke to him, learning that he was going to Jerusalem without money tried to dissuade him from the journey. They asserted with many arguments that it was impossible to obtain a passage without money. But he himself had so great an assurance in his soul, that he was unable to doubt but that he would find a way of getting to Jerusalem. He received the blessing of Pope Adrian VI and then left for Venice eight or nine days after Easter Sunday. However, he still had six or seven ducats which he had been given for the passage from Venice to Jerusalem. He had accepted them because he had been in some measure won over by the fears people expressed that he would not be able to obtain a passage in any other way. But two days after leaving Rome he came to realise that he had given in to a lack of trust, and the fact of having taken the ducats weighed on him heavily, and he wondered if it would be right to throw them away. Eventually he decided to distribute them generously to those whom he met, who were for the most part, poor people: This he did in such a way that when he arrived at Venice he had no more than a few quatrini left which he needed for the night.

41. During this journey to Venice he slept under the city gateways because of the preventative measures being taken against the plague. It once so happened that as he got up in the morning he came face to face with another man who fled in terror, at the sight of him, apparently because he must have seen how pale he was.

Travelling in this way he arrived at Chioggia. Together with some companions who had joined him, he learnt that they would not be allowed to enter Venice. His companions decided to go to Padua to obtain a certificate of health there, and he went along with them. But he could not keep pace with them since they walked very quickly and eventually left him behind at nightfall in a large meadow. There Christ appeared to him in the usual way we have described above and comforted him greatly. With this consolation he arrived on the following morning at the gates of Padua. He had not forged a certificate, as I believe his companions had done, but the guards let him in without asking any questions, and the same thing happened when he left the town. His companions were greatly amazed at this, for they had just obtained a certificate allowing them to go to Venice and he had not bothered about it in the least.

42. When they arrived at Venice the guards came to the boat to examine each and every person on board, and he was the only one they did not bother about. In Venice he lived by begging and slept in the Piazza of St. Mark. He never had any desire to go to the imperial ambassador's house, nor did he take any special pains about looking for the means of getting a passage. In his soul he had a great assurance that God would give him a way of getting to Jerusalem. This assurance gave him such confidence that none of the arguments people put up against him, nor their forebodings, could make him doubt.

One day a rich Spaniard met him by chance and asked what he was doing and where he wanted to go. Learning of his plans he took him to eat at his house, and afterwards put him up for a few days, until everything was ready for the departure. Ever since his time at Manresa the Pilgrim had the habit of not speaking at table when he was invited out, except to reply briefly. Instead he used to listen to what was said, and store up some of the remarks, which would give him an opportunity of speaking about God, which is what he did when the meal was ended.

43. That was the reason why the good man and his entire household became so attached to him, that they wanted to keep him with them and make him stay on in their house. It was his host, too, who took him to the Doge of Venice so that he could speak to him; that is to say, he arranged for him to be given an entrance and an audience. After hearing the Pilgrim, the Doge gave orders that he should be taken on board the ship which was carrying the government officials to Cyprus.

Although many pilgrims for Jerusalem had come that year, most of them had turned back home because of the new situation created by the capture of Rhodes. However there were thirteen on the Pilgrim ship whichsailed first, and eight or nine remained behind for the government ship. When the latter was ready to depart, our Pilgrim had a serious attack of fever. After giving him a bad time of it for some days, the fever left him. On the very day the ship was to sail he had taken a purge. His hosts therefore asked the doctor if he could embark for Jerusalem. The doctor replied that if he intended to be buried there, he could certainly embark. Despite this he went on board ship and sailed the same day. He vomited so much that he felt greatly relieved and from then on began to regain his health in every way. On board ship there was a certain amount of openly filthy and obscene behaviour which he reprehended with severity.

44. The Spaniards on board advised him not to do this because the crew were talking of leaving him behind on some island. But it was Our Lord's will for them to reach Cyprus quickly. There, after leaving the ship, they went overland to another port called Las Salinas, about ten leagues away, and here they embarked on the Pilgrim ship. He took with him for his sustenance nothing but the hope he had in God, as he had done on the other ship. During all this time Our Lord appeared often to him and that gave him great consolation and strength. It seemed to him that he saw a large round thing made as it were of gold, and that was what appeared to him. After leaving Cyprus they arrived at Jaffa and went from thence to Jerusalem riding on donkeys as was the custom. Two miles outside Jerusalem, a Spaniard called Diego Manes, a nobleman by all appearances, addressed the pilgrims with great devotion saying that since they would soon be coming to the place where they would be able to see the Holy City it was only right that each prepare himself interiorly and that they should go on in silence.

45. All agreed to this and each one began to recollect himself. Shortly before they came to the place whence Jerusalem can be seen they dismounted because they saw two friars with the cross already there waiting for them. On arriving at the city itself the Pilgrim felt great consolation and from what the others said, all had the same feeling accompanied by a joy that did not seem to be of the natural order. He experienced the same devotion continually whilst visiting the Holy Places.

It was his firm intention to remain in Jerusalem, visiting the Holy Places for the rest of his days, and in addition to this practice of devotion he had decided to help souls. With this in view he had brought letters of recommendation for the Guardian, and gave them to him declaring his intention of staying there out of devotion, but without revealing the second part of his plan, about wanting to help souls, because he had never told anyone about this, though he had often openly declared the former intention. The Guardian replied that he did not see how it would be possible for him to stay, since the house was in such want that it could not support the friars and for that very reason he had decided to send some of them back to Europe with the pilgrims. But the Pilgrim replied that he would not ask the monastery for anything except that they should hear his confession whenever he came to make it. Thereupon the Guardian said that if that was the case something could be arranged, but he would have to await the arrival of the Provincial, (I think he was the major superior of the Order in that land) who was at Bethlehem.

46. The Pilgrim was reassured by this promise and began to write letters to certain spiritual persons in Barcelona. He had written one letter and was starting on the second, it was the day before the pilgrims were to depart, when he was sent for by the Provincial, who had come back, and the Guardian. The Provincial told him in a kindly way how he had heard of his good intention of staying in these Holy Places and that he had given the matter careful consideration; but from his personal experience of others he did not think it feasible. Many had had the same desire, and such a one had been made prisoner, and this other had died, and the obligation of ransoming the captives fell upon the Order. For these reasons then he had better get ready to leave with the pilgrims on the following day. To this he replied that he adhered most firmly to his intention and determined not to let anything stop him from putting it into practice, politely indicating that although the Provincial did not share his views, as long as there was no question of his being obliged under mortal sin, personally he would not abandon his project through fear of anything. Thereupon the Provincial answered that they had authority from the Apostolic See to send away or keep whomsoever they wished, and power to excommunicate those who were unwilling to obey them, and that in the present case it was their opinion that he ought not to remain there.

47. When they wanted to show him the Bulls which gave them power of excommunication, he said that he had no need to see them, he believed their Reverences, and since they had made their decision with the authority they held he would obey them.

After that on his way back to where he had been, there came upon him a great desire to make another visit to Mount Olivet before he departed, since it was no longer Our Lord's will for him to stay in those Holy Places. On Mount Olivet there is a stone from which Our Lord ascended into heaven and even now his footprints can still be seen on it, and that was what he wanted to go back and see. So, without saying anything and without taking a guide, (and those who go without a Turk as their guide are in great danger) he slipped away from the others and went alone to Mount Olivet. The guards did not want to let him enter. He gave them a knife from the writing-case which he carried. After making his prayer with intense consolation he got the desire to go to Bethphage. Whilst he was there it came back to him that on Mount Olivet he had not noticed on which side the right footprint was and on which side the left, so he went back again. I think that this time he gave the guards his scissors to let him enter.

48. When it was known in the monastery that he had gone off without a guide, the friars set about looking for him. So it was that as he was coming down from Mount Olivet he came upon one of the Christians of the Cincture, a servant of the monastery, who was armed with a great club and evidently in a great rage, making signs as if he were going to hit him. Comng up to him he took him roughly by the arm and he allowed himself to be led along without resistance. But the good fellow was not going to let go of him for a moment. Going along in this way in the grasp of the Christian of the Cincture, he received great consolation from Our Lord in that he seemed to see Christ above him all the time, and this consolation lasted without interruption and in great abundance until he came to the monastery.

CHAPTER V

49. They left the next day.[2] When they arrived at Cyprus the pilgrims were divided up between the different ships. There were three or four ships in the harbour bound for Venice: one was Turkish, the second a very small vessel, and the third a magnificent and powerful ship belonging to a wealthy Venetian. Some of the pilgrims asked the owner of this last ship to take the Pilgrim on board. But having heard that he had no money the owner refused, although many people asked him, speaking highly of the Pilgrim etc. The owner replied that if he was a saint let him make the crossing as St. James had done, or some such remark. However, those who had spoken on his behalf easily obtained a passage for him from the owner of the little ship. They left one morning early with a favourable wind but in the evening a storm blew up and separated the ships from each other. The big ship went down near the same islands of Cyprus and only the crew and the passengers were saved, and the Turkish ship was lost with all hands in the same storm. The little ship was hard put to it, but eventually made a landfall at La Pulla. All this took place in the depths of winter: it was bitterly cold and snowing. The only clothes the Pilgrim had were a pair of knee-breeches of coarse cloth which left his legs bare, a pair of sandals, a shirt of black cloth open and much torn at the shoulders, and a short, very threadbare doublet.

50. He arrived at Venice in the middle of January in the year

2. September 23rd 1523.

1524, after being at sea since his departure from Cyprus, that is to say during the months of November and December and the first half of January. At Venice one of the two people who had received him into their houses before he left for Jerusalem found him again and gave him an alms of 15 or 16 julios and a length of cloth which he folded up many times and put over his stomach on account of the intense cold.

Since the said Pilgrim had understood that it was God's will that he should not stay in Jerusalem, he had been continually asking himself – "What is to be done?" Eventually he was more and more drawn towards studying for a time in order to be able to help souls and so he decided to go to Barcelona. Hence he set out from Venice for Genoa. One day in Ferrara whilst he was at his devotions in the main church, a beggar asked him for an alms and he gave him a marguete, a coin worth about 5 or 6 quatrini. After him another beggar came and to this one he gave another small coin worth a little more. Then since all he had left were julios, he gave the third beggar a julio. When the beggars saw that he was distributing alms they gave him no peace and in this way he used up all that he had. Eventually a whole crowd of beggars came asking for alms. He told them he was sorry but he had nothing left.

51. So he set off from Ferrara in the direction of Genoa. On the road he fell in with some Spanish soldiers who looked after him very well for that night. They were amazed that he was taking that road since it meant that he would pass almost between the French and Imperial armies, and they begged him to leave the highroad and take another safer one which they pointed out. But he did not follow their advice. Instead he kept straight on his road and came to a village which had been burnt and rased to the ground, so until night time he found no one to give him anything to eat. Then at sunset he reached a fortified town where the guards immediately seized him thinking he was a spy. They took him into a hut near the gate and began to interrogate him in the way they do when there is some suspicion. To all their questions he replied that he knew nothing. Then they stripped him and searched him examining his shoes and his whole body to see if he were carrying a letter. All their efforts led them nowhere so they bound him in order to take him before their Captain who was the one who would make him talk. When he asked them to take him clothed in his doublet, they would not give it to him and dragged him off as he was with only the breeches and shirt mentioned above.

52. On the way the Pilgrim had, as it were, a representation of Christ at the time of His being led away, although this was not a vision like the others. They took him down three big streets and he went along not in the least sad but joyful and content. His piety had led him to adopt the practice of addressing everyone familiarly no matter who they were, since Christ and the Apostles had spoken in that way etc. As he went through the streets it crossed his mind that it would be better to break with the habit in the present situation and address the captain as, Sir. This thought was accompanied by a certain fear of the tortures they might inflict upon him etc. Then realising that this was a temptation he said: Since it is like that, I will not call him Sir; I will not bow to him, nor will I doff my cap to him.

53. They arrived at the Captain's palace and he was left in a low room where, a little later, the Captain spoke to him. He, however, made no attempt to be polite and replied briefly with long pauses between each word. The Captain thought he was a madman and said so to those who had brought him along – "This man isn't in his right mind. Give him his belongings and throw him out." He was hardly out of the palace, when he met a Spaniard who lived in that place and who took him to his house and gave him a meal and whatever else he needed for the night. Next morning he set out again and walked until it was evening. Then two soldiers in a watch tower saw him and came down to arrest him. They took him off to their Captain who was French. Amongst other things the Captain asked him what country he was from and hearing that he was from Guipozcoa said, "I come from near there myself," he was from somewhere around Bayonne. Then he immediately added, "Take him away and give him something to eat and treat him well." On this journey from Ferrara to Genoa there were many other incidents of less importance, but he eventually arrived at Genoa. There he was recognised by a fellow Basque called Portundo, who had spoke to him in the past whilst he was serving at the Court of the Catholic King. This man made arrangements for him to embark on a ship going to Barcelona. During the crossing he was in great danger of being captured by Andrea Doria, then in the service of the French, who gave them chase.

CHAPTER VI

54. When he arrived at Barcelona he spoke with Isabel Roser of his desire to study, making this known also to a certain Master Ardevol who taught grammar. The plan seemed very good to both; Master Ardevol offered to teach him free of charge, and Isabel Roser to provide whatever he required for his upkeep. The Pilgrim had known a monk at Manresa, I think he was of the Order of St. Bernard, a very spiritual man, and it was with him that he wanted to study so as to be able to devote himself more easily to the spiritual life and also to help souls. So he replied that he would accept their offer if he did not find at Manresa the opportunities he expected. But when he went there he found that the monk had died. He returned then to Barcelona and began to study with great application. However, one thing was a great obstacle to him, namely, when he was doing his "by heart", as is necessary at the beginning of grammar studies, there came to him new insights into spiritual things and new pleasures, and this to such an extent that he was unable to learn by heart, and no matter how he fought against them, he could not get rid of these thoughts.

55. After repeated reflection on the matter he said to himself – "Not even when I am praying or at Mass do I get such vivid enlightenments;" and so little by little he came to recognise this for a temptation. After praying he went to Santa Maria de la Mar, near his master's house, having asked the latter to come to the Church to listen to him for a few moments. When they were seated there he gave him a faithful account of all that was passing in his soul, and of the little progress he had made up till then, for the reason mentioned. He further made a promise to his master saying – "I promise you never to miss one of your classes during the next two years as long as I can find bread and water enough in Barcelona to keep me alive." Because he made this promise with great firmness, he never again experienced those temptations. The stomach pains contracted at Manresa because of which he had taken to wearing shoes, had left him, and from the time of his departure for Jerusalem his stomach had been quite better. For this reason whilst he was still studying at Barcelona, he had the desire to take up again his former penances. Hence he began making a hole in the soles of his shoes. The holes gradually became larger and larger so that when the cold of winter came he was wearing only the uppers of his shoes.

56. At the end of two years of study, during which, as they told him he had made great progress, his master said that he could begin the Arts' course and that he should go to Alcala. Nevertheless he had himself examined by a Doctor of Theology, who gave him the same advice. Consequently, he set off for Alcala alone, although he already had some followers as far as I know. When he arrived at Alcala he began to beg and to live on alms. One day after he had been living in this way for ten or twelve days, a cleric and some others with him, seeing him begging for alms, began to make fun of him, shouting the sort of insults people usually hurl at strong and healthy beggars. Just at that moment, the director of the new hospital at Antezana was passing by, and, showing his disapproval of the incident, called him over and took him along to the hospital where he gave him a room an all else that he needed.

57. He studied for about a year and a half in Alcala. Now since he arrived at Barcelona in the Lent of '24 and had studied there for two years, it was in the year 1526 that he came to Alcala. There he studied the Logic of Soto, the Physics of Albert, and the Master of the Sentences. Whilst at Alcala he also occupied himself in giving spiritual exercises and explaining christian doctrine, and by these means brought forth fruit to the glory of God. He dealt with a number of people who came to have deep knowledge and appreciation of spiritual things. Then there were others who were tempted in various ways; there was one who wanted to take the discipline, but could not do so because it was as if someone were restraining their hand. Other similar occurences gave rise to public gossip, especially since people flocked to hear him wherever he explained christian doctrine.

Soon after his arrival in Alcala he came to know Don Diego de Eguia who was living in the house of his brother, a printer in Alcala and quite well-to-do. Both of them gave him alms to provide for the poor and they also received the Pilgrim's three companions into their house. On one occasion when he came to beg alms to meet some needs. Don Diego said that he had no money, but he opened a chest which contained a great assortment of things. Out of it he gave him some blankets of various colours, some candlesticks, and other articles. These were all bundled up in a sheet and shouldering the lot the Pilgrim went off to help the poor.

58. As has been said, there was a great deal of gossip circulating in the region about the happenings in Alcala, some telling one version, some another. The rumours went as far as Toledo to the ears of the Inquisitors. When these came to Alcala, the Pilgrim was informed by their host who told him that he and his companions were being called the sack-wearers, and I believe, "alumbrados", and that they would make mincemeat of them. The Inquisitors set to work making an investigation and enquiry into their lives and, at the end of it, since that was all they had come for, they went back to Toledo without summoning them. They left the legal process to the Vicar General Figueroa, (who is now at the Imperial Court). A few days later, Figueroa sent for them and explained that the Inquisitors had made an investigation and enquiry into their way of life, so that now they could go on as before without any hindrance. However, since they were not religious, he did not think it proper that they should all dress alike. It would be better – and this was an order – for two of them, he pointed to the Pilgrim and Artiaga, to dye their clothes black, and for the other two, Calisto and Caceres, to dye theirs light brown, as for Juanico, a French youth, he could stay as he was.

59. The Pilgrim replied that they would do as they were ordered, "But," he added, "I do not know what advantage these inquisitions are since the other day a priest did not want to give a certain person Communion because he received the Eucharist every eight days, and I have had similar difficulties myself. We would like to know if they found any heresy in us." "No," replied Figueroa, "But if they do you will burn for it." "They will burn you too," said the Pilgrim, "if they find any heresy in you." They dyed their clothes in obedience to his order. About ten or twenty days later Figueroa told the Pilgrim not to go about barefoot but to wear shoes and this he did without any fuss as he always did when ordered to do such things.

Four months later the same Figueroa again began an investigation about them. In addition to the usual charges, it was I think occasioned by the fact that a married lady of quality who had a special veneration for the Pilgrim, used to come to the hospital in the half-light of early morning wearing a veil so as not to be seen, as is the custom in Alcala de Henares. When she entered she uncovered her face and went to the Pilgrim's room. But on this occasion they did nothing to them, they were neither summoned after the investigation nor did anyone say anything to them.

60. After another four months when he was lodging in a little house away from the hospital, a constable came one day to his door, called him and said, "Come along with me for a little." Then having put him in prison, he said, "You won't get out of here until further orders." It was summertime and since he was not closely confined, many people came to visit him, and he carried on as if he were at liberty teaching christian doctrine and giving exercises. He never at any time wanted to have a lawyer or an attorney although many offered themselves. He remembers in particular D. Teresa de Cardenas who sent one to visit him and made frequent offers to have him released. But he never accepted and always gave the reply, "He for whose love I am here will get me out if it is for his service."

61. He was in prison for 17 days without being examined and without knowing the reason for his arrest. At the end of that time Figueroa came to the prison and questioned him about all manner of things going so far as to ask him if he enforced the Sunday observance; also did he know two certain women, a mother and her daughter. He answered "Yes." Had he known anything about their departure before they went away. He answered, "No," by the oath he had sworn. At that the Vicar General laid his hand on his shoulder and showing his joy said, "That was the reason why you were brought here." Amongst the Pilgrim's numerous following there were a mother and her daughter, both widows and the daughter very young and very pretty. Both were well advanced in the spiritual life, especially the daughter, and indeed although they were of the nobility they had gone on foot on a pilgrimage to the Veil of Veronica at Jaen, unaccompanied, and I am not sure whether they did not even beg. This had caused a great stir in Alcala. Doctor Ciruelo who was to some extent responsible for them thought that the prisoner had induced them to do this and on that account had had him arrested. When the prisoner heard what the Vicar had said he replied, "Do you want me to speak a little more at length about that affair?" "Yes," he answered. "You should know then," said the prisoner, "that these two women have frequently importuned me with their desires to go about the world serving the poor now in this hospital, now in that; I myself have always discouraged them from this idea in view of the youth and beauty of the daughter etc. I told them that if they wanted to visit the poor they could do so in Alcala and could accompany the Blessed Sacrament." At the end of this talk Figueroa went off with his notary, having put everything down in writing.

62. At this time Calisto, who was in Segovia, heard of his imprisonment. Although he had only recently recovered from a very serious illness, he came immediately to be with him in prison. But the Pilgrim told him that it would be better to go and report to the Vicar General. The latter treated him very kindly and said that he would order him into prison where he had better remain until the return of the two women, when it would be possible to see if they confirmed what he said. Calisto spent several days in prison but when the Pilgrim saw that his bodily health was suffering since he had not fully recovered from his illness, he had him released through the good offices of a doctor, a very great friend of his.

Forty two days passed from the time the Pilgrim went to prison until his release. At the end of that time now that the two devout women had returned, the notary came into the prison and read out the sentence to him; he was a free man again but he and his companions must dress like the other students; they must not speak about matters concerning the faith until they had completed a further four years of studies, since they were, as yet, without learning. In all truth the Pilgrim was the best educated of them all, and his own knowledge lacked real foundation, and that was always the first point he made when being interrogated.

63. The sentence left him rather doubtful about what he should do next, since it seemed that they had closed the door on him as far as helping souls was concerned without giving any other reason except that he had not done his studies. Eventually he decided to go and see Fonseca, the Archbishop of Toledo and put the matter into his hands.

He left Alcala and met the Archbishop at Valladolid. He gave him a faithful account of what had happened and added that although he was no longer under his jurisdiction and not obliged to observe the sentence, none the less he would do as he had been ordered in the matter. He spoke using the familiar form of address as he did with everyone. The Archbishop received him very well (and learning that he wanted to go to Salamanca) said that he had friends in Salamanca too and a college, and they were at his disposition. In addition he ordered that he be given four escudos on his way out.

CHAPTER VII

64. After arriving in Salamanca as he was praying in a church, a pious woman recognised him for one of the "compania" since the other four companions had already been there for some days. She therefore asked him what his name was and then took him to the place where his companions were lodging. In Alcala when they had been ordered to dress like the other students the Pilgrim had said, "When you told us to dye our clothes, we did so; but now we cannot carry out this order because we have not the wherewithal to buy clothes." So it was the Vicar General himself who provided them with clothes and caps and all the other students' attire, and it was in this dress that they had left Alcala.

In Salamanca he used to go to confession to a friar of St. Dominic at the monastery of San Esteban. Ten or twelve days after his arrival the confessor said to him one day, "The Fathers of the house would like to speak with you." "So be it in God's name," he replied. "In that case," said the confessor, "the best thing is for you to come to dinner here on Sunday; but I warn you about one thing, there's a lot they'll want to know from you." On the Sunday he went along with Calisto. After the meal the Subprior, the Prior was away, the confessor, and, I think, another friar, went with them into the chapel. There the Subprior began to speak with great affability, saying what good reports they had heard about their life and practices, that they went about like the Apostles preaching, and that consequently they would be glad to hear about all that in more detail. He first asked what studies they had done. The Pilgrim replied, "I am he who has studied the most," and gave them an account of the little he had studied and of the little grounding he had.

65. The Subprior went on, "And what do you preach about?" "We ourselves do not preach," said the Pilgrim, "but we speak informally of the things of God with certain persons, after dinner for example, with those who invite us." "But exactly what things of God do you talk about?" said the Friar, "That is what we would like to know." "We speak," replied the Pilgrim, "now of one virtue, now of another, praising them; or of this vice or that, reprehending them." "You are not learned men," said the Friar, "and yet you speak of virtues and vices. There are only two ways of being qualified to speak like that: either through learning or through the Holy Spirit; and if it is not through learning, then it is through the Holy Spirit." At this the Pilgrim became wary, for this style of argument did not seem good to him. Then after a brief silence he said they had better not talk about such matters. But the Friar was insistent. "There are so many errors today from Erasmus and so many others who have led the world astray. You do not wish then to reveal what you say?"

66. The Pilgrim replied, "Father, I shall say no more about what I have said unless it be to my superiors who can oblige me to speak." The Friar had previously asked why Calisto was dressed as he was; for he wore a short tunic, had a huge hat on his head, a pilgrim's staff in his hand and some sort of knee boots, and since he was exceptionally tall he looked all the more outlandish. The Pilgrim explained that they had been in prison in Alcala and had been ordered to wear students' dress, and that his companion had given his gown to a needy cleric during the very hot weather. At this the Friar plainly showed his displeasure and muttered under his breath, "Charity begins at home."

But to get back to the story. Since the Subprior was unable to get another word out of the Pilgrim he said, "Very well, stay here until we do what is necessary to make you tell us everything." Then all the Friars went out rather hastily. The Pilgrim had however first asked if they wanted them to remain in the Chapel or in some other place. The Subprior replied that they were to stay in the Chapel. Then the Friars had the doors bolted, and so it seems, got into touch with the Judges. However the companions remained for three days in the monastery, taking their meals with the monks in their refectory without a word being said to them about legal proceedings. Their room was almost continually filled with Friars who came to see them and the Pilgrim always spoke to them on his usual topics. The result was that there was something of a division in the community since many showed themselves favourable to them.

67. After three days had passed a notary came and led them off to prison. They were not put down below with the criminals but in an upper room which was in a filthy condition since it was old and never used. They were shackled together, each by a foot, with the same length of chain about ten or thirteen spans long, and the chain was secured to a post in the middle of the room. Whenever one of them wanted to do anything, the other had to go with him. They stayed awake all that night. On the following day when their imprisonment became known in the city, people sent bedding to them and an abundance of all that they required. They had a constant stream of visitors and the Pilgrim continued his exercises of speaking about God etc. The Bachelor Frias came in and examined them separately, and the Pilgrim gave him all his papers – that is to say, the Exercises – so that he could examine them too. Being asked whether they had any companions they replied that they had and told where they could be found. Soon these too were brought along by order of the Bachelor Frias. Caceres and Artiaga were put into prison, but they left Juanico who became a friar afterwards. However, they were not put in with the other two, but down below with the common criminals.

68. A few days later, he was summoned to appear before four judges; the three Doctors – Sanctisidoro, Paravinhas and Frias, and the fourth was the Bachelor Frias. All had already seen the Exercises. They asked him many questions not only about the Exercises but also about theology, for example, about the Trinity, and the Blessed Sacrament and how he understood these dogmas. He made his usual preliminary declaration, then at the order of the judges, he spoke and to such effect that they found nothing to correct. The Bachelor Frias, who had always been more persistent than the others in these matters, then gave him a case of canon law. He was obliged to reply to everything, though the first thing he always said was that he did not know what the Doctors had to say on such matters. Then they ordered him to explain the first commandment as he usually did. He began to do this and dwelt at such length on it and had so much to say about the first commandment that they had no desire to ask him for more. But before this when they were speaking about the Exercises they were most insistent about one point, which was in the beginning of the Exercises: about when a thought is a venial sin and when it is a mortal sin. The reason was because without any theological training he gave a definite opinion on the matter. He replied – "It is for you to decide whether or not it is true. If it is not true, condemn it." Eventually they left without condemning anything.

69. Amongst many others who visited him in prison there came one day Don Francisco de Mendoza, now known as the Cardinal of Burgos, and he came with the Bachelor Frias. He asked him in a friendly way how he was getting on in prison and if he found being a prisoner weighed on him. He replied, "I will give you the same answer I gave today to a lady who said how sorry she was to see me a prisoner. I said to her – "Those words show that you have no desire to be a prisoner for the love of God. Does prison then seem such a terrible thing to you?" "For my own part I can tell you that there are not so many fetters and chains in Salamanca that I would not wish for more for the love of God."

At this time it happened that all the prisoners broke out of prison, but the two companions who were in with them did not attempt to escape. When they were found there the next morning all by themselves with the doors open everyone was greatly edified and there was much talk about it in the town. The result was that they were given an entire palace nearby as their prison.

70. On the twenty-second day of their imprisonment they were summoned to hear their sentences. It was that no error had been found either in their way of life or in their teaching and they could continue as before teaching christian doctrine and speaking of the things of God but only on condition that they did not declare explicitly: such a thing is a mortal sin and such is a venial sin, before they had completed a further four years of study. When the sentence had been read out the judges gave them every sign of friendship as if they wanted them to accept it. The Pilgrim said that he would do whatever the sentence ordered, but that he would not accept it, since without condemning anything, they had closed his mouth and prevented him helping his neighbour in so far as he was able. No matter how the Doctor Frias insisted, and he showed great friendliness, the Pilgrim would say nothing more except that as long as he was under the jurisdiction of Salamanca he would do as he was ordered. They were immediately released from prison and recommending the matter to God he began to think about what he should do. He found one big difficulty about staying on in Salamanca, namely that with this prohibition against defining mortal and venial sin, the door seemed to be closed as far as doing good to souls was concerned.

71. So it was that he decided to go and study in Paris. When the Pilgrim used to reflect in Barcelona about whether he should study and for how long, his one idea was to decide whether after his studies he should enter religion or go about the world as he was. When thoughts of entering religion came to him he immediately got the desire to enter an order that was decadent and in need of reform, since his idea in entering religion was to be able to suffer more, and he also thought that God might help the others because of that. God gave him great confidence that he would be able to endure all the affronts and insults they heaped upon him.

During his time in prison at Salamanca these same desires of his – to help souls – had not left him. Accordingly, and in order to do that, to study first and to recruit a few men with the same ambition, and to keep the companions he already had, now that he had decided to go as far as Paris, he arranged with these companions to stay where they were whilst he went on alone to find out if it was possible for them to make their studies there.

72. Many important people were most insistent that he should not go, but they were never able to convince him. Instead fifteen or twenty days after coming out of prison he took a few books with him on a little donkey and set out alone. When he arrived in Barcelona all his friends tried to dissuade him from going across France because of the terrible wars that were raging there, giving him detailed accounts of what was happening and going so far as to say that Spaniards were being roasted on the spit there. But he never felt in the least afraid.

CHAPTER VIII

73. So he set out for Paris alone and on foot, and arrived in Paris roughly sometime in the month of February; and according to what he told me, it was in the year 1528 or 1527. He found lodging with some Spaniards and went to study Humanities at Montaigu. He did this since as a result of being pushed forward in his studies with such haste he now found he was deficient in the groundwork. So he went to school with the little boys following the syllabus and method of Paris. Immediately on his arrival a merchant gave him twenty-five escudos for a bill of change from Barcelona. He put the money in safe keeping with one of the Spaniards in the lodgings, but the fellow spent it all in a short time and had not the means of repaying him. Thus after Lent the Pilgrim was already without money since he had spent some himself and also for the reason mentioned. He was therefore obliged to beg and even to leave the house where he was staying.

74. He was received into the hospital of St. Jacques beyond the Innocents. This was very inconvenient for his work since the hospital was a good distance from the College of Montaigu, and if he wanted to find the door open, he had to be in on the stroke of the Angelus and could only go out after it was light. Thus he could not very well go to all the classes. Then there was the other difficulty of having to beg for alms for his livelihood. For almost five years he had been free from stomach pains and so he now began to practise more penance and greater abstinence. After living like this for some time, in the hospital and begging, he saw that he was making little progress with his studies and began to think within himself about what he would do. Then, noticing that some students worked in the colleges as servants of the Regents and still had time to study, he decided to find a Master for himself.

75. As he was thinking this over in his mind and making his plans, he found great consolation in imagining that his Master would be Christ our Lord, that to one of the students he would give the name of St. Peter and to another that of St. John and so on for each of the Apostles. When my master gives me an order, I shall think that it is Christ who is ordering me, and when someone else gives me an order I shall think it is St. Peter. He tried very hard to find a master; he spoke about it to the Bachelor Castro and to a Carthusian monk who knew many of the masters, and to others as well, but he never found an employer.

76. Eventually when he could find no solution, a Spanish friar said to him one day that he would do better by going to Flanders every year, since at the cost of two months or even less there, he could bring back sufficient money to enable him to study for a whole year. After putting this solution before God, he decided that it was the right one. Acting on the advice, he brought back from Flanders every year enough to enable him to get by somehow. Once he also went to England and collected more alms there than he had done in the previous years.

77. The first time he came back from Flanders, he began to devote himself more intensely than ever to spiritual conversations and gave exercises more or less simultaneously to three people, namely: Peralta, the Bachelor Castro, who was at the Sorbonne, and to a Biscayan, Amador by name, who was at St. Barbe. They all made great changes in their lives. They at once gave away all they had to the poor, even their books, began begging for alms in Paris, and went to lodge at the hospice of St. Jacques where the Pilgrim had formerly been but which he had left for the reasons already given. This caused a tremendous stir in the University since the first two were persons of distinction and very well known. Immediately, the Spaniards began a campaign against the two Masters, and being unable to persuade them by arguments and reasons to come back to the university, a considerable body of them went off one day armed, and brought them back from the hospice.

78. Taking them to the University, they made them agree to finish their studies before putting their other plans into action. The Bachelor Castro went to Spain later on and preached in Burgos for a time and then became a Carthusian in Valencia. Peralta set out to make a pilgrimage on foot to Jerusalem but on his way through Italy in this fashion, he met a captain, a relation of his, who took steps to bring him before the Pope and had him put under orders to return to Spain. These events did not take place immediately, but some years later.

At Paris, especially amongst the Spaniards, there was an increasing amount of talk against the Pilgrim. The Rector de Gouveia said he had turned Amador, who had been in his College into a madman, and that he himself had made up his mind and said it openly, that the first time he came to St. Barbe, he would have him beaten for seducing the students.

79. The Spaniard who had been one of his first acquaintances and who had spent his money without paying him back set off for Spain by way of Rouen. Whilst waiting for the boat at Rouen he fell ill. The Pilgrim learnt from a letter received from him that he was ill and the desire came upon him of going to visit him and give him help. He also had the idea that this meeting might win him over so that he would leave the world and devote himself entirely to the service of God.

(HERE THE ORIGINAL CONTINUES IN ITALIAN)

In order to obtain this result, the desire came upon him of walking the twenty eight leagues from Paris to Rouen barefoot and without eating or drinking. Praying about the matter, he felt very much afraid. In the end he went to St. Dominic's church and there made a resolution to do the journey in the way described and already the great fear he had of tempting God disappeared.

On the following morning when he was to set out, he got up very early and as he began to get dressed such a great fear came over him that he thought he would be unable to finish dressing. In spite of this repugnance, he left the house and was outside the city before it was fully light. However, the fear was still there, and followed him as far as Argenteuil, a walled town about three leagues distance from Paris in the direction of Rouen, where there is said to be the garment of Our Lord. He passed through the town with this spiritual labour and as he was climbing a rise in the road, the feeling began to leave him and there came upon him great consolation and spiritual force accompanied by such gladness that he began to shout out aloud in the middle of the fields and to speak with God etc. He lodged that night in a hospice with a poor beggar after having walked fourteen leagues in the day; the following night he found shelter in a barn, and on the third day he arrived in Rouen – and the whole time without eating or drinking and barefoot too, as he had resolved. At Rouen he consoled the sick man and helped him get a passage on a ship bound for Spain, and gave him letters introducing him to the companions who were at Salamanca, namely Calisto, Caceres, and Artiaga.

80. So that we shall not have to speak of these companions again, here is what happened to them:

Whilst the Pilgrim was in Paris, he wrote frequently as had been agreed, saying that there was little chance of his being able to arrange for them to study in Paris. However, he undertook to write to Donna Leonora de Mascarenhas and ask her to help Calisto by giving him a letter of recommendation for the court of the King of Portugal, so that he might obtain one of the scholarships the King of Portugal awarded for Paris. Donna Leonora gave Calisto the letters and a mule to ride on as well as some ready money for his expenses. Calisto went to the court of the King of Portugal but in the end he did not come to Paris. Instead he returned to Spain and went to Mexico* with a certain spiritual lady. Afterwards he returned to Spain and then went back to Mexico and returned to Spain this time a rich man, and caused great amazement in Salamanca amongst all who had formerly known him.

Caceres went back to Segovia, of which town he was a native, and began to lead a life which seemed to indicate that he had quite forgotten his former intentions.

Artiaga became a Comendador. Later when the Society was already established in Rome, he was given a Bishopric in Mexico. He wrote to the Pilgrim offering it to a member of the Society and receiving a refusal went to Mexico, was made a Bishop, and died there by a strange accident. He was ill and had two water carafes for his refreshment, one was full of water prescribed by the doctor and the other of water of Soliman, a poison. He was given the second by mistake and it killed him.

81. The Pilgrim returned from Rouen to Paris, and learned

*In the text: 'the Indies of the Emperor'.

that on account of what had happened with Castro and Peralta, great rumours had started about him, and that the Inquisitor had made enquiries about him. He did not want any further delay, and went to find the Inquisitor, telling him that he understood he was looking for him and that he was prepared for anything he might wish. This Inquisitor was our Master Ory, a Dominican friar. The Pilgrim asked him to expedite the matter quickly because he wished to enter the Arts course on St Remy's day. He wanted first to get this over, so that he could the better attend to his studies. But the Inquisitor did not call him back, but told him that it was true that they had spoken to him about his doings etc.

82. A short time afterwards, on the feast of St. Remy, which comes at the beginning of October, the Pilgrim enrolled in the Arts' course under a master named Master Juan Pena. When he enrolled he had the intention of keeping the companions who had determined to serve Our lord but he was not going to try to recruit any others, so that he would be able to study more easily.

When he began to attend the lectures of the course, he experienced the same temptation as when he had been learning grammar in Barcelona. Whenever he was at a lecture, he could not pay attention because of the spiritual thoughts which came into his mind. Seeing that he was making little progress on this account, he went to his Master, and promised that he would listen to the whole course without fail, so long as he could find bread and water enough to provide for himself. When this promise had been made, all the inopportune feelings of devotion which had come upon him disappeared and he went ahead with his studies in peace and quiet.

At this time he was in contact with Master Peter Favre and Master Francis Xavier, both of whom he later won over to the service of God by means of the Exercises.

During this period of his studies, he was not persecuted as before. The Doctor Frago once remarked upon the fact saying that he was amazed to see how peaceful his life was and that no one was causing him trouble. He however replied, "The reason is because I do not speak to anyone about the things of God, but once this course is over, we shall recommence our practice."

83. Whilst the two of them were talking together, a friar came up to ask Doctor Frago if he could find a house for him, since in the one where he was living there had been a number of deaths which he attributed to the plague because at that time the plague had broken out in Paris. Doctor Frago and the Pilgrim wanted to go and see the house and took with them a woman experienced in these matters. She inspected the house and confirmed that it was the plague. The Pilgrim also wanted to enter the house and finding a sick man, he comforted him, touching his sore with his hand. After giving him some little consolation and encouragement he went away alone. His hand now began to hurt so that he thought he had the plague; this imagination was so vivid that he could not overcome it until with a forceful gesture he thrust his hand into his mouth, turning it about inside and saying, "If you have the plague in your hand, you shall also have it in your mouth." When he had done this, the imagination left him and the pain in his hand as well.

84. But when he returned to St. Barbe where he had his lodgings, and was following the course, those in the college who knew that he had been into the house with the plague fled from him and would not let him enter. As a result he had to spend some days outside.

It was the custom in Paris for the third year Arts' students to "take a stone" as they say, in order to receive their Baccalaureat. Since this cost an escudo, many of the poor students could not afford it. The Pilgrim began to wonder whether it would be right for him to take a stone. He had serious doubts about the matter and was quite undecided so that he resolved to put the matter into the hands of his Master. The latter advised him to "take a stone" and he did so. Nevertheless there was no lack of critics and especially one Spaniard who made remarks about it.

In Paris he for some time now suffered from his stomach and every fifteen days he had stomach pains which lasted a good hour and brought on a fever. Once the pain lasted for sixteen or seventeen hours. At the time, he had passed his Arts' course, had studied theology for some years and had recruited the Companions. His illness grew steadily worse and he could find no remedy though he tried many. The physicians said that the only thing that would cure him was his native air. Moreover the Companions gave him the same advice and were most insistent about it.

85. At this time, they had all agreed upon what they were going to do, namely; to go to Venice and Jerusalem and to spend their lives helping souls. If they could not obtain permission to stay in Jerusalem they would return to Rome and offer themselves to the Vicar of Christ so that he might employ them wherever he judged to be most for the glory of God and the good of souls. They had also decided to wait for a ship in Venice for a year, and if in that year they had not obtained a passage for the Levant, they would be released from their vow to go to Jerusalem and would go to see the Pope etc.

In the end the Pilgrim allowed himself to be persuaded by the Companions, and also by the fact that those of them who were Spaniards had business to be settled which he could arrange. So they agreed that when he felt well again he would settle the affairs of the Companions and then make his way to Venice to wait for the Companions there.

86. This was the year 1535, and according to the agreement the Companions were to leave in 1537 on the Feast of the Conversion of St. Paul, though in effect they left in November 1536 because of the outbreak of war. When the Pilgrim was ready to set out he heard that he had been denounced to the Inquisitor and that they were making out a case against him. Hearing this and seeing that no summons arrived for him, he went to the Inquisitor and told him what he had heard and that he was about to leave for Spain and had companions, and requested him to pass sentence. The Inquisitor said that as far as the accusation was concerned, it was true, but in his opinion it was nothing of importance. He only wanted to see the manuscript of the Exercises. Having seen them, he praised them greatly and asked the Pilgrim to leave him a copy of them; and this he did. Nevertheless, he renewed his request that the proceedings should be advanced and sentence passed. The Inquisitor made excuses so he went to his house with a public notary and witness and had a statement made under oath of the whole affair.

CHAPTER IX

87. This done, he mounted a little horse which the Companions had bought for him and set off alone for his native country. He already felt better on the way. When he arrived in the Province, he left the main road and took a mountain road which was lonelier. After riding along it for a short time, he met two armed men riding towards him (the road had quite a bad reputation for murderers). These two passed him and then turned round and came back after him at a rapid pace and he was a little afraid. In spite of this fear, he spoke to them and discovered that they were servants of his brother, who had sent them to look for him. Apparently he had had news of his arrival from Bayonne where the Pilgrim had been recognised. The two rode on ahead and he followed them along the same road. Shortly before he arrived at the family estate, he met the same two again coming out to meet him. They made persistent efforts to lead him to his brother's house but they could not compel him to go there. He went to the hospital and later at a convenient time went about the region begging for alms.

88. At the hospital, he began speaking of the things of God by whose grace great fruit was produced. Immediately on his arrival he had determined to teach christian doctrine every day to the children, but his brother opposed this strongly, telling him that no one would come; to this he replied that one child would be sufficient. However, after he had begun, many came regularly to hear him, including even his brother.

Besides teaching christian doctrine, he also preached on

Sundays and feast days, to the help and profit of the souls who journeyed many miles to hear him. He also strove to suppress various abuses and with the help of God rectified one or two. For example: he had gambling effectively forbidden after winning over the administrator of justice to his views. There was also another abuse, namely this: the girls in that region always go about with their heads uncovered, and only cover their heads when they get married. But there are many who become concubines of priests and other men and remain faithful to them as if they were their wives. This practice is so common that the concubines have not the slightest shame in saying that they have covered their head for so-and-so and everybody knows them for what they are.

89. This practice gives rise to many evils. The Pilgrim persuaded the Governor to make a law that any woman who had covered her head for a man and was not his wife would be punished by the authorities In this way the abuse began to disappear. He also had a law made to provide regular public assistance for the poor; and yet another laying down that the Angelus be rung three times a day, in the morning, at midday, and in the evening so that people might pray as in Rome. Although in the beginning his health had been good, he now fell seriously ill. When he was better, he decided to go and settle the business which the Companions had entrusted to him, and to set off without any money. His brother was very annoyed about this and felt humiliated that he should set out on foot. In the evening the Pilgrim yielded to him to the extent of going as far as the border of the Province on horseback with his brother and relations.

90. But once he was out of the Province, he dismounted and without accepting anything, went off towards Pamplona. He went to Almazan the country of Fr. Lainez, then to Siguenza and Toledo, and from Toledo to Valencia. In all the places where the Companions had their homes he never accepted anything, though they insistently made him generous offers.

At Valencia he spoke with Castro who was a Carthusian monk. When he wanted to take ship for Genoa, his friends begged him not to do so, telling him that there were reports that Barbarossa was on the seas with a large fleet of galleys etc. But although they told him enough stories to make him afraid nothing could make him hesitate in the least.

91. He embarked on a big ship and endured the storm mentioned earlier on, when he said that he came closed to death three times.

On arrival at Genoa, he took the road to Bologna and suffered greatly on the way. There was one time in particular when he lost his way and took a path which ran along beside a river which was down below, whilst the path was on high ground. As he advanced along the road it became more and more narrow and eventually became so narrow that he could neither advance nor turn back. So he began to crawl on all fours and went along in this way for a good distance. He was terrified, because every time he moved, he was afraid of falling into the river. That was the greatest exertion and the hardest physical effort he ever experienced but in the end he came safely out of it. In order to enter Bologna he had to cross a little wooden bridge and he fell off it. As he picked himself up, covered with filth and wet through, many people standing around had a good laugh at his expense. Entering Bologna, he began to beg for alms but did not get a single quatrino, even though he went all over the city. He was ill for a time in Bologna and afterwards went on to Venice still travelling in the same fashion.

CHAPTER X

92. During this period in Venice, he occupied himself in giving the Exercises and other spiritual conversations. The most notable people to whom he gave them are Master Pietro Contarini, Master Gaspar de Doctis, and a Spaniard named Rosas. There was also another Spaniard there, named the Bachelor Hoces, who was in close contact with the Pilgrim and also with the Bishop of Chiete.[3] Although he had a certain inclination towards making the Exercises, he did not put it into practice. Eventually, he resolved to do them. After he had been in them for three or four days, he spoke his mind to the Pilgrim and told him that, on account of what a certain person had said to him, he had been afraid lest he should teach him some harmful doctrine through the Exercises. For this reason he had brought a selection of books with him so that he could refer to them in case the Pilgrim wanted to lead him astray. However, he received very considerable help from the Exercises, and eventually decided to follow the Pilgrim's way of life. He was also the first of the Companions to die.

93. The Pilgrim also suffered another persecution in Venice. Many people were saying that he had been burnt in effigy in Spain and Paris. This talk went so far that a legal trial was held and the sentence was given in favour of the Pilgrim.

3. In the original – Cette. Though some authorities suggest that this might refer to Ceuta in North Africa, Chiete (the diocese of Gian Petro Carafa) seems the more probable interpretation.

The nine Companions arrived in Venice at the beginning of 1537. There they split up and went to serve in various hospitals. After two or three months, they all went to Rome to obtain a blessing for their journey to Jerusalem. The Pilgrim did not go because of Doctor Ortiz and also on acount of the new Theatine Cardinal. The Companions came back from Rome with credit notes for 200 or 300 scudi, which had been given them as an alms to help towards their journey to Jerusalem. They did not want to accept money except in the form of credit notes. These they returned to their benefactors when they were unable to go to Jerusalem.

The Companions came back to Venice in the same way as they had left, on foot and begging their way, but divided into three groups in such a way that these were always composed of different nationalities. In Venice, those who were not priests were ordained and it was the Nuntio, aftewards Cardinal Verallo, who was in Venice at the time, who gave the permission. They were ordained "*ad titulum paupertatis*" and all made vows of chastity and poverty.

94. That year no ships went to the Levant since the Venetians had broken off relations with the Turks. So, seeing their hopes of a passage receding, they separated and went to different parts of the Venetian territory, with the intention of waiting for the year as they had decided. If at the end of this time they had not obtained a passage, they would go to Rome.

The Pilgrim's lot was to go with Favre and Lainez to Vicenza. There they found a house outside the city without a door or a window to it where they slept on a little straw they had brought with them. Two of them went twice a day into the town to beg for alms and they collected so little that they could hardly keep themselves alive. Their usual fare was a little cooked bread, when they had it, and the one who stayed behind cooked it. They spent forty days like this giving themselves entirely to prayer.

95. After the forty days, Master Jean Codure arrived and all four decided to start preaching. Each of the four went to a different public square and on the same day and at the same time they began to preach. They first of all shouted at the top of their voices and attracted the people's attention by waving their caps. These sermons caused a great stir in the city, and many people were moved to devotion and they themselves obtained in greater abundance what they needed for their bodily sustenance.

During the time at Vicenza, the Pilgrim had many spiritual visions and many almost regular consolations, in contrast to what had happened at Paris, especially when he was getting ready for the priesthood in Venice, and when he was preparing himself to say Mass; in all the journeyings he experienced great spiritual visitations of the sort he had been accustomed to have at Manresa. Whilst he was at Vicenza he heard that one of the Companions who was at Bassano was ill and at death's door. He himself was sick with the fever at the time. Nevertheless, he set out and walked so quickly that his companion Favre could not keep up with him. On the way he received an assurance from God and said so to Favre, that the companion would not die of this illness. When he arrived at Bassano, the sick man was greaty comforted and immediately recovered. Then they all returned to Vicenza and stayed there for some time, all ten of them. Some of them went out into the villages around Vicenza begging for alms.

96. Then, at the end of the year, since they had still not found a ship, they decided to go to Rome and the Pilgrim with them, since on the other occasion when the companions had gone there, the two persons about whom he had doubts had shown great good will towards them. They went to Rome in three or four groups, the Pilgrim with Favre and Lainez, and on this journey he received a very special visitation from God.

After being ordained, he had decided to remain for a year without saying Mass, preparing himself and praying to Our Lady that she might be pleased to put him with her Son. One day then, a few miles outside Rome, in a church whilst he was praying, he felt such a change in his soul and saw so clearly that God the Father put him with Christ his Son that he did not dare doubt about this fact that God the Father put him with his Son.

97. On their arrival in Rome he said to his companions that he saw that the windows were shut, meaning that they would have much opposition there. He also said "We need to be very much on our guard and not enter into conversation with women unless they be of high rank." It can be mentioned, a propos of this, that later in Rome Master Francis heard a lady's confession and visited her on several occasions to treat of spiritual matters, and who was later found to be pregnant. But it was the Lord's will that the one responsible for this misdeed was discovered. The same thing happened to Jean Codure with one of his spiritual daughters who was caught with a man.

CHAPTER XI

98. From Rome the Pilgrim went to Monte Cassino to give the Exercises to Doctor Ortiz and stayed there for forty days. During hs stay he saw on one occasion the Bachelor Hocez entering heaven and he wept copiously and had great spiritual consolation at the sight. He saw this so clearly that if he said the opposite it would seem to him that he was lying. He brought Francisco Estrada back from Monte Cassino with him.

On his return to Rome he occupied himself in helping souls. At that time they were still at the vineyard,[4] and gave the spiritual Exercises to several persons at the same time; one of them lived at Sta. Maria Maggiore and another at Ponte Sixto.

Then the persecutions began. Michael began to cause trouble and to speak ill of the Pilgrim, so he had him called before the Governor, having first showed the Governor a letter in which Michael praised the Pilgrim highly. The Governor examined Michael and the result was that he banished him from Rome.

Then Mudarra and Barreda began their persecution. They affirmed that the Pilgrim and his companions were fugitives from Spain, Paris and Venice. Eventually, in the presence of the Governor and the then Legate of Rome, both of them avowed that they had nothing ill to say of them, neither about their way of life, nor their teaching. The Legate ordered silence to be observed about the whole affair but the Pilgrim did not accept this and said that he wanted a final judgement. This pleased

4. The Companions' first residence in Rome.

neither the Legate nor the Governor nor even those who were at first favourable to the Pilgrim. At last after a few months, the Pope returned to Rome. The Pilgrim went to see him at Frascati and gave him his reasons. The Pope took the matter in hand and ordered a judgement to be pronounced; it was in favour of the Pilgrim.

With the help of the Pilgrim and the Companions, certain good works were begun in Rome as for example, the Catechumens, St. Martha the Orphans etc.

Master Nadal can tell the rest.

99. After these things had been recounted, on the 20th of October, I asked the Pilgrim about the Exercises and the Constitutions, desirous of knowing how he had written them. He told me that he had not written the Exercises all at one time. But when he observed certain things in his soul and found them useful, it seemed to him they could be of use to others too, so he put them down in writing, as for example about the examination of conscience with the method of the lines. He told me that he had taken the elections in particular from that diversity of spirits and thoughts he had had at Loyola when he was still ill with his leg. And he told me that he would speak to me about the Constitutions in the evening.

The same day, immediately after supper, with the look of one who is more than ordinarily recollected, he called me over and made a sort of protestation to me. The substance of it was to manifest his purpose and the simplicity with which he had narrated these things, saying that he was quite sure he had not exaggerated; that he had often offended Our Lord since he had begun to serve him but that he had never consented to a mortal sin; rather he grew steadily in devotion, that is to say in the ease in finding God, and at the present time more so than in his whole life. Always and at whatever time he wanted to find God he found him. That now too, he frequently had visions especially of the sort mentioned previously – seeing Christ like the sun. This happened often when he was dealing with important matters, and made him "venire in confirmatione."

100. He also had many visions when he said Mass, and when he was writing the Constitutions he also had them very frequently; he could now affirm this more easily since he wrote down every day what passed in his soul, and he found this written down. So he showed me a very large sheaf of writings part of which he read to me. For the most part they were visions which came to him in confirmation of some part of the Constitutions, sometimes seeing God the Father, at other times all three Persons of the Trinity, at other times again Our Lady, who was interceding, or on other occasions giving him confirmation.

In particular he told me about the deliberation over which he spent forty days saying Mass every day and daily with many tears, and the question was whether the Church should have any rents and if the Society could benefit by them.

101. The method he followed when he wrote the Constitutions was to say Mass every day and present the point he was dealing with to God and to pray about it, and he always prayed and said Mass with tears. I wanted to see all these papers on the Constitutions, and asked him to leave them with me for a short time; he did not want to.

translated by Fr. William Yeomans, S.J.

FOREWORD

The subject of this book, Ignatius of Loyola, was a Basque noble who served in the Spanish army, and who later went on to found a religious order for men, the Society of Jesus – known to most as the Jesuits. The Society has played a considerable role in the history of the intervening centuries since its foundation. What is perhaps less widely known is that Ignatius developed a distinctive way of praying and relating to God, to some extent articulated in his book, the *Spiritual Exercises*. This we have learned to call 'Ignatian spirituality'. The spirituality and the religious order are of course intimately linked with one another. For at the heart of the *Constitutions* of the Society of Jesus, which it took Ignatius several years to compose, lie the *Spiritual Exercises*. What is much less known is that in order to facilitate the promulgation of the *Constitutions*, Ignatius was asked by his fellow Jesuits to tell the story of his life. After considerable delay on his part, they finally teased it out of him. This story is the result of Ignatius's meditations on his own life, which is an integral part of the *Spiritual Exercises*. Thus the story of his life proves to be nested down in the heart of the works of Ignatius of Loyola. And it is this inner nest, this story, which is the subject of our book. In this commentary, I will be sharing with you my reading of his *Autobiography*. Together we will be looking at the life of this man, who discovered more and more freedom in so far as he discerned the ways of God and decided again and again to follow where they led him. He came to love these ways of discerning and deciding, as he came to love the way that God responded and surprised him again and again. Indeed, he came to love God. And as he came to discover the various ways in which God works, he also learned a variety of ways of cooperating with him. Paradoxically, as we shall see, he grew freer to the extent that he followed God more closely, bound himself to him, and abandoned himself to his will, which was his love and his desire.

This story, dictated in the middle of the sixteenth century, holds a considerable relevance for us in the twenty-first. The reasons may appear as we get into the plot of the story, into the transformations of the main character through a series of decisions which lead on from one to another, and into the themes that emerge. In the course of this paraphrase of the story, I will occasionally dwell upon various points which concern those transformations and themes, but we will find that it is in the way the plot moves on that the freedom of the man is revealed, and that this is more significant than any particular theme. The man himself is the story.[1] There is indeed a logic linking the themes as they emerge in the story, but it is not so much the logic of Aristotle, with the importance it gives to quantity (all, some, one), quality (affirmation and negation), and relation (of subject to object, major term to minor term, major premise to minor premise), but more like the logic of Hegel, in its attempt to affirm, negate, and then negate the negation. It is not my intention to discuss the merits of Aristotle's or Hegels's logic in itself, but only to point to the way Ignatius's story unfolds and develops.

This attempt to find the inner logic of the *Autobiography* may be of interest not only to Jesuits, but also to anyone who is studying Ignatian spirituality, as well as to those who practise it through following the *Spiritual Exercises*. It is my claim that there is a pattern playing just underneath the surface of Ignatius's story. The term 'pattern' tends to evoke a visual image, so it is frequently interchanged with the term 'rhythm', which, though more auditory, does introduce the notion of time. The pattern is also likened to a field of force, which draws the reader into the text and which surrounds the text itself with readers. The pattern itself emerges only gradually, and it would be doing some violence to the readers of this book if we were to pretend to give them an adequate summary of that pattern here. But, by way of introduction, an inadequate summary would perhaps be better than none, and may serve to alert the reader to what is to follow.

The pattern that emerges is one of oppositions that are eventually, temporarily and more or less completely, reconciled. The oppositions are sometimes between persons, even persons who are committed to the same ideals, but they are also within persons. The physical is opposed to the spiritual, the exterior to the interior, the active to the passive, the past to the future, hesitation to decisiveness, dynamic oscillation to static pause, day to night, chance to necessity, self to other, creature to creator, word to silence, excess to parsimony, and vice versa. But these oppositions often become appositions, that is, so positioned, so appointed with respect to one another within counterpointing rhythms, that a further level of pattern is revealed. This essay labours at revealing that pattern and sharing it with the readers. It attempts to go to the heart of the matter and stay there, by which I mean that it aims at going to the heart of the text and sharing what we find there. I have called this pattern a 'shy' pattern because, like a shy person, it does not reveal itself at the first encounter. In fact, it is only as we get to recognize the pattern over a period of time that we can come to know its true nature. At the heart of Ignatius's story, reconciling the oppositions listed above, beckoning him always onwards, teaching him to find his balance, is Jesus himself.

As we follow Ignatius in the twists and turns of his life, I shall on occasion stand back from the particular events of the story to view the picture as it is revealed so far.

Underlying themes will emerge, concerning the shy pattern, concerning Ignatius's own efforts to strip himself of all that could hinder him in his search and concerning the vision, which, whether explicit or implicit in his daily dealings with others, accompanied his pilgrimage. These themes will often be dealt with in short 'asides', printed in italics to differentiate them from the ongoing commentary on the episodes of the Autobiography. Clearly, the commentary and the 'asides' both concern the same story, and by the end of the book the two forms of writing will have merged.

Ignatius's experience is embedded in that of the human race, and, in order to illuminate it, I have occasionally made a comparison with other fields of human experience: art, music and literature, where what it is to be human is expressed with a particular intensity. Comments and references of this kind are mostly to be found in the *Notes* at the end of the book.

Chapter 1

THE CONTEXT OF THE STORY-TELLING

Ignatius died about nine months after he finished telling the story of his life. Two of his companions, Jerome Nadal and Louis Gonçalves da Camara, had been instrumental in getting him to tell that story. Some years after he died, they composed Prologues relating how and why they had pressed him to begin it and to complete it as soon as possible. At the end of the story, there is a brief Epilogue (*Autobiography*, paragraphs 99–101), in which Camara describes his final interview with Ignatius. A careful reading of these Prologues and the Epilogue shows that they contain various themes that are also found in Ignatius's story. In addition to the themes, there is also a certain continuity of plot. From the relationship between Ignatius's story and the stories of those who succeeded in getting it out of him, there emerges an almost hidden drama that unites the whole book.

1. *The Prologues and the Epilogue*

Both the Prologues show that Ignatius was sometimes spontaneously drawn to tell particular incidents of his life to his Jesuit companions. When Nadal first pressed him to tell the whole story, Ignatius resisted; later he agreed to the request, but he put it off again and again until pressing events finally brought the story to its end.

The final interview in the Epilogue not only ended the story, but led to a further revelation. For in the course of answering questions about the way he composed his two books, the *Spiritual Exercises* and the *Constitutions of the Society of Jesus*, Ignatius volunteered the information that he was writing another book, a *Diary*, which he kept to help him in his composition of the *Constitutions*. This *Diary* was part of a large pile of 'notes' that Ignatius referred to in the course of the conversation. The context of the final interview also revealed the determining role that letters played in the life rhythms of Ignatius. For it had often been more urgent affairs that had kept Ignatius from dictating the story of his life. It was the more urgent sending of letters that would limit the amount of time that he could give to his companion during the final interview.

Thus, the further revelation was not just that there was another book, the *Diary*, as well as the letters, but that the *Diary* and the letters were part of a rhythm that encompassed the compositions as well as other activities. It was the ordinary urgency of keeping up with the daily mail that made the end of his narration of the past resolve itself quite simply into the everyday tasks of the present, in view of a future that depended upon them. In other words, although both the notes and the letters are previously mentioned in the story, it is only at the end that the written medium of the letters takes precedence over the dictation and writing of the *Autobiography*. The point of paramount interest is not that one activity takes precedence over the other, but that one alternates with the other. At certain times the more distant communication took precedence over the more proximate; and the more particular took precedence over the more general. At other times, the opposite was true. The higher truth was grasped in the recognition that there was an oscillation, a relay or rhythm, that arose in going from one part of the pattern to another: there was a time to speak, and a time to write; a time for the story of one's life, and a time for the diary; a time for writing letters, and a time for posting them.

This rhythmic pattern is not thematized in his story. This is not because Ignatius was unable to thematize. On the contrary, the *Spiritual Exercises* and the *Constitutions* are proof of the degree to which he could abstract from his personal experience the themes and structures that he had found there. But in this instance his companions didn't want him to follow that tendency. Instead the whole *Autobiography* was the result of their efforts to get him away from his more abstract work on the *Constitutions*, and away from the demands of daily meetings and correspondence, long enough for him to give his full attention to narrating the concrete experiences of his life. They were trying to get him to tell a personal story that could accompany and counter-balance the *Constitutions*, and flesh them out, thereby creating an equilibrium that neither text could have by itself. There was a need for this which Ignatius did not seem to have noticed, but which some of his companions considered to be essential to the founding of their group. This is part of the drama which is now to be outlined.

2. *A dramatic framework*

The drama was not just that the companions needed the concrete story, but that, as two of them composed their Prologues and Epilogue, they were varying some of the same themes which governed the story that Ignatius had told them, and which they had taken such efforts to obtain and transcribe. Did they realize this? Have readers of the book ever realized this? For it is as if the book of the *Autobiography*, as it stands there with its two Prologues and its Epilogue, contains a pattern that is 'shy', that doesn't appear on a first and easy reading. The shy pattern remains there, like a figure in the carpet on which we walk without noticing it. And yet it is asking us to notice it, to listen to it, and to respond to it. It is imperative to catch on to the rhythmic pattern contained in the *Autobiography*, if one intends to read the book at the level on which it was written. The *Autobiography* of Ignatius of Loyola is not just a story, and yet it is a story. It is not just the story of a pilgrim, but the story itself is a sort of pilgrim trying to reach a place somewhere inside its readers. And that is why this book about a book refers to it as *The Pilgrim Story*.

Why is it imperative to catch on to the rhythmic pattern of the book? For whom is it so imperative? First of all for Ignatius's companions, since the story was written for them as a sort of testament by their founding Father. But the book may also interest other persons and groups, since it is imperative for any group which wants to be faithful to its original purpose and founder, to know the story of its origins. And it is of great help to anyone who has chosen Ignatius as their guide in the spiritual life to understand how he came to write about his life. The story of how two of Ignatius's companions finally got the story out of him, and of how Ignatius acted towards them and for them in the process, and what God was doing with them all, is not only interesting in itself, but casts light on and receives light from the content of the story Ignatius himself told.

Reflection and Conversion: Las Meninas

Roman Jakobson, the distinguished literary theorist, has written that every great work of art does nothing but tell the story of its birth. Great works of art may do much more than that. The Autobiography *of Ignatius of Loyola is a work of art, not only because it is telling the story of its own birth in a highly condensed yet strictly constructed way, but also because it is a collective effort, deeply set within a framework of Prologues and Epilogue that reflect and deepen the dimensions of the original story. To give a comparison: in Velasquez's well-known painting* Las Meninas *we see a number of people either looking at us or concerned with those who are looking at us. Actually, in the fiction of the painting, they are in the studio of a painter who is painting two persons occupying the place where we are looking from, and who are reflected in the mirror on the back wall of the studio. They are the King and Queen of Spain, and we are standing in their place, having their view – not only of the artist and the great room behind him, but of their daughter, the Infanta Margarita, with her attendants and dwarves and dog. It is the mirror on the back wall which tells us whom they are all looking at, whereas it is we who are looking at them. The King and Queen are standing at a place where we might expect to see our own faces. They are standing for us. Such a painting puts the whole art of painting into place, precisely here where it affirms this capacity of the artist to bring about this almost magical reversal of roles, heightening our awareness and appreciation of who we are, who they are, and how we are. Bach did something quite similar in the* Art of Fugue, *as we shall see. My contention is that the Autobiography of Ignatius brings about a similar reflection and conversion. It contains its 'mirror' or reflection which questions the reader – just as Ignatius began to question himself when he was confined to bed and spent time reading over books and wondering at their effects upon him.*

This testament that Ignatius left to his companions may not yet have been fully understood – reading his *Autobiography* is a 'spiritual exercise'. In order to discover the vitality of that testament, I will describe the inter-connected drama of the two Prologues. Then, after retelling and commenting on Ignatius's story, I will show how the Epilogue complements and completes the Prologues by repeating one of the major themes of the story itself.

3. *Nadal's Prologue*

According to his Prologue, Fr Jerome Nadal was the first of the companions to take the initiative of asking Ignatius to tell the story of his life. This occurred in August, 1551. Nadal had been delegated to promulgate the *Constitutions* of the 'Companions of Jesus', and thus he took particular interest in the progress of the composition of the text. Ignatius had been working on this text since 1544. Although it was not definitive, and only partially approved by the assembled companions, this was the text that Nadal had been charged to explain and discuss when he travelled from one community to the other.

3.1 *The initial request*

On that day in August, 1551, Nadal heard Ignatius refer to an extraordinary insight that he had just received. Ignatius said: 'I have just been higher than heaven!' When Nadal asked him what he had seen, Ignatius changed the subject of conversation. Nadal pressed him on the point, saying that his life story from the time of his conversion would be like a testament or fatherly instruction that would greatly help the Jesuits. Ignatius claimed that he was too busy. He added however that Nadal, Polanco, his secretary, and Cogordan, the treasurer, should say three Masses, during which they could raise the matter before God. Afterwards they should tell him if they still thought that the matter was important.

The companions did as Ignatius asked. They said their Masses, and found their desire for his story as firm as before. They repeated their request that Ignatius write down the story of his life, as a sort of testament for the future companions. On hearing this, Ignatius agreed to tell his story, but he didn't do so immediately. We do not know why. A brief presentation of the context may clarify his deferment of the matter.

3.2 *The context of the request*

In order to understand the pressures on Nadal, it is necessary to outline four distinct stages in the composition of the *Constitutions*: the Sketch, the Formula, Text A, and Text B.

Late in 1537, the companions arrived in Rome, coming from Venice, as Ignatius would describe. Their plan to go to work in the Holy Land had been frustrated, due to the political tensions between Venice and the Ottoman Turks. No pilgrim ship left during that year.

During the following year the Jesuits worked in various apostolates in Rome, but, in order to obtain official approval of their work, in early 1539 they composed a Sketch on the nature of their group and its apostolate. This was developed into what was called a Formula.

In 1540, on the basis of this Formula, the group received Papal approval as a new group of religious men. In the spring of 1541 they met to discuss the composition of a first draft of their *Constitutions*, and this draft was signed in late March or early April. That same April, Ignatius was unanimously elected the first General of the Society, and among other duties he was required to oversee or compose a final draft of the signed *Constitutions*.

Ignatius began to undertake that task in 1544, and worked on it for seven years. The completed draft, Text A, was examined by the assembled Jesuits in 1551. This is the version of the *Constitutions* which Nadal was delegated to promulgate. Text A was not yet fully approved by the companions, however, and Ignatius continued to work on it, in what is referred to as Text B, during the remaining five years of his life. His health continued to be very fragile. In 1550 he was ill to the point of death. The uncertainty of his ever completing Text B added to the concerns of Nadal. This brings us up to the time of Nadal's request for Ignatius's life story.

The reader may be curious to know what eventually happened to these efforts of the companions to compose a final text, to approve it fully among themselves, and to obtain official and written approval from ecclesiastical authorities. Two years after Ignatius's death, Pope Paul IV orally confirmed the Institute of the Society, and that same year the congregation of the Jesuits approved the Spanish text and the Latin translation of the *Constitutions* (presumably Text B). Twenty-five years later, in 1583, Pope Gregory XIII approved the Institute of the Society, including its *Constitutions*, in a special bull.

3.3 *Reasons for the request: Nadal's dilemma*

In view of the possibly imminent death of Ignatius, the unfinished state of the composition of the *Constitutions*, and Nadal's request for a 'testament' for future companions, I would offer the hypothesis that Nadal had found the *Constitutions* a rather abstract text to promulgate. Where had the vitality of the companions disappeared to? Why was it that the *Constitutions* seemed to be undoing what was better done in the Formula? What was it about this literary genre that tended to kill and then embalm the very body whose life it was trying to preserve and to further? Nadal saw something from the viewpoint of his apostolic work that Ignatius perhaps did not notice in his office: Ignatius was thinking the 'Companions of Jesus' back into an abstraction.

Or *was* he? Could it not also have been that Ignatius was just simplifying his design, and that it required great distance to see the single-minded sweep of the *Constitutions*, as they began from the admission of postulants (Part I) and ended in the description of the Superior General who had the task of over-seeing 'how the whole body of the Society can be preserved and developed in its well-being' (Part X).

However that may be, Nadal must have asked: What ever happened to the Ignatius who once read Amadis de Gaul? What happened to the chivalry, to the lives of the saints, to the life and mission of Jesus? Nadal was interested in reversing the series: peeling away the *Constitutions* to find, not just the *Spiritual Exercises*, but the man who discovered them in his concrete life; not just the life of the wise saint, but the life of the sinful fool: the one who experienced a conversion that continued through the different periods of his life, across events that Ignatius could speak about in such spontaneous and moving ways. Nadal was reaching for something deeper than *Constitutions* because he needed to. He needed some of the vitality that came from Ignatius when he spoke of his personal experiences, such as the great insight or grace that he casually mentioned one day, and then refused to enlarge upon. Nadal needed a story that would relate in a concrete and vivid way the searching experiences and the discoveries from which the companions and their *Constitutions* arose. Ignatius's story must bear his character, his signature; it must transmit something of his fire, his contrasts, his spirit. It would be in touching upon what was more particular and even unique to him that he would allow the most valuable general truths to emerge concretely and freshly.

Such is my hypothesis on the dilemma of Nadal and the reasons that pushed him to encourage Ignatius to tell his story.

3.4 *The second request*

Two years later, in 1553, when Nadal returned to Rome from Sicily on his way to Spain, he asked Ignatius if he had done anything on his *Autobiography*. 'Nothing at all,' Ignatius replied. Faced with this 'nothing', Nadal changed his approach to the subject and in a typically Ignatian way he said something like this: 'Very well. For two years I've been asking you to tell the story you promised us, and I assure you it will be more useful than ever. But since you don't want to do it, I can tell you that we are perfectly resigned one way or the other. If you do it, we will know how to make good use of it. If you don't, it doesn't matter. We will have the same confidence we would have had if you *had* written it.'

Ignatius did not answer. But Nadal believed that on that same day Ignatius began to dictate his life to Camara, the administrator of the house.

Thus ends Nadal's Prologue. It describes a succession of contrasting episodes: from the initial exaltation of Ignatius about some 'great graces', to his refusal to say more about them; from his request that Masses be said on the request, to his agreement to tell his story; from his doing nothing about it for two years, to his sudden decision to do so.

Why did Ignatius finally yield? Nadal thought he had the answer: it was because he himself had shifted from pressing Ignatius on the project, to professing a radical indifference to it. Thus he gave Ignatius the freedom he needed. In a sense, Nadal disarmed Ignatius by using his own arm: the indifference mentioned in the opening paragraph of the *Exercises* in the 'Principle and Foundation' [23]. (Throughout this book, references in square brackets are to the paragraphs of the *Spiritual Exercises*).

> To attain this, we need to make ourselves indifferent towards all created things, provided the matter is subject to our free choice and there is no prohibition. Thus for our part we should not want health more than sickness, wealth more than poverty, fame more than disgrace, a long life more than a short one – and so with everything else; desiring and choosing only what conduces more to the end for which we are created.

But this may not be the only answer. Another even more practical and immediate reason for Ignatius's change of mind is given by Fr Louis Gonzalez da Camara, the administrator of the house. In his Prologue, he would show that the telling of Ignatius's story would not only be of use for the companions in the future, but it would be most helpful for Ignatius's companions in the present. Of those companions, Camara names first of all himself.

4. *Camara's Prologue*

Camara was the man to whom Ignatius dictated the story of his life. First I will describe the initial incident which led Ignatius to this choice, followed by an outline of the three periods of dictation. Then I will analyze possible reasons for Ignatius's behaviour towards him, in view of what Camara relates about himself. We can then draw certain conclusions from the two Prologues, when they are combined. This will help us to understand what is at issue in the Epilogue.

4.1 *The initial incident*

Camara's Prologue is slightly longer than Nadal's. It confirms and complements Nadal's information, but at times it stands in counter-point to it. His Prologue begins with all the precision of time and place that justifies his reputation among the companions for retaining details. His talent in this respect made him a likely choice as a faithful transcriber of Ignatius's story. But this does not seem to be the reason why Ignatius chose him for that task.

The choice came about in the following way. One morning in early August, 1553, Ignatius was in the garden of the Roman house with Camara. He was counselling him on a personal problem of vanity, or vainglory, that Camara had raised. As in the initial incident with Nadal, Ignatius spontaneously told Camara of an episode in his own life. It was not the story of an extraordinary grace, but rather the story of a difficulty. Ignatius told him how he too, when he was a pilgrim, had had to fight against the vice of desiring to impress people. He told of his days in Barcelona, when he was begging for sea-biscuits to take with him on his voyage to Italy. He made deliberate efforts not to mention that he intended to go to Jerusalem, lest people be impressed, and lest he bask in their good impressions. When he mentioned Rome as his destination, however, he once received a humorous and unexpected reply from a woman who refused to give him any alms for Rome because people seldom returned changed in any way. The very first lines of the *Autobiography* announce the theme of Ignatius's vanity, and it is central to the whole book:

> Up to the age of twenty-six he was a man given over to the pleasures of the world. Out of a vain, vehement desire to win renown, he took special delight in the career of a soldier.

An hour or so after this conversation in the garden, Ignatius was at the dinner table, and he raised the subject of his *Autobiography*. As he would relate later, in recounting his pilgrimage to the Holy Land, it was not typical of him to raise subjects at meals, unless they were comments on what had already been said. He recalled that although several companions had asked him to write the story of his life, he had never got round to it. But after the conversation with Camara that morning, and after having recollected himself in his room, he had been so interiorly moved that he had decided to begin telling his story. He would do so, not by writing it himself, but by dictating it to Camara. Thus he would satisfy Nadal's request to help companions in the future, and he would also be helping Camara now. By telling his story to one man, he could answer the request of the other. This kind of combination of parallels and opposites is the signature of Ignatius. It forms a kind of baroque knot, a friendly dialectic, which is at the heart of the shy pattern in Ignatius's life.[2]

This happened in early August, 1553, almost two years after Nadal had asked Ignatius to write his life as a testament or fatherly instruction. Again, however, Ignatius deferred the story-telling, claiming that ill health or urgent business demanded the delay. Then one day in early September Ignatius called Camara and began to tell the story of his life.

4.2 *The three periods of dictation*

Nadal and Camara disagree on the date of that day in September, the former claiming that it occurred in 1554, the latter being sure that it could only have taken place in 1553, since Nadal had spent 1554 in Sicily. What seems to have occurred is this. After their conversation in the garden, Ignatius chose Camara to be the transcriber of his story. That occurred in early August. Nadal came through Rome shortly afterwards and learned that Ignatius had done nothing on his *Autobiography*; he thereupon changed his approach and expressed his indifference. The same day, in early September, Ignatius began to dictate his story to Camara. The initial incident of Camara's story dove-tails into Nadal's story, between the latter's first and second requests. Thus the actual dictation only took place after Ignatius had twice rebounded from one man to the other: first, from Nadal in 1551, when he agreed to tell his story, to Camara in August, 1553, when he chose him as transcriber; secondly, from Nadal the following September, when he agreed to begin the dictation to Camara, to Camara on that same day, when he actually began. Ignatius seems to have been waiting patiently for a convergence of conditions and opportunities, yet he was also gathering momentum amidst the other pressures of his life so that the energy built up by his very resistance might become a positive force when the opportunities finally converged.

The first period of dictation, that September of 1553, stopped shortly afterwards, and Ignatius excused himself for the usual reasons: his poor physical health and the urgent demands of the apostolates. The excuses continued for more than a year!

When Nadal returned to the house in Rome in October 1554, Camara says that Nadal was delighted to learn that the *Autobiography* was under way, and he urged Camara to keep pressing Ignatius to finish it, because this was truly 'to found the Society'.

The dictation did not continue until March 1555, but that period also was soon interrupted, for toward the end of the month Pope Julius III died; this was followed shortly by the death of his successor, Pope Marcellus II. The result of this was that Cardinal Carafa – a man with whom Ignatius had had difficulties in Venice back in 1537 – was elected Pope; he took the name of Paul IV. Still a further irony is that it was this man who confirmed the Institute of the Society of Jesus in 1558, two years after Ignatius's death. Due to the great heat that summer of 1555, and many urgent affairs, Ignatius put off continuing his story until the autumn.

The third and last period began on September 22, 1555, and it ended less than a month later on October 20. On that date Camara had his final interview with Ignatius, as related in the Epilogue.

Ignatius died the following summer on July 31, 1556. In view of the obstacles that he often had to overcome in order to continue and complete his narrative, the dictation was completed none too soon.

4.3 *Reasons for the deferment: Camara's behaviour*

The question arises: To what degree was Ignatius's deferment of the dictation a way of correcting Camara's vanity and curiosity? For Camara admitted to three weaknesses. A conversation with Ignatius about his vanity was the initial incident which led to the first period of dictation. He would speak of his tardiness and curiosity in the course of describing the third period. It is true that Ignatius gave specific reasons for putting off the dictation: his bad health, his heavy administrative work as General Superior, and his concern over the rapid succession of Popes. But we must take a longer look at Camara and what he says of himself, for he is also indirectly revealing something about Ignatius.

Camara had his strengths and weaknesses. His precision in noting times and places was quite the opposite of Nadal's. Nadal, for instance, said that it was on his return from Sicily in 1554 that he was finally able to get Ignatius to begin telling his story; but from other sources it is clear that Nadal spent that year in Sicily. It was Camara who remembered the correct date of his return, which coincided with his own role in the process of getting Ignatius to begin.

But Camara's weaknesses require further attention. At first, vanity and curiosity seem like a strange and unrelated set of weaknesses. But on second thoughts, they are deeply related: curiosity is one of the expressions of vanity. An excessive interest in certain subjects reveals some defect in one's own self-appropriation. The periods of dictation reflect certain difficulties that Camara has in his relations with Ignatius. Before the first dictation began, the difficulty was one of vanity; during the third and last, the problems centre around tardiness and curiosity.

❖ Camara's vanity

Camara had spoken of his vanity to Ignatius on August 4, 1553. Ignatius advised him to get into the habit of frequently referring everything to God, and to offer to God everything in him that was good, acknowledging that it came from God, and thanking Him for it. Three things can be noted about this advice. First, this advice is identical with the act of grateful and loving recognition which is found at the end of the *Spiritual Exercises*, in the 'Contemplation for Obtaining Divine Love' [230–237], where the exercitant contemplates the source and end of the graces of his or her whole life. Secondly, this act of offering all to God and retaining nothing for oneself is at the heart of Jesus's way of offering himself to God for the sake of others on the cross and in the Mass. Thus, Ignatius's advice to Camara to offer himself gratefully to God, thereby repeating the offering of the Mass, repeats in a discreet way the advice he gave to Nadal and the two other companions, when he asked them to say three Masses to see whether he should really set himself to writing an *Autobiography*. Thirdly, in the final interview Camara learned that the Mass was an integral moment in the method Ignatius used to compose the *Constitutions*. The cure of Camara's vanity was to be found in his recognition of the true source and end of everything and anything he might be tempted to be vain about.

Perhaps it was Camara's ability to be so scrupulously retentive of whatever he heard that constituted the matter of his vanity. Perhaps Camara was tempted to vanity because Ignatius chose him to be the transcriber of his story. But, in so far as Ignatius kept putting it off, Camara's vanity must have been sorely tested.

❖ Camara's tardiness

It was only at the beginning of the third period of dictation, on September 21, 1555, that Camara learned that he had been delegated to take the mail to Spain. Thus his departure from Rome was imminent. Perhaps it was after he learned that he was to leave for Spain that he asked Ignatius to conclude the story before he left. No one was sure whether Ignatius would still be alive when he returned. However the events may have succeeded one another, this was to be the third and last period of dictation, and Camara knew that he must try to get the full story before he left.

Despite the urgency of the situation, Camara admits that he was late for the appointment with Ignatius. For some reason, he thought that Ignatius would be late. On finding that Camara was not at the meeting place on time, Ignatius decided to call off the session for that day. Camara and others insisted so strongly, that Ignatius reconsidered his decision and returned to the appointed place. Thus the final dictations began, as they walked back and forth in the garden – the same garden where two years before Ignatius had told Camara the story about his begging in the streets of Barcelona.

It is not only surprising to find Ignatius more punctual than Camara, but it is even more so to find him reconsidering his decision to break off the appointment. Could it be that Ignatius was trying to communicate something to Camara that he could do in no other way? Was he both correcting Camara and consoling him, to strengthen his accuracy and obedience for the future? After his long deferment of the dictation, could he not have been more patient? The point is that it was not a time for patience, but for action; and Camara was not there. Ignatius acted in consequence: when Camara arrived late, it was Ignatius who was not there. This was Ignatius's character, his signature, as he had come to shape it over the years. If one wants to understand him and his story, one must learn to read them.

❖ Camara's curiosity

Camara, however, goes on to tell how he made yet another mistake that same morning. He was saddened that soon he was no longer to see Ignatius, since he himself was leaving for Spain and Ignatius's bad health led them all to believe that he could die at any time – a belief that Ignatius shared. Camara describes how, as they walked side by side in the garden, he drew his face closer to Ignatius's, the better to observe his expression. Ignatius told him that this bothered him, and asked him not to stare at him. Shortly afterwards, thoughtlessly, Camara approached to stare once more. Ignatius not only repeated his request, but went away! We don't know who or what may have caused him to return, but later that same morning he came again to a corner of the garden and finished the story.

Camara admitted his own weaknesses, probably because they led to further revealing details about Ignatius. Ignatius's contrasting and abrupt behaviour may be signs of a sick man, but they may also be signs of his effort to reach Camara at a deeper level. This is what will emerge from the final interview.

5. *Ignatius's combination of the two requests*

Ignatius's refusals and agreements, his deferments and yet his insistence on precise coordination of appointments, his corrections of Camara, his leaving and then returning – all this indicates that a struggle was going on among these men. Was Ignatius playing with both of them, or playing one off against the other? Or were they all playing out some game with God? As already mentioned, Ignatius combined the request of Nadal for a written text with the need of Camara to overcome his vanity and certain other weaknesses that Camara did not hesitate to mention.

This struggle and combination can be defined with more accuracy. The two Prologues express two different kinds of men, with two different kinds of needs. They form two poles: Nadal is more general in his concerns, while Camara is more particular; Nadal is planning ahead for what will be needed later; Camara has a stronger sense of the past, and can be late for an appointment. These polarities of universality and particularity, of past and future, are found in every person and in every society. They were unified to a high degree, but always fragilely and temporarily, in Ignatius himself, and this was partly due to his living in community and in communication with companions. These companions who surrounded him in the last years before his death are successors of his previous comrades: from the soldiers with whom he defended the besieged castle of Pamplona, to the fellow pilgrims with whom he travelled to the Holy Land, to the groups of students with whom he lived in Barcelona, Alcala, Salamanca, and Paris.

But these latter companions were not just 'companions of Ignatius'; they were members of the 'Company of Jesus'. Something had happened to them: they had come, as a group, to believe in Jesus and in his way of moving in their midst. This is what the Mass meant: it was Jesus's way of moving among them, and of moving them towards him. It was a way of bringing them into intimacy with God, so that they could continue creation, as they had been created in the image of a creative God. If Ignatius and his companions had any creativity, it was due to their approach to that creative source. The various polarities that they managed, in some instances, to combine in a juggling way in their apostolic works, had first been combined by Jesus, with Peter, James, John, Paul and the other apostles. They were especially united by the promise and covenant Jesus made with his apostles at the last supper, and in the death by which he kept his word. This is what is recorded and transformed in the various genres of the writings canonized in the *New Testament*. It is impossible to get at the heart of what animates Ignatius and his companions, if one overlooks the meaning that Jesus gave to his death. For it was there that these various polarities were combined, crossed, and held unto the end.

One can describe the three men as follows:
– NADAL grasped the grand vision of Ignatius and the essence of his method and style.
– CAMARA, with his excellent memory and talent for languages and writing, had a grasp of the fine detail.
– IGNATIUS worked out his combination of both of these tendencies, and he needed both. He needed companions in order to be himself. He was not a superman, an autonomous individualist, who could find his inner equilibrium and purpose by depending only upon his own resources and upon God. He had learned long before of his need for companions. They were not just tactical supports or means for achieving projects that he alone had designed.

One of the major achievements of Ignatius's life was his eventual success in forming a group of men animated by the same spirit and work. The attitudes of Nadal and Camara, as revealed in their Prologues, testify to the degree to which the spirit of Ignatius was also theirs. It is moving, and not sentimental, to realize that these two Prologues were written only some years after the death of the man whom they had so pressed to tell his story. The Prologues witness to the difficulty in doing so, as if they were fighting with a strong fish who wasn't going to give up easily, and whose resistance was going to bring out the best in them all, not just individually, but together. Ignatius seems to have used the differences between Camara and Nadal to make them complement one another, in order to propel both himself and them farther along toward the realization of their goal.

We have reached the end of the Prologues, and stand at the beginning of the story that Ignatius related to Camara.

Chapter 2

PAMPLONA: THE FALLEN FORTRESS

– NO! The story begins with a shout of refusal as Ignatius looked down from the castle fortress of Pamplona on the French troops who surrounded it with their cannons. He, his Captain and his fellow soldiers were outnumbered, but the King of Spain had commanded them to defend the fortress. Despite the odds Ignatius succeeded in convincing the Captain that the fortress must not be surrendered, the attack must be resisted. As dawn approached Ignatius confessed his sins to a fellow soldier, as there was no priestly confessor among them. The French siege began as the cannons fired. The defence held for a while, but when a cannon ball smashed into the legs of Ignatius, his comrades lost courage and the Captain thought it best to surrender. The French entered the fortress and treated the conquered Spanish forces with appropriate formality. They treated the wounded Ignatius with courtesy. One leg was slightly wounded, but the other was severely broken. After twelve to fourteen days at Pamplona, Ignatius was transported in a litter to his family home in the castle of Loyola, some seventy miles away.

Chapter 3

LOYOLA: THE CASTLE HOMESTEAD

The leg did not mend properly. The journey overland had undone the previous setting. The doctors and surgeons decided that the leg must be rebroken and reset. Ignatius agreed to this. His only sign of resistance to the pain during the operation was to clench his fists tightly.

After the operation his condition declined. The doctors found him so close to death that they thought he might not survive. They claimed that if his condition did not improve by midnight, there would be no hope for him. It was the vigil of the feast of Saints Peter and Paul, June 29, 1521. During those dangerous days of illness, Ignatius confessed his sins to the local priest and received the Last Sacraments. He had always had a special devotion to St Peter, and now on this vigil of his patron, he called upon him with special urgency. In response to his prayer, or so he believed, he survived the night and in a few days was out of serious danger.

As the days passed, and as bandages were changed, he discovered that a bone protruded from his slowly mending leg. This physical deformity would severely limit his military career, so he insisted that he be operated upon once more. Despite the protestations of his older brother Martin, and despite the warnings of the surgeons about the surpassing pain to be endured, he persisted in his decision. Once again the clenching of his fists was the only sign of his resistance to the pain. Afterwards, his health did not decline as it had after the first operation. He had to keep to his bed, absorbed in the care of his slowly mending leg. He used every means he could, from ointments to a traction of weights, to make sure that the once broken leg would not be too much shorter than the other.

It was during this long period of his convalescence, from July until the following March, that Ignatius underwent a profound change. He had to stay in one spot, and within the limits of that space he discovered things he had never noticed before. This change took place in four stages. First, he experienced an oscillation between his previous projects and the new perspectives opened by his reading. Secondly, he made a discovery about his own inner life. Thirdly, he had a vision which confirmed him in that discovery. Fourthly, the previous experiences led him to new levels in his social relationships and took the shape of a new project. These stages resulted in his making a decision which was to guide the rest of his story: he decided to go on a pilgrimage to Jerusalem.

1. *The oscillation between previous projects and reading*

Although his condition improved, he was forced to keep off his leg. Confined to his bed, he thought over his personal projects. To distract himself, but also to maintain himself within the world of his values, he asked for his favourite books: the tales of chivalry that were popular at that time. But not a single such tale was to be found in the castle. Two books, however, were found: a Life of Christ and a book on the Lives of the Saints. He did not refuse them, but read them frequently and was increasingly attracted to them. When he interrupted his reading, he noted two after-effects:
– he found himself thinking about what he had just read;
– he found himself returning to his own personal concerns:

those previous projects that had occupied him before he asked for reading material. He became aware of an oscillation between these two poles.

One of the previous projects he entertained was the service of a great lady. He imagined in his heart all the services he intended to perform in order to please her, the various means he would use to reach her country, the verses and declarations he would compose for her, and the feats of arms he would accomplish in her service. His presumptions were so great that he didn't see that the project was unrealizable, for the lady was of a rank of nobility even higher than that of duchess. The woman was an unattainable goal. But the unreflecting immediacy, or vanity, in which he lived blinded him to his limits. The whole thrust of his personal dreams was toward the future, toward action in word and deed, and toward the achievement of honourable recognition. He had yet to discover the present. Once he began to do that, he would become captive of his past, but only for a time, until he finally found his balance in time: a balance always difficult to maintain.

Other thoughts also came to his mind. 'Our Lord' came to his help by bringing thoughts to his mind from his reading. These thoughts oscillated with the 'worldly and vain' preoccupation with his former life and values. He began to think and say to himself that he would do what St Francis and St Dominic had done. The book on the life of Christ gave him an example of a full response to the Father's will and plan. The book on the lives of the saints gave him examples of a variety of responses to Jesus's way of responding to the Father. His reading led him to imagine his own responses. His desire to beg as St Francis did and to preach as St Dominic would later bring him into confrontation with the Franciscans in Jerusalem and with the Dominicans in Salamanca, leading him to decide to go to Paris, where he would assemble a group of men to go about realizing his Jerusalem project in a new way.

2. *The great discovery*

These aspirations to imitate Jesus and the saints lasted for a certain time, but they were succeeded by eating, sleeping, conversing, caring for himself and exercising. Then his worldly preoccupations would return to mind. These two trains of thought shifted back and forth, not just in succession but as an oscillation from one pole to another.

He came to notice a further experience he had been undergoing; he reached a deeper degree of awareness. He noticed the emotional effects and duration of these thoughts. He noticed that his dwelling on a life of saintliness, with its barefoot pilgrimage to Jerusalem, its begging, its meagre diet, not only gave him a certain joy at the time of his thinking about them, but the state of joy tended to last for some time afterwards.[3]

By contrast, the pleasure he had first found in thinking of his worldly preoccupations and plans led to a state of tiredness, dryness and discontent. His new preoccupation with his personal response to Christ's life led him to a prolonged state of joy. One day he simply noticed this; his eyes opened 'a little', and he set about reflecting on this new data. He was no longer reacting so immediately, but he was thinking about his feelings and feeling about his thinking. He had noticed not only the oscillation from one train of thought to another, but he had noticed the different emotional states and their durations, and then he worked his way up to their sources. He came to the conclusion that he was not alone, but rather a field of contending forces – a sort of battlefield – open to the diversity of spirits or moods. These moods were not just psychological, but ontological. That is, there was something – someone – behind them. He concluded that at times he was agitated by the demon, or a spirit against God, and at other times he was moved by a spirit which was for God. One spirit's action tended to cease after a time, whereas the other spirit's action tended to remain longer with him.

Ignatius's habitual tendency to act immediately and

impulsively had broken down. A certain facade had been broken into. He discovered that he himself was a sort of fortress that was under siege. After this discovery, which expanded his sense of time in the present, and which revealed deeper dimensions or levels of present experience, he sank to a deeper truer level of himself; he began to reflect on his past life and his great need to do penance for it in order to be freed from its effects. The stages of the discovery were traceable. He had grown aware of the alternating succession of inner movements which resulted from his reading. That led him to search out the sources of those movements and to identify them as the contrary spirits which were also tempting and inspiring the characters in the books he was reading. It was in this context of doing penance for his past life that he conceived the plan of going to Jerusalem as soon as he was healed. He had discovered a new goal and a new means, a new weapon in his struggle: his own body, and its as yet barely discovered soul. Though he later admitted that his spiritual life was very superficial and external at that time, it was his new awareness of his body and his soul as a battlefield with temporal dimensions of past, present, and future, which was at the origin of his liberation.

3. *The vision*

Immediately after describing his desire to do penance for his past life, his past imaginings of a possible future were forgotten and 'chased away' by his holy desires for another kind of future. This was confirmed for him by a 'vision' that he experienced one night when he could not sleep. This was the first vision of his story. It was the vision of 'Our Lady and the Holy Child Jesus'. At this sight he experienced for a considerable length of time such an extreme consolation, as well as such a revulsion at his past life, especially the disorder of his sexual life, that it seemed to him as if all the images engraved in him up to that time were erased from his soul.

At this point in the story Ignatius reinforces the strength of that past experience by a shift to the present, saying that from that night in 1521 down to the August of 1553 when he recounted the story, he had not consented to a sexual temptation. When Ignatius breaks the continuity of his narrative to bring the reader up to the present time, he is witnessing to the duration of the experience.

What precisely happened? Our hypothesis is that since he had been bedridden for such a long time, and given to such dreams as that of the great lady whose recognition he sought, he experienced some sexual stimulation which came into contact with the stream of thoughts and feelings related to his new spiritual experience. Thus this normal male physical response came to be seen and experienced in a new light. The presence of 'Our Lady and the Holy Child' gave him such an insight that he experienced in himself a new order and peace. The vision was not simply spiritual, but had a physical effect: his body's impulses and his soul's aspirations were integrated in a new creative way, from another level of himself, which was his heart. He accepted himself more deeply in his present, in their presences.[4]

4. *Social relationships and projects*

Ignatius's discovery of his existence as a battlefield of opposing spirits led him to a deeper integration of his spiritual and sexual life. The discovery continued to expand beyond himself into his relationships with others. He did not just bide his time during the last phase of his convalescence, but he wanted to share what he had been given. Other people in the house began to notice that some interior change had occurred in him. He spent more time speaking with his relatives about 'the things of God'.

He was less immediately impulsive now, and more present to himself and to the spirits inside him. He was less inclined to lunge into the future. It was this which made him more present to others, and it was of this that he conversed with others. Having learned to listen to himself, he was learning to listen to others, and to speak from a listening heart. It was a domestic apostolate that would develop into an apostolate of larger dimensions.

In addition to this, since he had grown to savour the books he had been reading, the idea came to him to summarize the most important things he had found in the lives of Jesus and the saints. As he began to write such a summary with exceeding care, he also began to get up from bed and move about the house. As he put his pen to paper and wrote across the pages, he put his feet on the floor and moved about the house.

Ignatius's writings would expand to fill various genres for different circumstances: letters, the *Spiritual Exercises*, the *Constitutions of the Society of Jesus*, his *Spiritual Diary*, and the *Autobiography*. These notes from his reading, begun in the bedroom of Loyola, are the core of that 'large pile of notes' that his biographer, Camara, will be allowed to see in the room in Rome more than thirty years later.

These notes were the subject of special care. Ignatius used different colours to distinguish certain persons: red for the words of Christ, blue for those of Mary. In narrating this later, he describes the smoothness and lines of the paper, as well as the beautiful calligraphy. The service he had once intended to offer to that very noble lady, by means of verses, declarations, and feats of arms were here channelled into a writing of another order, aiming at another form of service, in honour of another Lady and her Son.

Ignatius's bedside apostolate took both an oral and a written form, and it was as he wrote that he also found the strength to get up on his feet. It was in the context of this expanded space that he describes the order of his days and nights, an order which helped him to see more clearly the alternatives of his future. His day included the two previous activities: one part of his time for writing, another part for prayer. This rhythm had taught him a new equilibrium. At night, however, he found his greatest consolation in looking at the stars. He did that frequently and for long periods of time. The months of immobility in his bed had given him time to appreciate the movements of the stars and the grandeur of the heavens – time and space in their largest dimensions. When he looked at the stars, he felt a deep desire 'to serve Our Lord'. It was no longer only the example of the saints which was leading him to respond to God, but nature itself – in this instance, the stars. In the same way he had begun better to appreciate God in the nature of his sexuality, his masculinity.

Ignatius had first noticed an oscillation when he was reading: how his mind went from his old projects to his new desire to imitate Christ and the saints. He now set up another form of oscillation: from his work on the summary to his prayer, from his ordered day to his contemplation of the stars at night. With his life thus ordered, he thought often of his decision to go to Jerusalem on pilgrimage. Beyond that immediate project, he hesitated about what he would do on his return. He sketched his future in the following way: he intended to live a life of penance for his past sins. He hesitated between two life-styles: withdrawal to the Charterhouse of Seville, or wandering about the world where he would be freer to give full rein to his self-renunciation. He even asked a house servant who was travelling to Burgos to bring back information about the Charterhouse there. But Ignatius was getting ahead of himself. He would eventually fix on a third possibility which would come to mind at Montserrat. There he would deepen his pilgrimage project to the point where he resolved to stay permanently in Jerusalem. In this resolution he chose neither the fixed Charterhouse in Spain nor the life of a constantly moving pilgrim, but the life of a permanent pilgrim in Jerusalem. He would not be dislodged from that resolution except in Jerusalem itself. But at the present time, toward the end of his stay in Loyola, he was not able to see clearly what he would do after his pilgrimage, so he limited himself to his immediate project and began his preparations to leave the castle homestead.

He had told no one of his intention to go to Jerusalem.

Without speaking of that ultimate destination, he told his older brother Martin that he had to go to Navarette to report to his former employer, the Duke of Najera, with whom he had been engaged since 1517 as a military accountant. His brother led him from one room to another, and with great emotion appealed to him not to leave, using all the arguments he could. But Ignatius resisted such pleading, and without deviating from the truth (for which he said he always had a scrupulous respect), he succeeded in leaving his older brother.

In the company of another brother who wanted to go with him as far as Onate, Ignatius mounted a mule, with his project in his heart and his notes in his saddlebags, and left through the castle gate. He had arrived there on a litter at the end of the previous June; now in March 1522 he was on the road to Jerusalem.

Chapter 4

MONTSERRAT: THE MOUNTAIN MONASTERY

1. *Towards Montserrat*

Ignatius hoped to be at Montserrat for the vigil of the feast of the Annunciation on March 25. Four episodes occurred on the way, and in each of them there is a reference to Our Lady.

The first episode relates that he persuaded his brother to make a detour from the road to Onate, so that they could spend the night in vigil at a local shrine to Our Lady at Aranzazu. He claimed that he wanted to do this to gain fresh strength for his journey. The vigil completed, he left his brother in Onate at the house of one of his sisters and continued on to Navarrete.

The second episode occurred at the Treasurer's desk in the household of the Duke of Navarrete. When he tried to collect the few ducats that were owed to him, he was told that the treasury had no money for him. When the Duke learned that the Treasurer had refused the money, he proclaimed that there might not be money for anyone else, but there was no lack of money for a Loyola. The Duke even offered him a good position, but Ignatius refused it, collected his money, distributed it among certain persons to whom he was indebted, and saw that a part of it was spent to repair a badly appointed statue of Our Lady. He then dismissed the two servants who had come with him, and set out on his mule for Montserrat.

The third episode is related after a short parenthetical paragraph which describes Ignatius's interior attitude toward outward penances. He speaks of his soul as 'still blind', though greatly desirous of serving Our Lord as far as he knew he could. Thus he had decided to do great penances, no longer to expiate for his past sins, but simply to please God in the present. When he recalled some penance that the saints had performed, he proposed not only to do likewise, but to do even more. From the retrospect of his narration in 1553, he notes that his consolation on that road across the north of Spain in 1522 was found solely in his external emulation of the saints, and not in anything interior. He claims that he had no knowledge of humility, charity, patience, or the discretion that regulates those virtues. His whole intention was to do great external works for the glory of God, without taking into consideration any more particular details. This was not just a disordered state to be in, but it was a dangerous state to bring into human relations. Ignatius makes a detour with this parenthetical paragraph because it leads into his fanatical behaviour in the last episode.

Ignatius was used to persuading people and to having his own way. Whether against the French at Pamplona, or against the doctors and his brother at Loyola; whether convincing his brother to make a vigil at Aranzazu, or getting the Treasurer at Navarrete to pay him his ducats; Ignatius had the habit of overcoming obstacles. In the last episode Ignatius would come up against an obstacle that would not yield to him. He would be tempted to follow his instincts, to defend the honour of Our Lady, but something would happen to stop him. The episode is as follows.

Ignatius met a Moor who rode along at his side. They engaged in conversation on the virgin birth of Jesus, agreeing that Mary was a virgin before child-birth, but disagreeing over whether she remained a virgin afterwards. Ignatius gave as many natural arguments and reasons as he could, but he could not change the position of the Moor. The Moor rode off quickly, leaving Ignatius behind in a state of muddled discontent. He describes his inner feelings: his frustration at not doing his duty, his indignation against the Moor, the supposed dishonour to Our Lady. Should he pursue the Moor and give him a few sharp stabs with his dagger? That is what he would have done to allay such troubled feelings only a few months before. But now he was uncertain about following that ethical code of honour. All the elements were there, but he had a new consciousness of them. His feelings were there; the honour of Our Lady was there; the Moor was there; the dagger was there; and the mule was there. What was he to do? The Moor had ridden off to a village only thirty or forty paces away. Should he pursue him there? Something made him hesitate. There was a conflict between the immediate response required by the old code of honour and another code that was implied in the very 'honour' that he wanted to defend. Those interior motions lasted for a long time – so long that he actually grew tired of examining what would be best to do. In this state he did something that shows us a new side to his personality: he decided not to decide. He decided to let himself be passive and to let someone else decide: to let the mule decide. He let the reins go slack as he approached the turn off to the village, so that it would be left to the mule either to continue on the King's Highway with no village in sight, or to pull into the nearby village where Ignatius would settle the argument with his dagger. Although the road to the village was broad and good, the mule took the King's Highway.

Later Ignatius made other decisions in this way: putting himself in the hands of natural forces, and in the hands of human authorities such as teachers, soldiers, priests, bishops, inquisitors, and the Pope. Those instances are further expansions of the lesson that the mule taught Ignatius on the road to Montserrat. (The implication is that the mule was wiser than Ignatius! If we take this incident as an example of Ignatius's self-mockery, we won't be misled into believing that, telling his story all those years later, he is actually recommending this as a model of discernment.)

But it was not only the mule, but also the Moor who taught him a lesson. Safe in the village by the roadside, he represented one of the edges of the Muslim world off which Ignatius rebounds. He would rebound off another edge of that Muslim world during this pilgrimage, at the other end of the Mediterranean, on the Mount of Olives in Jerusalem. The breakdown in the relations between the Venetians and the Turks was also to play a determining role in the future of the young 'Society of Jesus' at a much later stage of this story. The presence of this Muslim world around the western, southern, and eastern shores of the Mediterranean is an essential part of the environment in which Ignatius lived. The various European wars between France and the Hapsburg Empire of Austria and Spain have to be understood in the larger context of the various wars (and other happier and more lucrative relations) between the Christian and Muslim worlds – not to mention the Jews who lived in both, when they were not expelled from or persecuted in one, the other, or both.

The fourth episode that he recounts before climbing up the steep road to Montserrat is his entrance into a large town in order to buy the prickly sackcloth he needed for his pilgrim's robe. He had the robe made before he left the town. It was a long garment that reached to the feet. This is a strange detail to retain, unless one notices that later costumes sometimes reach only to the knees. The true meaning of these descriptions might lie in their covering or their indifference to showing the once broken wounded legs. He also bought his pilgrim's staff and a small gourd, loaded these things on his mule, and then worked his way up the steep switchbacks to Montserrat, the Benedictine monastery high in the saw-toothed peaks that gave the place its name.

Before describing his arrival at Montserrat, Ignatius makes another interior detour to inform us of the attitude of mind that he brought to this stage of his journey. He says that he was always thinking of the exploits he would perform for the love of God. He explicitly admits that his mind was still full of the tales of Amadis de Gaul. This was what led him to decide ahead of time to keep a vigil of arms during one entire night, without sitting or lying down, but standing for a while and kneeling for a while, before the altar of Our Lady of Montserrat. On the occasion of that vigil, he laid aside his normal clothes and put on the 'armour of Christ', the pilgrim's sackcloth. He was the kind of dreamer who was so lost in his own future that he did not see how this could cause trouble for others. It was not really an open future, expressing an inner freedom; it was still deeply conditioned by the past – not only his own past, but his past as perceived through the values of Amadis de Gaul. He was more or less programmed by his reading, which had not really freed him from itself. He was not very quick at catching on to this. But once he had caught onto it, he had an unshakeable sense of priorities. This is why he gave so little importance to recounting his life, compared to more urgent decisions to be taken. In the Epilogue we will see that this is what he was somehow trying to tell Camara in that last interview before Camara left for Spain. But his attitude of mind before arriving at Montserrat was such that he knew that something was wrong with him. The episode with the Moor had shown him that he no longer had the conditioned reflex that once dominated his life. But he did not yet have what he needed to replace it. This was what led him, after his vigil at Montserrat, to make his prolonged detour at Manresa. It was both a physical and spiritual detour, and it was a detour from which he would never return.

In these episodes on the road to Montserrat Ignatius describes himself as something of a fool. His parenthetic remarks about his interior life are ironic and even humorous, as they reveal how deep was the cleavage between what he wanted to be and was pretending to be, and what he really was. He tells his story in this way precisely to make the readers dissociate themselves from this automatized or programmed pilgrim.

2. *At Montserrat*

Once he arrived at the monastery, he began to put his plan into execution: he prayed, he fixed an appointment with the confessor, and he made a general confession in writing. The confession took place in sessions that extended over three days. It was not just a rapid over-view, but a thorough examination and confession, giving both the penitent and the confessor time to experience and reach the full benefit of the sacrament. It was with this confessor that he arranged to have his mule taken in charge, and his sword and dagger placed at the altar of Our Lady. It was to this confessor that he revealed for the first time his decision to go to Jerusalem. He finally shared this decision with another. He did not put himself in the confessor's hands and ask what he should do. He was not at the crossroads of the Moor and the mule. He was communicating a decision he had taken when he was back in bed at Loyola – a decision in which he had persevered from Loyola to Aranzazu, from Onate to the crossroads, from the town where he bought the sackcloth to the confessional at Montserrat. Armed with this decision, Ignatius performed his vigil before the altar of Our Lady on the eve of the Feast of the Annunciation, March 24, 1522. He may have recalled that vigil of the Feast of SS Peter and Paul the previous June, when he passed through midnight and came out alive. He may have recalled that vision of Our Lady and the Holy Child, when he persevered patiently through a sexual experience in a new way. He had just spent three days examining his past life, and he had also communicated the decision that sketched out his immediate future. Having confessed his sins and been forgiven, there seemed to be nothing to keep Ignatius from settling down into his present. But such was not to be the case. There he stood in his pilgrim robe, having stripped off all his former garments and given them secretly to a beggar. How perfectly he seemed to be imitating the combined examples of the saints and Amadis de Gaul. What could possibly go wrong? He stood, he knelt, his pilgrim staff in hand. Thus the night passed, and just at daybreak, early enough for his departure to go unrecognized in his new disguise, he took to the road that led to the town of Manresa. There, in a valley slightly behind the saw-toothed mountains of Montserrat, he planned to spend only 'a few days' in a hospice in order to note some things in 'his book'. Here we learn for the first time that he carried this book around with him very carefully and was greatly consoled by it.

Then the plan started to come undone. About a league from Montserrat a man came running after him to ask if he had really given his clothes to a beggar, as the beggar claimed. He answered that he had, and found that tears of compassion came to his eyes for the beggar who had been harassed by those who thought he had stolen them. Ignatius's secrecy had backfired, not on him but on a beggar whom he had used as part of a plan that couldn't have been more ideal. Somehow, reality had intruded. His symbols were still too imaginary and not yet fully in tune with the real world.

He also discovered that his reputation had followed him to Manresa. He tried to avoid favourable notice, but news of the events of Montserrat had followed him to the town, expanding the truth until it was no longer recognizable, spinning tales of the large income he had forfeited.

His plans backfired in surprising ways. He was surprised that he had been recognized; surprised at the contrary effect that his generosity had on the life of the beggar; surprised at the tears that came to his eyes; surprised in retrospect at the ironic and humorous consequences of his slavish imitation of the saints, when it was confounded with the model of Amadis de Gaul.

After this incident Ignatius had all the more reason to take time off from his pilgrimage in order to devote himself to 'his book', which was an account of his progress. He needed more than 'a few days'. It is this book which we are now reading. It is the germ of the *Autobiography* he dictated and of the *Spiritual Exercises* he composed. For the story of his life, its sins and its graces throughout a lifetime of movement from place to place, from task to task, was the concrete content of certain meditations in the *Spiritual Exercises*. His decision to spend some time at Manresa was a sign of his need to come to deeper terms with himself, and with the spirits that were wrestling in him, before he continued on his road to Jerusalem.

The tears of compassion for the beggar in Montserrat constitute the first mention of tears in the story. This will not be the last. In fact, Ignatius last mentions tears in the final interview with Camara in Rome when he describes how often tears came to his eyes as he said Mass, while composing the Constitutions of the Society of Jesus. Was he weeping for his beggar Jesuit companions, and for himself, knowing that the ideal would necessarily break up in encounter with the real world at a later stage?

Stripping Down to an Identity (1)

Ignatius's change of clothes is a clear instance of his effort to strip off the marks of one identity and to assume another. But all along the road he has been leaving things behind. At Montserrat he left not only his clothes, but his mule and his sins. In his conflict with the Moor, he left his first impulse behind and let the mule take the lead. At Navarette he sought out his salary, but only to leave it behind by paying certain debts. At Onate, he left his brother and sister behind. At Loyola he left his brother and the rest of his family behind. He also left behind certain other options, such as going immediately to a Charterhouse or deciding to wander about as a beggar. 'Leaving behind' is one way of speaking of what is decided against. Stripping down to an identity is not just a choice of good over evil, but a choice of what is better over what is good. It is also a choice of what is best over what is better. Here we touch on the source or origin of a person's identity, which is a constant self-transcendence: a constant freedom to go beyond what has already been attained, in response to a higher call. In George

Bernanos's novel, UNDER THE SUN OF SATAN, *an old priest counsels the young priest who is the protagonist with these words: 'When you are called, you either go up or you are lost.' There are such defining moments in a person's life; from our viewpoint, they challenge us to an ultimate decision, although, of course, on God's side there is no limit on the offer of love he extends.*

Chapter 5

MANRESA: THE HOSPICE, THE CAVE AND THE RIVER-BANK

Ignatius stayed in Manresa for almost a year, from March 25, 1522 to February 1523, when he finally left for Barcelona. This period is so rich in detail that an over-view of the various episodes is helpful. The episodes oscillate, as might be expected, from a preoccupation with the physical order of his life to a preoccupation with the spiritual. The first episode shows his concern with the physical details of his new life. This is followed by a strange vision, where the spiritual and the physical are combined. The third episode is an interior detour, which describes the effects of this oscillation and vision upon Ignatius. This kind of detour is his signature, a typical aside or withdrawal whereby he waits to grasp the unity of what has just preceded. In the *Spiritual Exercises* it is the recollection after the meditation, a quarter of an hour spent in reflecting on what one received during the hour of meditation. As a result of this interior detour, in the fourth episode Ignatius looked for people with whom he could talk about these new experiences. In looking for spiritual conversation he was showing his need and his willingness to learn from others. The fifth episode recounts the ordering of the spiritual details of his life, but this effort did not meet with success, and he broke down into a prolonged crisis of scruples. This crisis, the sixth episode, is described in great detail, for the order he has established between the physical and the spiritual exercises falls apart completely. Once the crisis of scruples is resolved, Ignatius establishes a more open order to his life in the seventh episode. This includes not only the physical and spiritual activities, but a further activity which is concerned with others: his apostolate or ministry, services he renders to certain people in the town. After the seventh episode, concerning his apostolate, the eighth relates the five great 'lessons' that he learned from Our Lord. Some of them are visions, but one of them is a grace which leads him to distrust one of these visions. The ninth episode relates two illnesses, one of them being more mental or imaginary in its effects, the other more directly physical. The tenth and last episode, like the fourth, tells of his search for spiritual conversations with others. Although the overcoming of his scruples had freed him for service to others, (and this service reveals his concern with giving), and although he had received certain great graces during the course of his stay in Manresa, he still experienced the need for spiritual conversations. This reveals his need not only to 'receive' from God, but to receive through spiritual persons some form of spiritual direction.

This brief sketch of the narrative ahead reveals a pattern:

1. The ordering of physical details
2. Spiritual visions and voices
3. Effects of oscillation between the physical and spiritual orders, resulting in perturbations
4. Spiritual conversations
5. The ordering of spiritual details
6. The crisis of scruples
7. Apostolates towards others: a new equilibrium
8. Five spiritual lessons
9. Two physical illnesses
10. Spiritual conversation.

The Shy Pattern (1)

The pattern that emerges from this outline of his experiences at Manresa is a field or structure of opposed terms, which refer to areas of experience in a man who is not only in search of meaning, truth, and goodness, but who is increasingly in search of more meaning, more truth, and more goodness. This 'more' is not only quantitative, but qualitative, and relational, that is, in increasing relationship with other people. 'More' in one area or relationship might require 'less' in another. The place from which one goes about such discernment and decision is the place in Ignatius which is struggling dialectically and dialogically as it goes through a conversion to the foundations from which his life can more freely flow. The physical and the spiritual orders are the first two such opposed or ap-posed areas that appear in the pilgrim story. Vision occurs there at the centre where extremes meet. The inadequacy of his spiritual conversations with others leads to his crisis of scruples: he falls into an excessive, obsessive, preoccupation with his own past, after which his apostolate or ministry is a further effort to reach out to others in the present. This leads to greater spiritual gifts but also to physical illness. In that state his spiritual conversations take a further step forward.

We should note that it is in conversation with 'spiritual persons' that Ignatius seeks direction in his life. This search will continue until his return from Jerusalem, where it will broaden into the relations with others outlined in the *Spiritual Exercises* as the relationship between the giver of the Exercises and the exercitant, a different relationship from that of sacramental confession. Finally his need to relate to others will settle on the form of a permanent community that will be called 'the Society of Jesus'.

1. *Physical details*

The physical details that Ignatius describes at the outset of the Manresa narrative are not ends in themselves but means toward the end of breaking habits which he sees as obstacles on his path. Behind each of these details lies its opposite; to choose to do each task in one way was to decide not to do it in another way. The areas in which he experimented and verified his hypotheses were in begging for alms, in eating and drinking, and in caring for his hair and nails.

Each day he begged alms in Manresa. He did not eat meat or drink wine, even if they were offered to him. He did not fast on Sundays, but on that day he did drink a little wine if it were offered to him. To break himself of his fastidious vanity, he did not cut or comb his hair, nor did he pare his finger and toe nails.

The general area of exterior or physical details will continue to play an important part throughout the story. Certain sectors of this area such as finance (revenue and expenses), food and drink recur constantly; other sectors such as care of hair and nails will disappear rapidly. This is because the end has been achieved. This area will come to include the sectors of vigils, transportation, alms-giving, clothes, housing, speech, and even proper pronunciation and grammar. These are not just physical means to spiritual ends. In trying to control these sectors, Ignatius was trying to free himself from habits that had imprisoned him. He was trying to expand, not just his consciousness, but his power to decide. He advanced from one sector to another, in one area or another, like a piano player who learns how to play one new note after another until he discovers a whole new octave: somehow the same, yet different, really different, and inviting him to go farther.

These areas of the physical and the spiritual, the apostolic and the academic, the sense of the whole and the detail, together with passivity and activity, are the most general areas of experience referred to in this study. They are areas that Ignatius learns to combine, to expand, to contract, to transform, in his relations with himself, with others and with God. Each area contains its sectors, as Ignatius moves from stage to stage, from episode to episode within each stage, from relationship to relationship. These areas are foundational, in so far as they have emerged from the experience of conversion resolving dialectical oppositions.[5]

This alternation discovered in his own life is incorporated in the *Spiritual Exercises* as a passage from the spiritual duties of the day to the more physical duties which are outlined in the 'Additions', and which vary for each of the Four Weeks. It is by creating a field of moderate tensions between the interior activities and the exterior – which includes contact with the director of the retreat (a 'spiritual person') – that the 'ascending' or 'descending' movements of the spirits are experienced and discerned. [10]

Pierre Favre, Ignatius's earliest companion in Paris, and one of the first members of the Society of Jesus, was highly esteemed by Ignatius as a director of the *Spiritual Exercises.* In his *Memorial* which combines his brief autobiography with a spiritual diary, Favre writes of the importance of getting the exercitant to the point where his spirits start to operate, that is, to oscillate. In his opinion, one of the more effective ways of doing that is to propose a change in the state of life of the exercitant. He noted this on April 28, 1543, as he was giving the *Spiritual Exercises* to a brilliant young theology student, who later became St Peter Canisius.

2. *The 'vision' and the 'voice'*

While he was staying in the hospice, Ignatius began to see, in broad daylight, something in the air near him. Even though he could not discern very clearly what it was, its beauty gave him great consolation. It had the form of a serpent, covered with glittering points that were like eyes, but were not eyes. Each time he saw it his pleasure increased, and when it disappeared he experienced displeasure.

This vision lasted for many days. During the days that it lasted, or just a short time before it began, he was shocked by a rude thought that suddenly intruded into his consciousness. The manner of its rude entry was as remarkable as its message, for up until that time he had remained in an interior state of very steady joy, although he admits that he had no real knowledge of spiritual interiority. The thought came to him as he was entering a church where he attended High Mass, Vespers, and Compline each day. He had been taking great comfort in these devotions, and during Mass he had the habit of reading the passion of Christ, always advancing in the same state of serenity. The thought came to him as a questioning voice:

'How will you be able to endure this life for the seventy years you have to live?' Ignatius perceived immediately that this voice came from the enemy, so he answered interiorly with great vehemence:

'Wretch! Can you promise me one hour of life?'

It was thus, he said, that he overcame the temptation and maintained his peace. He noted that this was the first temptation he had experienced since the one previously mentioned. That was probably the sexual experience he had at Loyola, or else the temptation to stab the Moor on the road to Montserrat. Although he resisted the temptation and kept his peace, and although he continued to see the consoling vision of the glittering serpent-form, Ignatius once again was experiencing breakdowns in the execution of the plan for a well-ordered life, such as he had thus far conceived it. He did not yet see the connection between the tempting voice and the beautiful vision which, despite the consolation he experienced from it, would prove to be no less than a temptation from the evil spirit.

3. *Perturbations: effects of the oscillation between the physical and spiritual poles*

It was soon after the temptation to quit his new way of life that he began to experience great changes in his soul. Suddenly he found no more consolation in his prayers, at Mass, or in other devotions. Just as suddenly the opposite feelings returned, and he took great joy in his spiritual exercises. In his own words, sadness and desolation followed joy and consolation as abruptly as a cloak is laid over one's shoulders and then snatched away. Ignatius did not just experience these changes, but he became perturbed in so far as his reflections and efforts to control them led him nowhere. He said to himself:

'What new life is this that we are now beginning?'

It is in this context that he mentions his conversations with spiritual persons. Although he describes them as people who had regard for him and wanted to talk with him, he himself was looking for help in dealing with his own interior motions and perturbations.

4. *Spiritual persons*

Even in this context of being sought by 'spiritual persons' who wanted to speak with him, Ignatius admits that he did not pretend to have any knowledge of spiritual matters. His speech however did reveal his great fervour and eagerness to advance in the Lord's service, and it was this contagious fervour that attracted some people to him.

He specifically mentioned a very old woman at Manresa who came to see him. She had a great reputation for being a servant of God and was known in many regions of Spain. Even the King had once summoned her in order to communicate something. One day when she had been speaking with Ignatius she said to him: 'Oh may my Lord Jesus Christ deign to appear to you some day!' Ignatius was startled, he said, because he took her words literally. He responded: 'Why should Jesus Christ appear to me?'

Yet at Loyola Ignatius had already had a vision of Our Lady and the Holy Child. He now wanted less to see Jesus Christ than to serve him. His recounting of this conversation with the old woman would seem to indicate that there was a certain maladjustment between him and others. As with the Moor and the beggar at Montserrat, so the conversation with the old woman fell short of a fuller spiritual exchange.

A further aspect to note in this scene is his reference to himself as 'the new soldier of Christ'. It may be that it was in the presence of this woman who had met with the 'Catholic King' that Ignatius was reminded that he himself had once been a soldier in the army of that King. He has since changed Masters. Since he has already had a vision of Our Lady and the Holy Child, the prayer of the old woman has already been answered. He does not share that experience with her, but deflects her exclamation. This indicates that there is a considerable distance between what he says to others and what he feels. That distance leads to the crisis of Ignatius's scruples over his past life: he falls through the broken present into the depths of his past. It is in this crisis of scruples that he makes a fundamental discovery: he is in a dialectical relationship not only with himself and with others, but with Satan and Christ, and with God himself.

5. *The ordering of spiritual details*

There is no one particular episode where Ignatius describes his spiritual exercises and devotions during this period before the crisis of scruples. When he relates the incident of the 'voice', he notes that it occurred as he was entering a church; and it is then that he mentions that he attended High Mass each day, as well as Vespers and Compline. When he speaks of his perturbations, he refers to his prayers and Masses. After he tells the story of the old woman's words and his immediate response, he adds the simple line:

'He kept up his usual practice of confession and communion every Sunday.'

Thus, well before the crisis of scruples begins – a crisis that the old woman's prayer may have precipitated – a certain pattern has emerged: the concern with ordering the physical details of his life, interwoven with his spiritual exercises of various sorts; the beautiful consoling vision and the tempting, disturbing voice which occur more or less at the same time, once the spiritual and the physical ordering has been established; the abrupt oscillation from consolation to desolation; his sharing of these experiences with other persons leading spiritual lives. The plan for the order of his life has become more complex than the simple transactions at Montserrat, yet we can still recognize something of the order he came to discover and maintain when he was bed-ridden in Loyola. The oscillations are now going to stop, however, with his descent into a crisis of scruples which almost exhausts his resources.

6. *The scruples*

Ignatius's willfulness and initiative at the fortress of Pamplona, as well as in his bed at Loyola, show that he was a person who was used to taking action, in order to fight his way into the future. His experience of the spirits, which began to act upon him in his reflections after his reading, brought him into a deeper sense of his present. But after the confession of his past sins at Montserrat, and after he had settled down to execute the plan of a more ordered life at Manresa, his past caught up with him.

Although he went to confession and communion each Sunday, he began to be deeply troubled, for it seemed to him that he had not accused himself of certain sins. The means that he took to cure himself of these scruples, and the failure of almost all of them, constitute the whole point of telling the incident.

First he had recourse to other people: he confessed his sins again, but found no satisfaction. He sought out spiritual persons who could advise him on his scruples, but found no help. Finally a 'doctor', a university graduate at the cathedral, a spiritual man and preacher at the cathedral, told him one day in confession to write down every sin he could remember. Ignatius did that, but after the confession the scruples returned in an even subtler way.

He thought that the ultimate remedy might be obedience: he would ask his confessor to command him, in the name of Jesus Christ, to cease to confess anything of his past life. Although he desired to receive such an order, he didn't dare to ask his confessor to do such a thing. Nevertheless, without having been asked, the confessor did order him not to concern himself further with any one of his past sins, unless it was a matter of something very clear. But since everything appeared very clear to him, he drew no profit from this order.

After these four efforts to be helped by others, he switched to other means, counting more upon himself and turning directly to God.

He remained faithful to his programme of seven hours' prayer on his knees each day, even rising at midnight for an hour of prayer. Yet the penance and self-denial that such a programme of prayer demanded of him had no effect on his scruples. His effort was a combination of both the physical and spiritual poles, which are essential elements of the basic pattern.

One day he cried aloud in his prayer, humbling himself to the utmost, protesting that he found no remedy anywhere, and that he was willing to accept any suffering in order to be freed from these scruples. He claimed that he would even follow 'a little dog', if only the dog would lead him to find a remedy. This is the most extreme form that his prayer takes.

As these thoughts occupied him, he was frequently

tempted to abase himself even further by throwing himself down into a great dark hole which was in the room of the Dominican hospice where he was staying. He stopped short of this, recognizing that he should do nothing to offend God, but he repeated his protestation of willingness to do anything, even the most humiliating act, provided that he didn't offend God. Even this prayer, however, had no effect on his scruples.

After having prayed his most extreme prayer, which took him to the temptation of suicide, he was inspired by an extreme form of penance that he had perhaps read about in the lives of the saints: he resolved not to eat or drink until God came to his aid, or until he found himself very close to death. It was a form of hunger strike against himself. He didn't give a thought to the fact that once he was that close to death, he would be too weak to ask for help and to receive it. This resolution was taken on a Sunday after communion. All during the week he kept his resolution faithfully and yet missed nothing of his attendance at the Divine Office, nor did he shorten his hours of prayer.

After these four personal efforts to overcome his scruples by prayer and fasting, another person once again intervened unexpectedly.

On the following Sunday before Mass, when he confessed his life – for he confessed not only his sins, but all the details of what he was doing – he mentioned his current week-long fast. The confessor told him to break the fast. Although he felt he had the strength to continue, he obeyed, and he was freed that day and the following day from the scruples he had previously known. But on the third day, Tuesday, during his prayer, he began once again to recall his past sins. One sin suggested another, and soon he was in the same state of believing himself obliged to confess his past sins once again.

However, at the end of such reflections, he felt an extreme disgust, not just for his past, but for the very life he was living at present.

In this state of disgust he felt a strong desire to abandon

this form of life completely, as the 'voice' had once suggested as he entered church.

At that moment, he says, the Lord woke him up as if from a dream, and he realized that – thanks to the lessons God had already taught him in his experience of the diversity of spirits – the spirit which had just tempted him to abandon his new life was thereby revealed to be the evil spirit. He began to reflect on the way in which this spirit had finally come upon him. He thus resolved with complete lucidity to confess no longer any past fault. From that day on he was freed from scruples, and he held it as a certainty that Our Lord, in his mercy, had deigned to save him from them.

This struggle with his scruples recalls the great discovery Ignatius made when he was convalescing at Loyola. There he realized that he was actually wrestling with the same spirits that he was reading about. He had also recognized in the 'voice' that discouraged him as he entered the church in Manresa the same evil spirit whom he was resolved to expel from his life. He now recognized the same evil spirit discouraging him from continuing his present life by constantly raising his scruples about the past.

What becomes so transparent in this episode is that finally Ignatius has to do his own discerning and make his own decision. The directions of the oscillations are unmistakable: he moves back and forth, from four efforts at finding help from others to four efforts that he undertook without the help of others. The last of those efforts brought him back in touch with a confessor who ordered him to stop his week-long fast. Despite his obedience to this order, his scruples returned, and it was *then*, when he was thrown back on his own resources, that he experienced the disgust which became like a dark cloud in which the evil spirit tempted him to abandon his new life. This disgust with the whole situation was the context in which he was finally able to discern with one part of himself what was going on in another part of himself. It was not just that his past had accumulated to the point where he saw enough of the 'material', so to speak. It was that the past and his efforts to be free of it kept recurring, to the point where he was so disgusted at his failures that the experience took an imperative form.

The 'declarative' mood became so dark that it changed into the 'imperative'. He knew how to deal with such imperatives: he counter-responded by going exactly in the opposite direction. A pattern of relationships finally reached the critical mass that allowed breakthrough. He had tried all the means he could find, with others and with himself, until he rebounded back to his confessor, then back to himself, and finally things resolved into the opposition between the evil spirit and God. This is thematized in the *Spiritual Exercises* as the Meditation on the Two Standards [136–1248] which occurs about one third of the way through the Second Week. The only way through to the revelation of the Two Standards is to resolve to be a person who belongs to the 'Third Class of Men' [155], and who is not only ready but resolved to follow and accompany Jesus, even when Jesus appears to make a fool of himself or to be made a fool of. This is what Ignatius means by 'the third degree of humility' [167–168]. It was not enough to 'follow a little dog' or to throw oneself down a dark hole. One had to follow Christ, and not just follow him, but accompany him. This meant that one had to become the little dog, to become the donkey, to wear the crown of thorns, to take up the cross. It is from that cross that reality takes on its truest proportions, and the world is seen for what it is. Ignatius's scruples are not just another episode in his life; they go to the heart of his life. This crisis throws light on the whole landscape of his journey.

A further point remains to be made. Ignatius tried every means he knew in order to be free of his past: oral confession to a priest; conversations with spiritual persons; a written confession, remade at the advice of both a learned and spiritual confessor; obedience to the order of a confessor who commanded him to confess no past sin unless it were very clear. But he made no progress in ridding himself of his scruples, so he switched to more personal tactics. He not only remained faithful to his combination of long periods of prayer and penance, but he found himself addressing the most extreme prayers to God, accompanied by his willingness to perform the most degrading acts of self-abasement. Unanswered in his prayers, he undertook a most extreme form of penance: his week-long fast. Thanks to the honesty and thoroughness of his weekly confession, he was ordered to stop his fast, but his obedience did not solve his basic problem. It is only when he reached such an intense degree of disgust with his *present* life and experienced the temptation to abandon his way of life that he detected the work of the evil spirit. His failures to find help led him toward the moment for which there can be no substitute: his own personal decision within his personal relation to God, revealed in his direct opposition to Satan, yet surrounded and helped to a degree by his relations with others. He *had* to continue his discernment through to the recognition of the 'serpent's tail', revealing the presence of the Evil One. But his discernment had to include not just the data of the past, but the data of the present situation as well: the presence of the past in his scruples, ie their disorder, as well as the source of their disorder: the 'prince of this world'. The immediate struggle with his scruples had to become dense enough, be repeated frequently enough, be patterned and polarized enough for him to see in this struggle the bias that had misdirected him previously in the matter of his previous sins – at least, of those sins which had the scrupulous habit of returning to his mind and blocking his advance into the future. Once his disgust reached this point, he saw the scruples themselves as a means that Satan had used to end his life. It was not just his physical life which was threatened, by thoughts of suicide that came in his prayer, but especially his new spiritual life, by a more subtle form of death that would result from his extreme penance and his disgust at his situation. His programme of weekly confession saved him from reaching the point of death by fasting, but Ignatius's obedience did not save him from the scruples. Nothing short of his own discernment of the total sequence of the experience, from the earliest scruples down to the present temptation to leave his newly chosen life, and nothing short of his own resolution no longer to confess any past faults, could release him from the grip of the Evil One, who was using Ignatius's own past to keep him from moving with confidence into his future. It was in that discernment and resolution that God's grace worked.

The underlying direction of this scene is its gradual focus on the grace of God which is found in discerning that the pattern of the past is being repeated in the present. It is recognized, and either rejected or embraced, for good, for the future. As a resolution, it will move into the future as a continual negation of the false present, and a persevering affirmation of the presence of God. Like the presence of God which moved with the Ark of the Covenant as it was carried by the twelve tribes through the stations of the desert from Sinai to Jerusalem, like the presence of God which moved more mysteriously from Jerusalem to Babylon and back, and like the presence of God that returned after the desecrated Temple was rededicated in the days of the Maccabees (*Babylonian Talmud*, 'Shabbat', 21b), so Ignatius's experience at Manresa will become disengaged from that particular place and he will carry it with him to Jerusalem and back, and on to the very moment of this dictation of his story to Camara.

The Shy Pattern (2)

In terms of the structure of basic notions, Ignatius has finally grown out of his past, and into a more liberated and liberating present through the long struggle with his scruples, which has hollowed out his interior life more than any previous trial or grace. Though it is still only on a very personal level, he has had an experience which permits the temporal axis of past-present-future to become disengaged or exorcised of a sort of obsession with only the past or the future. This is what happened with the last Passover of Jesus, whereby the Passover became portable or transferable, not only in space and time, but even with respect to its participants, in so far as faith in Jesus as the Christ opens the entire set of Jewish feasts to all the nations who believe, without dispossessing the Jews of their covenant, and without negating the salvific value of their tradition. Passover leads not only to Jerusalem, but beyond Jerusalem to the ends of the earth and back again, rebounding, circulating, enheartening. The whole movement circulates through the centuries, toward the final feast of Tabernacles: the feast of the End-time.

7. *The new equilibrium*

Once Ignatius experienced this breakthrough from the past into the future, various areas of his physical and spiritual life were affected, and he reached a new equilibrium. It is from this new equilibrium that his concern for others takes on the form of a work, a ministry with a mission.

Besides his seven hours of prayer, he helped certain 'souls' who came looking for him. He thus continued the same sort of service that he had been rendering before the crisis of scruples, when spiritual persons – such as the old woman – sought him out.

In addition to his prayer and his apostolate, he says that he spent the rest of the day thinking about the things of God that he had meditated upon or read that day. Thus he was organizing his day, as he had done at Loyola.

This description of his daytime passes into a description of his nights. When he tried to go to sleep, he often had such great illuminations and spiritual consolations that they made him lose a good part of the time he had decided for sleep – a time which was purposely not very long. After examining the matter several times, he concluded that since he had many hours to converse with God during the day, the illuminations that came at night may not have been from the good spirit. Finally he decided to ignore the nightly illuminations and sleep during the time he had allotted for it.

> <u>*The Shy Pattern (3)*</u>
> *The temporal axis within the pattern that gradually emerges is not a simple line of past-present-future, but a sort of dialectical equilibrium between the physical and spiritual aspects of his daily life, in so far as he can control them as well as learn from them within temporal limits. In the present instance, he decides to limit the time of his illuminations; he refuses to give too much time to the spiritual, if it interferes with what has been previously decided for the physical. The decision is taken with a new self-confidence, as if the major battle with his scruples has given him the experience of a truth that can now be deployed on different issues, in different areas, as they arise.*

Ignatius also tells a story in which his firmest resolution not to eat meat is countered by a 'vision' of meat. The vision was so real to him that he did not hesitate to change his resolution and he decided to eat meat henceforth. The incident happened in the following way. On awakening one morning he saw the meat very close to him, although he had no previous desire to eat it. At that waking moment he did not experience a physical appetite for the meat, but a strong inclination of his will to eat it. He recalled the firmness of his previous resolution, but that did not deter him from the new decision to eat meat. He couldn't bring himself to hesitate on the issue. After telling the story to his confessor, the latter told him to examine whether the vision was not a temptation. But Ignatius, having considered the whole incident carefully, did not have the least doubt that he was meant to eat meat. He now had confidence in his discernment of the proportion, or discretion, to be kept in both his spiritual and physical lives, so that these two sides of his personality might be more united into a single life. Although this confidence had grown deeper and wiser than before, one can still recognize the basic character of the man who insisted on defending the fortress of Pamplona.

In this description of his experience, Ignatius is careful to distinguish his recall of the past (an act of memory), his past decision (an act of will), and his present reflection and effort to understand (an act of intellect). The vision of meat influenced his will in a direct way, without his being able to understand how or why. Ignatius would not have been able to describe this experience at Manresa in these terms when he was actually living there. It was during his later studies of scholastic philosophy in Paris that he learned the classical categories and the faculties of the soul that would give him the means to articulate the experience of previous years. In the story-telling of 1553–1555 we are listening not just to the story of events that once happened, but to the interpretation of those events that has been formed by a life-time of prayer and study, community life and ministry or work.

The reader of the *Autobiography* may not realize it, but Ignatius's story is no more nor less than the summarized result of his meditations on his own life as he himself made them in the *Exercises* that he wrote for others. These are his sins and his graces, his ups and his downs, his regressions and his progressions, his breakdowns and his breakthroughs. By telling them to his listeners and readers, he himself takes the position of the 'exercitant' or maker of the *Exercises*, and it is the reader or community of readers who are listening to them, to him, who are called to discern in them what Ignatius is learning from his Lord. In other words, the readers themselves are put in the role of the one 'giving the *Exercises*', though in an informal way, despite the historical separation. This is precisely why the painting of *Las Meninas* is so helpful in making us realize where we stand with regard to what we are reading and how we are invited to appreciate and respond to it.

Although Ignatius did not link them, the last two incidents in the areas of sleeping and eating contain similarities and differences. They are both instances where Ignatius decided to go against his initial inclination, for he obviously enjoyed those 'nightly illuminations', and he explicitly says that he had not experienced a desire to eat meat. In both cases he makes a decision that goes in the opposite direction to a state of feeling. But in the case of his sleep, he examines the matter for a considerable time, and it is on the basis of his intellectual reasons that he takes his decision. In the case of eating meat, he decides instantly: he knows he must eat meat, even though he doesn't understand why; nor can his confessor dislodge him from his certitude. There is a contrapuntal contrast between the two incidents: the first is a reaction against too much illumination; the second is a reaction against too little meat. Both are implicated in the greater equilibrium of the spiritual and physical aspects of his new life.

8. *Five lessons of the Master*

After the crisis of his scruples, Ignatius once again describes his life by going over the same major areas as before the crisis: details of his spiritual life, details of his care for his body, and conversations with spiritual persons. Now that he has reached a new equilibrium, marked by his confidence in his own judgements and decisions, he describes the five spiritual experiences or 'lessons' he learned at Manresa. Then he switches to the physical side and describes the two major illnesses. The final episode that he chooses to tell touches on his search once again for spiritual direction from spiritual persons. Obviously he has spent much time in prayer reflecting over the various episodes of his life. If the crisis of scruples and the temptation to suicide represent the lowest point of this period, the set of 'lessons' represents the high point.

He prefaces these remarks by saying that God treated him at this time just as a schoolmaster teaches a child. He dwells on this subject and protests that he does not really know why God treated him in such a way, but he is absolutely certain that God was teaching him as if he were a child. He searches for reasons for this, but he admits that he has never found rational satisfaction. Nonetheless he is certain it is so. This certainty recalls the certainty with which he decided to eat meat, without knowing precisely why. This is the kind of experience of immediate decision-making that he incorporated in the *Spiritual Exercises* where he treated the three times for making a correct and good choice of a way of life during the Second Week [175].

It is in this context of the five 'lessons' that Ignatius uses a construction that occurs for the first time, and which will recur in a few other rare contexts: he says that he is so certain, that if he were to doubt this, he would think he had offended the Divine Majesty. This is also the first time that Ignatius refers to God as 'the Divine Majesty'. Only then does he begin to describe the five 'lessons', numbering them as 'points'. This is similar to the 'points' in each of the meditations of the *Spiritual Exercises*. For the points are central, concentrated experiences of such density that they require one's meditation, that is, one's taking time to think round them, over them, through them, recognizing one's feelings toward them, recalling how they affect one, intending and willing to get to the heart of them, and to appropriate them in a real and not just a notional way, until one reaches the real presence of God, which Ignatius calls 'colloquy' – or speaking together, conversation. The five lessons or points form a kind of scale, descending from God to creation; from the way Christ is in the Eucharist to a sense of the humanity of both Christ and Our Lady; and finally to an experience that touches on many things, both spiritual matters of faith and profane matters as well. Ignatius relates how often each lesson recurred, by what sense or faculty he received it, where it occurred, what constituted the content of the lesson, and how it affected him. He describes not only the different subjects of the lessons, but also how he entered into them, to the degree that his understanding was opened even further until it was confirmed by a 'vision', often accompanied by tears.

Visions and Tears

'Visions' and tears occur when Ignatius is very close to the heart of the pattern. The internal spiritual vision brings tears to his physical eyes. The experience integrates the spiritual and the physical at a deeper level of the heart. Tears can also spring from a deep spiritual 'hearing' of a word. Augustine in his Confessions *speaks of the ears and eyes and even of the mouth of the heart. Lawrence Durrell recounts a telling experience of the depth and importance of a child's tears in* Sebastian, *the fourth volume of his* Avignon Quintet.

THE FIRST LESSON concerned the Holy Trinity. Each day he prayed to the three Persons separately, but since he also prayed to them together as one, the thought came to him: Why do I say four prayers to the Trinity? It was a curious question, he says, and hardly important. Yet why does he tell his readers about it? Because it was a preparation for what followed: Logically, there had to be four prayers to the Trinity, if the three Persons were really distinct from one another, and yet one. His mind is working at the logic of the subject. His question and his value judgment on its relative unimportance were proof of the extent of his awareness, although they were also proof that he had not yet *experienced* the 'Trinity and Unity' of the God whom his words were addressing. When that experience came – and it came only once – it took the form neither of a question nor simply of a 'vision', but more of a 'hearing' which affected him so deeply that he broke out in many tears and uncontrollable sobbing. The 'system of control' that he had built up broke down – gracefully, and most fortunately. What happened?

One morning while saying the Office of Our Lady on the steps of the Dominican monastery, in whose hospice he was lodging, his understanding began to be raised to the point where he 'saw' the Most Holy Trinity in the form of three musical (organ) keys. This led him to break down in tears. Three distinct keys were held as one. For the rest of that morning, even during a procession, he could not hold back his tears. After dinner, he seemed to have oscillated to the opposite pole of his feelings: he was so joyous and consoled that he could not keep himself from speaking about the Trinity, using as many comparisons as he could. In fact, this joy is not the opposite of the tears, but their source, for he had wept tears of joy. Extremes meet. This single experience, he said, had a *lasting* effect throughout the rest of his life: he always experienced 'great devotion' when he prayed to God as the Trinity.

THE SECOND LESSON also occurred only once. He does not say exactly where he was when this happened, but it came to his understanding in the form of 'something white, from which some rays were coming, and God made light from this.' It was a 'vision' of how God had created the world. He did not know how to explain it, nor did he remember too well the 'spiritual enlightenment' that God was imprinting on his soul at that time, but he experienced great spiritual joy.

Neither his mind nor his memory are able to cope with the experience, but his feelings of joy are unquestionable. The way he sees the actual operation of creation is interesting, for it is as if God were an artist or craftsman, who works from some source of material (something white) out to the parts of the whole (rays coming from it). From that source and its rays God created light. It is a gradual process, in steps, similar to the steps of the lessons by which Ignatius felt himself being led further into the revelation of the Creator.

THE THIRD LESSON is introduced by a remark on physical details that at first might seem out of place. He says that *after* he had begun to be consoled by God, and *after* he saw the fruit which he had borne in dealing with souls (his modest apostolate of conversing with people on spiritual things), he abandoned some of the physical practices he had deliberately undertaken at the beginning of his stay at Manresa. He began again to cut his nails and his hair.

It was as if in response to this physical adjustment that he had a 'vision' during Mass. Again, this seems to have happened only once. In the church of the same Dominican monastery, at the elevation of the Host, he saw 'with interior eyes' something like white rays coming from above. Again he protests that he could not explain this very well after so long a time; and he thereby repeats his admission of the limits of his mind and memory, but he says that he saw clearly with his understanding how Jesus Christ was there in that Most Holy Sacrament.

A few details of this story help us to appreciate it further. First, his vision or 'hearing' of the Trinity had taken place outside the Dominican church. The vision of Jesus in the Eucharist takes place inside the same church during the Mass itself. Ignatius at this stage is a layman, a former soldier, a man going on thirty, who is on an early stage of a pilgrimage to Jerusalem. We do not know when he began to hear the call to become a priest, but we do see how the sacraments of Penance and the Eucharist were central to his personal life and to his apostolate. The Eucharist was Jesus's ultimate act of self-giving: a state he remained in from the Upper Room, through his agony, his arrest, his trials, his execution and death. Ignatius somehow has a vision into this prolonged act. This third 'lesson' is Ignatius's first mention of a really outstanding experience at Mass. And the heart of the experience is that 'Jesus Christ our Lord' is in 'that most Holy Sacrament'. The inwardness, however, is described in terms of a descent, or a coming from above. This leads to the second detail.

Ignatius explicitly says that it was with his 'interior eyes' that he saw how Jesus was in the Eucharist. The actual inwardness is likened to rays coming from above. These rays are coming from a source of light which is above. This is similar to the image he saw in his 'vision' of the creation of the world. Although both of these 'visions' are described as a source from which rays are coming, the visual image is also similar to the experience of the Trinity, which is described in auditive terms as three distinct notes struck together. The 'white rays' come from the source of light and do not detach themselves from it. Like the rays of light that sparkle off a glittering object, they are both radiating from the source and yet totally related to the source from which they come. As the Host, the Body of Christ, is lifted up at the elevation in the Mass, Ignatius has a vision of a movement in the opposite direction: a coming from above. The coming from above is joined with the elevation from below through an inwardness that Jesus brought to this act. Having come from above, it is in his offering of himself up to the Father that he reveals the depths of the love at the heart of his relationship to the Father. It is when he is 'lifted up' that he will draw all men to himself (John 12:34) and give eternal life to whoever believes in him (John 3:14–15). The combination of the ascending and descending movements is effected through an interior act which is expressed on the cross. Just as Jesus puts himself into the Eucharistic act and offerings, so he can only be received through an interior act or with 'interior eyes', the eyes of faith.

Vision and Hearing

The vision and hearing in the first three lessons lead to Ignatius's seeing through the false vision and hearing in the fifth lesson. The discovery of the false vision and hearing (the serpent-form, the voice on entering the church) is the same discovery as was made in the Meditation on the Two Standards.

Ignatius has worked his way down from his thoughts to his feelings and their duration, and also up to their source.

This movement from brief summary statements or 'points' up to the colloquy – an experience of speaking to the Lord and listening to him – is what is meant by a meditation. It might be argued that a meditation is more of an active effort on a person's part to reach the stage of colloquy, whereas a contemplation is more passive, less of an effort on one's part, and more of an experience of seeing rather than of listening, of showing rather than of speaking, of being with and in and for another. Similarly, the application of the senses is an imaginative effort to touch and to be touched according to the senses one applies. Thus the body is involved in the application of the senses, the soul in meditation, and the heart in contemplation. This distinction of types of prayer is used by Ignatius thoughout the Spiritual Exercises, *and it is clearly from this time at Manresa that the terms are derived.*

Ignatius communicates with the Body and Blood of Christ through his interior eyes. He describes how sensitive his physical eyes have become to the grace he received through the image of the three musical notes; he says that he broke out in uncontrollable tears. He might equally have spoken of a perception through his 'interior ears'. The whole point here is that both his body and soul – both his senses and his interiority – are being increasingly refined through the lessons of his schoolmaster.

THE FOURTH LESSON was learned through a 'vision' that occurred more than once. Not only did it occur often, and in various places, but it lasted for a long time. He saw it often at Manresa, and for the second time he added the short contrapuntal phrase that is characteristic of him: if he should say that he saw it twenty or forty times, he would not dare judge it a lie. In other words, if he said that he saw it less than twenty or forty times, he would be lying. He had used this phrase before when he said that God was teaching him 'lessons', and that were he to say otherwise, he would be offending the Divine Majesty. He relates only two other episodes where this 'vision' appeared to him: near Padua and in Jerusalem.

What was the 'vision'? It was a vision of the humanity of Christ, and Ignatius repeats that he saw it with 'interior eyes'. It was not the Eucharistic Christ who offers himself up to the Father in the Mass and on the cross, but it was rather the human Christ, the most ordinary Christ – merely 'Jesus', we might say – moving among us as one of us, a pre-

Eucharistic Christ, who does not yet reveal his divinity. There is a very subtle and clear presentation of this interplay between Christ's outward humanity and hidden divinity in the *Spiritual Exercises* in the meditation of the Third Week:

> Fifth point: This is to consider how the divine nature goes into hiding, that is to say, how Christ as divine does not destroy his enemies, although he could do so, but allows himself in his sacred human nature to suffer most cruelly. [196]

This point is reversed in the meditation of the Fourth Week, which is concerned with the apparitions of Jesus after his resurrection from the dead:

> The fourth point is to consider how the divine nature, which in the passion seemed to go into hiding, now in his holy Resurrection appears and reveals itself so miraculously in its true and most holy effects. [223]

This kind of baroque twist is characteristic of Ignatius's way of thinking and expressing himself, as noted above, when he says that were he to say the opposite, he would be lying.

It may at first seem strange that Ignatius mentions this vision of the humanity of Christ only *after* his mention of Christ in the Eucharist. The series of lessons begins with the Trinity, then moves to the creation of the world, and so one might expect a chronological order to be followed, moving to the Incarnation, and only then the Eucharist. But Ignatius does not follow a strictly chronological order, leading from before to after. He is interweaving the temporal order with a movement from the source to its full ramifications, from the whole to its parts, from the Trinity and the creation down *through the Eucharist* to the humanity of Christ. It is through the Eucharist, after or beyond the Eucharist, that Ignatius has the visions of Christ in his humanity; and this vision occurs often, and not briefly but 'for a long time'. It was also in all-too-human contexts in Ignatius's life that he experienced these visions of Jesus's humanity.

The vision took the form of something 'like a white body, neither very large nor very small, but he did not see any distinction of members.' He says that he also saw Our Lady in a similar form, without distinguishing parts. The two other 'visions', and the 'audition' as well, comprise both a unity and a multiplicity, both a whole and its parts. The absence of distinct members in these visions of Christ and of Our Lady may be due to the presence of an aspect that is lacking in the others: the aspect of duration. For these visions last for a length of time that makes them unique among the lessons that Ignatius learned. 'Time' may be the most invisible of dimensions, but when we are confronted with something that remains in our presence, without changing, we tend to become more aware of what is changing in us. It could be that Ignatius's vision of the humanity of Christ and his Mother is a vision which restores him to his own humanity, to himself. The vision of the humanity of Christ and his Mother is a vision, with interior eyes, into their accompaniment of him in the duration of his humanity, in his space-time. It was a 'vision' of Our Lady and the Child that had so affected Ignatius in his bed at Loyola that he never afterwards assented to a sexual temptation, that is, never fell short of a complete sexual experience. If ever a vision had an affect on the 'humanity' of a man, it was that one. The strange 'vision' of meat, which appeared so near to him one morning when he awoke, was also immediate, lasting, and unshakeable in its effect. The particularity or 'radiation' of this vision is experienced in one's own humanity as it 'endures', as it exists in our time. It is an absolutely necessary bridge to the fifth and last lesson.

<u>*Time, Unity and Multiplicity*</u>

The unity and multiplicity of a form takes place in time. The unity of a structure is only revealed in the multiplicity of its variations. The unity, vitality, and particularity

> *of such a structure in time can be illustrated by listening to Bach's* Art of Fugue. *The first subject or melody is repeated successively, but with subtle variations: in faster and slower rhythms, with delayed or precipitated entries of the voices, with inversions of the subjects, with surprising reversals of the responses, with changes of instrumentation from strings to winds or both simultaneously in counterpoint, and finally with the introduction of two, and then three rhythms of the same melody at the same time. Only after he has revealed these variations inherent in the very nature of the music of a single melody does Bach introduce a second subject or melody, which takes its time to combine with the first and to try out a few variations. Then Bach introduces a third subject, to interplay with the first and second. Finally he introduces the fourth, which is constructed on the notes corresponding to the letters of his own name. We are not just introduced to an extensive display of the technical possibilities of the fugue, but our hearing and consciousness are expanded to fuller and fuller ranges of appreciation of the depths that can co-exist in time. This is what Ignatius was doing when he headed toward the 'Contemplation for Obtaining Divine Love' at the end of the* Spiritual Exercises. *This is also what was unwittingly yet gracefully achieved in the corporate work of the* Autobiography, *as prefaced and concluded by his fellow Jesuits.*

THE FIFTH AND LAST LESSON occurred outdoors, and it occurred only once. Ignatius was going to pray in a church about a mile away. Years later he believed that the church was dedicated to St Paul the Hermit. He was walking in that direction, absorbed in what he calls his 'devotions', and then sat down for a while with his face toward the river which ran beside the road. As he sat there, the 'eyes of his understanding' began to be opened. He explicitly says that he saw no 'vision', yet he learned so many things, in spiritual matters, in matters of faith and profane things as well, that the enlightenment made everything seem new to him.

Ignatius's way of referring to the content of his vision is curious. One might expect spiritual matters and faith to form one side of the dichotomy, and profane matters the other side. But here spiritual matters are distinguished on the one hand, and matters of faith and profane things are understood in a new unity. It may be that the matters of faith and profane things are what he now understands more spiritually and more subjectively. He does not give any further details on the content of this vision, but he makes the sweeping statement that if he were to combine all the graces he had received from God during the sixty-two years of his life, with all the things that he had learned on his own, these would not equal the clear illumination of his understanding that occurred just once there at the riverside.

After this experience had lasted 'for a good while', he went to kneel before a nearby roadside cross to thank God for the grace he had just received. It was there that he once again saw the beautiful vision of the serpent-form with many eyes. He noted, however, that its usually beautiful colour had faded, and he realized that this was due to his own proximity to the wayside cross. He says that he knew immediately, and 'with a strong agreement of his will', that it was the demon. The reference to both his understanding and his will imply that it was with his whole soul, with his whole interiority, that he experienced this. He does not say that the vision was from the devil, or that it was a ruse of the devil, but that it was the devil. Even though it would later continue to appear to him for a long time, in this instance he took a staff he used to carry in his hand – the staff he had bought, together with the sack-cloth and gourd, in the town he had passed through before climbing up to Montserrat – and with contempt he used it to drive the Devil away.

The fifth lesson was more comprehensive than all the previous visions and all the succeeding graces, although it was not strictly speaking a 'vision' that he had seen with 'interior eyes'. Yet it is this experience which enabled him to see through the false 'vision' of the demon. It was not just the enlightenment of his understanding which helped him to see through the falsity of the vision; it was only after he had chosen to approach the wayside cross to express his thanks for the new understanding that the many-eyed serpent appeared, no doubt to distract him from his personal act of gratitude. It is in that two-fold context of the great grace given, and of Ignatius's practical physical response to it, that the serpent-form appeared, and it was in Ignatius's movement toward the cross that he noticed the serpent, perceived the contrast of colour, realized the identity of the Devil, and raised his staff to drive it away. It is in this scene where there is no divine 'vision' that Ignatius finally sees through the demonic 'vision' which has accompanied him on the road. This scene of the greatest of all Ignatius's illuminations did not occur in a church, but outdoors in natural surroundings. He had a comprehensive understanding of spiritual matters and matters of faith and profane things; this was a way of saying that all his past spiritual experiences came together in a new way and formed him in such a way that all his future spiritual experiences would find their places within it. It was not some special vision of Jesus that strengthened him, but the presence of an ordinary wayside cross sufficed to let him recognize the lie that underlay the consoling beauty of the many-eyed serpent-form. The final lesson of the Master disillusioned Ignatius of a false consolation, which had at least partly faded due to the new illumination he had had, to his gesture of gratitude toward the cross, and to his use of the staff as a weapon to drive off the enemy detected beneath his disguise.

9. *Two illnesses*

After the detailed descriptions of these five spiritual experiences, Ignatius switches back to the physical aspect of his life and relates certain details of two illnesses.

The point of the story of his first illness is that it was accompanied by a temptation to vanity and presumption. He was so sick that it appeared that he was going to die, as had been the case back in Loyola on the eve of the feast of SS Peter and Paul. But here in Manresa the thought came to him that he was a just man, and sure of his salvation. He did everything he could to reject the thought, and he countered it by recalling his past sins. This thought and the memories that he used to oppose it tired him out more than the fever itself. But despite all his efforts he could not succeed in driving away the idea. When he was a little better and no longer in danger of death, he began to cry out to certain visiting ladies that, for the love of God, should they ever again see him in danger of death, they should cry out with all their strength that he was a sinner, so he could better recall his offences against God.

In this episode Ignatius increasingly admits that he needs other people to help him 'to save his soul'. His own memory, understanding, and will are not enough. There is considerable contrast between this man in Manresa and the man who, a few months before, would only clench his fists when he underwent the operations on his leg.

Although the point of the story may be his vanity and presumption, and his need of others to help him overcome the temptation to complacency in his salvation, the context of this story gives it further relevance. Only shortly before, his scruples over his past sins were so great that he was tempted to suicide in order to be free of the past. Now, however, he is so freed from his past that, even though he is in real danger of death, he cannot recall his own past sins enough to counter a temptation to presumption.

Before recounting the story of the second illness, Ignatius makes a detour to relate two other incidents where he was in danger of death. Once, after his studies in Paris, when he was sailing from Valencia to Italy, it seemed certain that the ship was going to sink. As he prepared for death, he could not feel any fear due to his sins, nor did he fear damnation, but he did experience a great confusion and suffered much because he esteemed that he hadn't used well the many gifts and graces God had given him. In this instance he was not worried by his lack of fear about his past life or about his possible damnation in the immediate future. Rather, his confusion stemmed from his regret at not having used more fully the gifts he had been given. The spiritual experience went in the opposite direction from the temptation to vanity; it was a regret, not for what he had done, but for what he had not done.

A similar baroque twist is found in the third instance when he was expecting to die, in Rome in 1550. At the thought of death he experienced such lightness of heart and spiritual consolation that he broke into tears. The tears became so frequent that he avoided thinking of death so as not to expose himself to such an intense consolation. Whereas the shipboard scene had led him to confusion and desolation over not having well employed his gifts, the Roman scene brought him to intense consolation. Here again, confronted with the same concrete experience, the imminence of death, Ignatius experienced the opposite reactions which are his signature. For it is in the tension of the opposition that a new force appears. Neither of these experiences left him in the state of interior powerlessness that he knew at Manresa, but the danger of the situations led him to experience feelings of a deeper nature: feelings of confusion, related not to past sins but to past graces, and feelings of joy, related to future work which awaited him, but without the presumption of claiming to be just.

After this detour into the future, Ignatius returns to his story to describe his second illness at Manresa. The first illness was described more in its interior aspects, leading him nonetheless to call upon the help of others who were absent when he was undergoing the temptation. But the second illness is described more in its exterior aspects, with many details of the kindnesses he received from others who were present:

– the municipality arranged for him to be lodged with a family;

– the family took great care of him;

– many ladies of society came to visit him, and even kept watch at night by his bedside, and

– they gave him clothes, shoes and a beret, since winter was approaching, and he was both weak and subject to frequent stomach pains.

In these descriptions of his illnesses Ignatius is ordering his experiences according to the pattern referred to: interior and exterior, spiritual and physical, self and others and God, day and night. In addition, certain areas of the physical side of his existence recur faithfully: his body with its hair, nails, food, and sexual life; its need for clothes, lodging, transportation. Similarly, areas of his spiritual life recur: temptations, personal prayer, Mass, the sacrament of Penance, the Office, 'visions'. There is a definite progress in the integration of these two aspects of his personality, with an awareness of the classical faculties of his soul: his memory, feelings, understanding, and will. His tears and more comprehensive understanding are unmistakable signs of his development. Especially significant is this series of lessons which led this controlling man to 'uncontrollable' tears and to recognizing the demon in something that had previously given him pleasure.[6]

10. *Spiritual persons*

The last sentence of the story of his Manresa period recalls that during all this time Ignatius was very eager to find people with whom he could have spiritual conversations. Thus he returns to that desire which he had already mentioned before he fell into the crisis of scruples, but which proved to be as inefficacious as confession, prayer, and penance. It was not just other people who sought out Ignatius for spiritual direction, but he also sought out others for the same purpose. This desire remained with him until shortly after his return to Barcelona from Jerusalem. It disappears from the story at this point, probably because his desire was satisfied by the life he lead with certain student companions. After the group of companions formed in Barcelona and Alcala, and then dissolved in Salamanca, another group formed in Paris, and this group became known as 'the Companions of Jesus'. Parallel to this emergence of a group of companions after the pilgrimage, there is an increasing tension in Ignatius's relation to both civil and ecclesiastical authorities. The Manresa period ends on this note of seeking spiritual persons, showing Ignatius's need for others, both physically in his illnesses and spiritually in his interior life. His life with companions in the future, his efforts at forming and living in community, fall apart if the conditions of its unity are not fulfilled. The basis of that unity is the desire to communicate with those one loves the good things that one has received, and to receive from them the good things that they have received. This is precisely the point he makes in the opening note of the final 'Contemplation for Obtaining Divine Love' in the *Spiritual Exercises* [230–231].

But before returning to Barcelona, where Ignatius will begin to lay the foundations of his intellectual life and learn to integrate it with his spiritual life and the physical limits imposed on his daily life, and where he will start to gather companions in view of an apostolate, there lies the polarizing experience of his pilgrimage to Jerusalem. For it was not only a most consoling experience and the partial realization of his dream, but it was a great disappointment whose meaning he had to discern.

Chapter 6

JERUSALEM: FORWARD AND ABOUT FACE

On the road from Barcelona to Jerusalem and back, two major facts stand out. First, Ignatius insists on travelling alone, without any companion, so that he may learn to put all his trust, his hope and his affection in God alone. Secondly, his plan to stay in Jerusalem fails, not due to his lack of courage or trust in God, but due most probably to his failure to express all of his intentions to the Franciscan Provincial Superior. Although the Provincial might still perhaps have refused, for financial or political reasons, Ignatius felt that it was because he had not shared all of his project with the authorities. This may be linked to the fact of his travelling alone: if he had had close companions with him, he might have had the presence of mind and the counsel to speak his mind completely. The return to Barcelona, the undertaking of studies, the assembly of a group of companions who intended to return to Jerusalem with Ignatius: all of this was a second attempt to reach the goal – the citadel of the castle – from which he had been sent away, under the papal authority held by the Franciscan Provincial. The failure of the second attempt in 1538, and the return of the group from Jerusalem to Rome, is but another, longer way of returning to Jerusalem.[7]

The story describes one long movement toward Jerusalem, followed by Ignatius's return to Europe in view of preparing himself for another attempt at getting there. Although the first trip to Jerusalem is the geographical centre of the story, the magnetic pole is found in the experiences of Manresa. It was there that he learned the basic lessons which he brought to each of the stages on his way, whether he met with success or failure. His energies had found there an equilibrium which was still rather crude, but which became all the more evident as it was refined.

It may be that, had he travelled with companions, they would have counselled him to trust the Franciscan Superior with all that was in his heart. But the fact is that Ignatius was really not ready for companionship yet. He truly had to learn to trust, hope, and centre his affections on God alone during this pilgrimage. In the final confrontation with the Franciscan Provincial he appears to have been very close to getting permission to stay in the Holy Land, but he expressed only the subjective half of his personal intention: his desire to remain in the Holy Land for his own 'devotion'. He did not mention his more objective and interpersonal intention: to 'do good for souls'. He learned only later how to open himself completely to persons in authority, although never relinquishing his judgement, his liberty, and his discernment, which were necessary in order to reach beyond the relationship to the point where Christ might appear (or 'come') in the 'colloquoy' of the conversation itself. (See the final conversation between Ignatius and Camara, as recounted in Camara's Epilogue.) Thus, the interpersonal factor was an element, though unexpressed, in Ignatius's intention of staying and working in the Holy Land. The mere fact that he chose to travel alone does not mean that the interpersonal factor was missing. In summary, on his first trip to Jerusalem, Ignatius came alone, with the unexpressed intention of working for other people. On his second proposed trip to Jerusalem, after his years of study in Europe, as we shall see, he set out with a group of fellow religious and priests with the expressed intention of working with them for other people. In other words, the interpersonal factor is found in his group and in its objective. Ignatius will grow in that direction, thanks largely to the kind of companionship that he finds with God during that first pilgrimage.

It may seem out of place for us to take note of these interpersonal factors at this stage of Ignatius's journey, since he himself deliberately excluded them at this point. But since he later changed his mind about companions, and since he told the whole story for the companions themselves, our attention to the eventual inclusion of companionship enables us better to appreciate the purpose of their exclusion at this stage of his journey. For their absence prepares him for the graces that he sought: trust in God alone.

1. *In Barcelona*

Despite the brevity of the description of Ignatius's activities in Barcelona, it is easy to recognize the rhythm of the pattern which moves from other people to himself, from the physical to the spiritual aspects of his life, and then back to other people.

Even though he didn't know Italian or Latin, he resisted all offers of companions who could translate for him. Thus he stripped himself of any facility with language.

He had also decided to go without any provisions of food. Although the owner of the ship was so generous as to be willing to transport him to Italy for nothing, he insisted that the pilgrim bring his own sea-biscuits. Ignatius had so many scruples about doing this that he simply put himself in the hands of his confessor, who told him to take the biscuits that were necessary. This is the first time since the great crisis at Manresa that his scruples recur. Although he describes the incident of the sea-biscuits as causing him 'great scruples', since he saw good reasons on both sides of the argument, he solved them simply and swiftly by taking counsel. His indifference to the result recalls his decision to release the reins of his mule on the road to Montserrat, although there the decision was not between two equally good courses of action. This deliberate passivity is an attitude he takes toward a decision to be made: not a decision between good and evil, but a decision between two actions that are equally good. In the case of the sea-biscuits the crisis does not drag on as it did at Manresa. Since then Ignatius has learned how to deal with this kind of problem.

The root of his reasons for *not* bringing sea-biscuits was simply that he wanted to put his complete hope and trust in God. The same was true of his reasons for not taking a companion with him; he would expect help from him when he was hungry or otherwise in need, he would trust him, he would take him into his affections. Ignatius was resolved to free himself from all such relations. The single-mindedness of that resolution was nakedly apparent in his readiness to go aboard the ship without any food. It was the refusal of the ship's owner which made him rebound to the confessor, who then told him to take the sea-biscuits.

Ignatius's story about himself at this point seems designed to show how foolish he was. Not only did he make a fool of himself – a 'fool for Christ' – but his telling of it shows that he has overcome any desire to hide the foolishness of such behaviour. In its own way, the telling of the story continues to witness to the truth and wisdom behind the foolishness.

When he went to beg for the biscuits, he feared to succumb to the vain glory of receiving people's admiration for him, should he say he was going to Jerusalem, so he would say that he was going on pilgrimage to Rome. In one instance, the lady to whom he told this answered in amazement: 'You want to go to Rome? But the people who go there come back in I don't know what sort of state.' Although she did not have a high opinion of the spiritual benefits Ignatius sought in Rome, he does not say whether or not she contributed to his fund for sea-biscuits. But he treasured this memory, which it would be hard to keep if one didn't have a sense of humour and an appreciation of paradox. Nadal later described the spirit that surrounded Ignatius's quarters in the years he knew him in Rome: 'Those who were in his room were always cheerful and laughing.'[8]

His fear of vanity was so great that he would tell no one the name of the country or of the family to which he belonged. This reticence concerning both his origins and his destination may have protected him from vanity, but it would work against him in his interview with the Franciscan Provincial in Jerusalem. It is also this reticence, practised during his pilgrimage, that he shared with Camara many years later in Rome: this deliberate act of *not speaking* is the kernel from which came the whole story which he later told. The time finally came to tell the story of his silence. But as Camara learned and later related in his Epilogue, there were still limits to his story telling.

After buying the biscuits, Ignatius had some extra change: five or six 'blancas'. Just before boarding the ship, he left them on a bench by the shore. Perhaps no gesture in the whole story speaks more eloquently of Ignatius's desire to have nothing. To leave his sword, his mule, his noble clothes before the altar of Our Lady at Montserrat is the stuff of high drama. To steal away early in the morning, dressed in one's pilgrim robe is equally dramatic. But to leave one's spare change on a bench that happens to be in a port, just before boarding ship, is an act of another order. The ordinariness of the surroundings makes the gesture stand out as all the more extraordinary. Who would ever have noticed such an insignificant act? Yet the act bespeaks the intimate conviction that the God who created the universe is also the God who controls sea-transport, food provisions, financial systems, and the generosity of those who give to beggars. The gesture is Tolstoyan in its implications. There is something God-like in the confidence that it expresses, and in the reaction that it still elicits. In the text, at least, the money is still lying there on the bench, and no one will ever pick it up.[9]

Ignatius recalls at this point, just before his departure, how he sought for spiritual persons in order to speak with them, even if they were hermits who lived far from towns. But neither at Manresa nor at Barcelona did he find as much help as he desired, not even from the old woman in

Manresa who had cried out her prayer that Jesus Christ might appear to him. After his return to Barcelona from Jerusalem, he had grown out of this excessive dependency on finding spiritual persons.[10]

2. *Passage to Italy and the road to Rome*

A strong wind made their passage to Italy particularly swift. Once they landed in the region south of Rome, there was fear of the plague. He refused to be afraid and set off immediately for Rome. His complete lack of fear of the plague would recur in Paris several years later, but in that later instance the overcoming of his fear and imaginings is described with more complexity of detail and more attention to his interior struggle. At this stage of his pilgrimage to Rome, Ignatius mentions the strong wind and the plague as if he were rapidly listing the great obstacles found in the biblical model of the lives of Elijah and Moses.

He relates another instance of overcoming his fear when he tells how he defended a mother and her daughter from drunken soldiers who threatened to molest them in a barn. His strong words of protest and indignation were enough to shake everyone in the house and farm where they were lodged. His immediate initiative and confidence were enough to bring fear and reason to the lusty soldiers.

This incident reveals more than Ignatius's fearlessness. It was out of gallantry that he had accompanied the mother and daughter who were also on the road to Rome. They and a youth had been passengers with Ignatius on the voyage from Barcelona. The mother had dressed her daughter in boy's clothing, evidently to discourage passing men from taking undue notice of her. (It is as if we were in one of those roadside inns among variously disguised characters, such as we find in Shakespeare and Cervantes.) The four fellow passengers – Ignatius, the youth, and the mother and daughter – found lodging at a place where there were also many soldiers, gathered around a great fire. The soldiers gave them something to eat and coaxed them to drink a good deal of wine, as if to warm them up. Then the mother and 'son' were put in an upstairs room, while Ignatius and the youth were quartered in a stable below. At midnight Ignatius heard loud cries, and found the mother and daughter (still disguised, or undisguised, Ignatius does not tell us) in the courtyard below, wailing that someone had attempted to violate them. At this point Ignatius shouted out with such force that everyone in the house was alarmed. The youth had fled, thereby indicating possible culpability, as he may have figured out the disguise of the mother's 'son'. Ignatius took the mother and her daughter and left the lodging immediately to continue on their way. Ignatius did not hesitate to spring to action, but the assailant had already fled.

Next he came to a town where the gates were locked, but he appealed for help to the lady of a nearby castle who was entering the town. Surprisingly, she agreed to his request, and through her good offices he entered the town. Moreover, his begging in this town resulted in his receiving many 'quatrini', coins of small value.

In this incident, it is not so much Ignatius's strong initiative which triumphs over the difficulty, but his quiet patience. He recounts how he and the mother and daughter had to spend the night in a leaky church, because the gates of the nearby city were closed and they were forced to find some shelter outside the gates. In the morning they were not allowed to enter the city, nor did they have any success in receiving alms outside. In search of alms they went to a nearby castle outside the city walls, but they found no alms there either. Ignatius was so tired that he could go no farther, so he decided to remain there, but the mother and her daughter left him to continue on their way to Rome. It was in this weak state that he approached the lady of the castle, who was leaving for the nearby city. He explained that he was ill only from weakness, not from the plague, and he asked her to let him accompany her into the city to seek some cure. Unexpectedly she readily granted his favour.

At the end of a long series of obstacles, a final obstacle is suddenly overcome. It was out of a sense of honour that he left the first lodging; after a night in the leaky church with the women he had protected, and after unsuccessful attempts to obtain alms, he was finally too tired to move; then the very women whom he had defended took it upon themselves to continue their journey and leave him alone. Alone, as alone as he had chosen to be, he made a simple reasoned request, and received a ready response. In addition, Ignatius's begging results in his gaining plenty of small coins, as if the 'blancas' he had left on the bench in Barcelona are now falling into his hands as Italian 'quatrinis'. Ignatius no longer thematizes his stories with a moral, underlining how God was continuing to treat him as a schoolmaster does a child, for he considered it obvious that the One he had chosen as his companion was indeed taking care of him with His surprising sense of humour. After two days of recovery in that city, Ignatius went on to Rome. He entered Rome on Palm Sunday, 1523. He had left Manresa in February and sailed from Barcelona in mid-March. His arrival in Rome for Easter, like his arrival at Montserrat for the Annunciation, shows that Ignatius was continuing to fit his new life into the cycle of the feasts of the Christian year. The momentum of those feasts was helping him to move out of his old habits and to discover in the events that the feasts were celebrating a new rhythm for his own progress. On what we call 'Palm Sunday' we commemorate Jesus's entrance into Jerusalem, riding on a donkey. Ignatius did not compare himself to Christ, nor to the donkey, but his life had taken on ironic twists. Whether he actively took the initiative to defend the frightened women, or patiently depended on others and begged from the lady in the castle, events had a way of accumulating around him, as if gathering their own momentum, leading him finally to arrive at his chosen destination. One event led to another until a whole set of events had been put into motion, involving chaos, chance, and surprise, and then everything suddenly stopped. But wherever it stopped, it was tending toward the place where he was going. Pamplona, Loyola, Montserrat, Manresa, Barcelona, Rome ... Ignatius was catching on to the chance element in his life.

3. *From Rome to Padua and Venice*

After receiving the papal benediction for his pilgrimage, he set out from Rome about a week after Easter. He carried with him six or seven ducats that had been given him for his voyage from Venice to Jerusalem. He had accepted this money because so many people in Rome had tried to dissuade him from his determination to make the passage without money. He was absolutely certain that he would find the means to go to Jerusalem, yet he was persuaded to take the money. Two days after leaving Rome, however, he concluded that it was basically his lack of trust in God that had led him to accept the ducats, so he asked himself if it would be good to get rid of them. He finally decided to give the money as alms to those who begged from him. In this way he arrived in Venice with only a few 'quatrini' in his pocket, and he spent them on his first night's lodging.

As he approached Venice with a group of other travellers, they were informed that since there was fear of the plague in the area, they must all obtain certificates of good health at nearby Padua. As he walked more slowly than the others, it happened that he found himself at nightfall abandoned by them in the countryside. In this isolation he had a 'vision': Christ appeared to him as he had at Manresa, like a white body, neither very great nor very small, but he could not distinguish the members of his body. Ignatius was deeply consoled by the vision, and the next day when he came to the gate of Padua he entered very simply, without having obtained a health certificate and without being questioned by the guards. The same thing happened when he left Padua. His companions were astonished, for he hadn't bothered about the certificate. Similarly, when the Venetian police came aboard the boat for Venice to check the passengers, he was the only one that they overlooked.

The Vision of Christ

The vision of Christ takes this particular form in only three places during Ignatius's life story: at Manresa as many as forty times, at Padua this once, and once at Jerusalem. Why did Christ appear to him in such circumstances?

A first characteristic common to all three visions is that Ignatius was isolated, without companions (at his own wish), and Christ came to him as though to be with him, to accompany him. In a later episode of this story, in the chapel at La Storta, a town outside of Rome, Ignatius was not alone, but with his companions. There he prayed a prayer which is the complement of this: he did not ask Christ to come to him or to appear to him, but he asked Our Lady to intercede with the Father so that he might be put with Christ. In other words, in that later circumstance, Ignatius took the initiative.

A second characteristic of all three visions is that they are consequent on a decision to abandon something, so that he may rely only on God.

It is also noteworthy that the false 'vision' of the serpent-form was linear and curled, with many eyes; it even proved to have a voice which tempted him to abandon his life of abandonment. The 'vision' of Christ is round, and is not articulated into distinct members. Ultimately, as in Ignatius's last interview with Camara, Ignatius had 'visions' of Christ when he was in conversation with real persons who had eyes and voices of their own.

4. *At Venice*

Ignatius's description of his days in Venice covers the same areas of his physical needs and his spiritual dispositions.

His behaviour oscillated from activity to passivity, as he adhered to his goal and his means.

• He lived by begging, after he had spent his last 'quatrinis' on his first night's lodging, and henceforth slept on St Mark's Square.

• He refused to go to the Imperial Spanish Ambassador, who was his relevant authority in Venice. He thereby refused the ordinary channels that a Basque nobleman would be expected to use.

• He made no special effort to find out how to make passage to the Holy Land. In his soul he was certain that God would not fail to find the means for him to go to Jerusalem, and he was so sure that none of the arguments and fears that people expressed could make him doubt his conviction. He was all the more wary of being moved by other people's fears for him, since only as recently as at Rome he had yielded to the temptation to save five or six ducats for the passage to Jerusalem. It was only after he had decided to abandon his trust in his savings that he experienced the vision of Christ outside of Padua. In Venice Ignatius kept a very low profile, as if he understood that the lower the profile, the greater the chances of God's will being worked out.

In fact, one day a rich Spaniard approached him and asked him what he was doing, and where he wanted to go. Once informed of his intention, he brought him home to dinner, and then lodged him for several days until everything was ready for his departure. The threads of the pattern have tightened once again: a chance encounter, followed by food, lodging, and arrangement of passage. His host was especially fond of a habit Ignatius had acquired at Manresa, of not speaking during meals, except to respond briefly. Instead, he listened to what was said and retained certain points that would give him the opportunity to speak of God at the end of the meal. The Spaniard and his family were so fond of Ignatius that they wanted to delay his departure and even force him to remain with them. His host took him for an audience with the Doge of Venice, so that

Ignatius could speak to him. Having heard him, the Doge gave orders that he was to be put aboard the Governor's ship bound for Cyprus.

Meanwhile many other pilgrims were arriving in Venice looking for passage to the Holy Land, but most of them returned home because of the new situation created by the fall of Rhodes to the Turks in 1522. Their fear, of a political and military nature, did not affect Ignatius. Thirteen pilgrims boarded the pilgrims' ship. Eight or nine were to board the Governor's ship, to which Ignatius had been assigned by the Doge himself.

Shortly before setting sail, however, Ignatius fell ill with fevers that rose for several days and then fell. The ship was to leave on the very day he had taken medicine. The doctor whom his Spanish hosts had consulted said that if he boarded the ship, he was going to his grave. Nevertheless Ignatius boarded the ship and left that same day. He says that he vomited so much that he felt greatly relieved. That was the beginning of his return to good health.

After his total abandonment to God's will at the beginning of his days in Venice, having spent the last 'quatrinis' that remained of his Roman ducats, and after receiving such warm hospitality and favours through his Spanish host, Ignatius nevertheless describes the last days of this episode as being dominated by the fears of others for his physical safety and by his physical illness. Neither fear of the political situation nor fear of a more or less certain death could shake his decision to trust totally in the only companion he has allowed himself: God.

5. *Passage to Cyprus and Jaffa*

Hardly had his health improved, as he was sailing to the destination he so deeply desired, than he noticed certain openly licentious forms of behaviour on board. Just as he had reacted so immediately to the behaviour of the man or men who tried to molest the mother and her daughter on the road from Gaeta to Rome, so here too Ignatius censured this behaviour severely. The Spaniards on board advised him to be quiet, since the crew were talking of abandoning him on an island. But they soon arrived at Cyprus where the passengers on the Governor's ship were transferred to the pilgrims' ship.

During this time on board ship, Ignatius says that Our Lord appeared to him often, consoling and strengthening him. He believed that he saw a large round object, as if of gold. This representation of Christ seems to be different from the one he saw so often at Manresa, and once only at Padua and Jerusalem. When he tells Camara during the last interview that he still has many visions, especially of Christ, he describes this vision as if it were a 'sun'. That later image may refer to this 'large round object, as if of gold'. Whatever the link may be, the vision on board ship confirmed him once again in a situation where he was isolated from others by his own disapproval of the licentious behaviour, and by the determination with which he refused to be intimidated by other people's fears for the crew's reaction to his disapproval. The same two characteristics as in the situation mentioned above are present here as well: his isolation and his firm determination to rely on God.

They sailed from Cyprus to Jaffa without further incident, and they mounted the donkeys that they rode to Jerusalem.

6. *In Jerusalem*

Ignatius's experience in Jerusalem was a major turning point in his life. It began positively enough, for when the pilgrims dismounted from their donkeys at the traditional site where they caught their first view of the Holy City, Ignatius felt great consolation. Indeed, all the pilgrims admitted to being seized by a joy that did not seem natural. This consolation at the beginning of the visit to the holy places should be compared to the great consolation he experienced at the end, in such contrasting circumstances. The 'great consolation' persevered, even though Ignatius's entire project had been reversed. But to return to the narrative, he felt this same devotion throughout his visits to the holy places. This devotion would confirm him in his intention to remain in Jerusalem, continually visiting the holy places and helping souls.

At this point it is best to follow the series of scenes he describes.

FIRST SCENE: He called upon the Franciscan Custodian of the Holy Places and presented him with letters of recommendation, telling him of his intention to remain in the Holy Land for his own devotion. It is at this point that he admits to Camara that he did not tell the Custodian of the second part of his intention: about his wanting to help souls. Nor had he told anyone of this apostolic intention, although he had frequently made public the first part.

After he told the Custodian of his personal intention, the latter answered that he did not see how the Custody could support him in such a project, since it could hardly support the Friars themselves. Ignatius replied that he required nothing of the Custody, except a confessor on occasion. The Custodian admitted that such an arrangement might work, but he would have to wait for the return of the Franciscan Provincial Superior, the head of the order in that area, who had gone to nearby Bethlehem.

SECOND SCENE: While waiting, Ignatius wrote letters to certain persons in Barcelona with whom he had shared conversation about his spiritual experiences. He was reassured by the Custodian's promise to arrange an interview with the Provincial. He informed his correspondents of the good news of God's will for him in the Holy Land. This may have been one of the subjects that he sought to discuss with those spiritual persons whom he had so avidly sought, yet failed to find. Many years later he still remembered that he had already written one letter and was busy writing another when, on the eve of the departure of his fellow pilgrims for return to Jaffa, he received a summons from the Custodian and the Provincial, who had arrived from Bethlehem.

THIRD SCENE: The Provincial spoke to him kindly, telling him that he had heard of his intention to stay, but having given it much consideration, he thought it expedient for Ignatius to leave with the other pilgrims. Many other pilgrims had shared Ignatius's desire, but history proved that some were captured, others killed, and the Order had been obliged to ransom the captives. Ignatius was told to prepare himself to join the other pilgrims for the return trip to Jaffa.

Ignatius, however, replied that there was no question of his returning. His decision was firm, and he would allow nothing to keep him from carrying it out – neither fear of death, nor a life of unransomed captivity. He gave them to understand that even though the Provincial thought otherwise, he would not allow any fear to make him abandon his intention, except the fear of sin. Since that was the case, the Provincial replied that he had been authorized by the Pope to tell anyone to leave the place, or remain, as he judged best, and to excommunicate anyone who disobeyed. In this instance, he had judged that Ignatius was to leave, or to suffer excommunication for the sin of disobedience. The Provincial wanted to show Ignatius the papal bulls giving the Franciscan Custody the power to excommunicate, but Ignatius stopped him by saying that he did not need to see them. He believed their reverences' words.

By the style of his quick-witted obedience, it is clear that Ignatius had obtained something more important than a residence permit in Jerusalem. He had learned to press on, further than he had done with any other authority. He had pressed up to the very limit of being under pain of sin. But when that point was reached, and the authority refused his request, he submitted. He knew how to obey in a way that did honour to the force he was resisting. He insisted that he did not have to see the papal bulls; he trusted his ears, and the words of the authorities, whom he explicitly called 'their reverences'.

This confrontation might recall Ignatius's meeting with the commander at Pamplona, whom he succeeded in convincing to defend the fortress despite the great odds against them. One important difference between the two scenes is that the firmness and fearlessness of Ignatius's resolution in Jerusalem was controlled by his sense of the moral and religious limits and responsibility of those in ecclesial authority.

FOURTH SCENE: After Ignatius's tense exchange with the authorities and the failure of his deeply and long determined plan, the next episode comes as a release. Suddenly realizing that he had to leave the next day, Ignatius didn't return to finish the interrupted letter, but he headed out to visit the Mount of Olives and the site of Jesus's ascension for the last time. He had just learned, through the Custody with its papal authority, that Our Lord did not want him to stay in the Holy Land. He desired to go up one last time to the place from which Jesus ascended into heaven, to see again the imprint of his feet in the stone there. This desire sprang from a deep source in him. For he really believed that his resolution to stay in the Holy Land was God's will. It was during his convalescence at Loyola that he had decided to make the pilgrimage to Jerusalem. It was during his time at Montserrat, his year at Manresa, and the episodes of his voyages and journeys from Barcelona to Gaeta to Rome, from Rome to Padua to Venice, from Venice to Cyprus to Jaffa and Jerusalem that his determination to remain in the Holy City gradually took shape. The swiftness with which he accepted the reversal of such a long-conceived intention is proof of the depth of his sense of sin – a sense that can only be acquired by having an even deeper sense of the graces one has received, and is indeed receiving within each present situation. Ignatius's insistence and ability to accept reversal in the name of the only higher authority he will recognize, are proof of his profound attachment to the Source of the project, and not just to the project itself. When the Franciscan Provincial referred to the papal bulls, he was referring to the authority of St Peter, conferred upon him by Jesus. It is this chain of command, within the Church, that proves to be at the heart of Ignatius's inner attitude. Just as this presence of Christ in the Church is found at the centre of the episode in Jerusalem, so it will be found at the centre of the later episode where Ignatius and his companions are frustrated in their attempt to return to Jerusalem a second time.

To return to the pilgrim's story, Ignatius decided to revisit the site of the ascension. He said nothing to anyone, as was his custom also regarding his intention of helping souls in the Holy Land, and he took no guide. Was it not his wish, during the whole pilgrimage, to have no companion but God? So he headed out fearlessly, even though it was dangerous to go out without a Turkish guide. The guards at the site of the ascension would not let him enter until he had paid his way in by some form of exchange. He gave them his knife from his writing kit. He laid down one of his new-found arms. The writing-kit had long since taken the place of the weapons that he left at the altar of the Virgin at Montserrat. This gesture is fraught with meaning. He who had been so confidently writing letters only a short time before, he who was so confident in his determination to stay in the Holy Land, was now giving up one of the very instruments of his writing-kit in order to go farther: to know more accurately and more intimately the supposed print of a foot in rock. After praying there by the footprint and experiencing intense consolation, Ignatius pressed on farther down the road to Bethpage, the place of still another stone: the rock on which Jesus stood to mount the donkey that carried him into Jerusalem on Palm Sunday for his last Passover. Once Ignatius had finished his devotions there, he realized that he hadn't noticed in what direction Jesus was facing as he ascended. In what direction were the footsteps pointing? This need for knowledge of the details may have been an effect of the reversal just experienced, as if he were looking for some sign, some new indication of the Lord's will for him: Where was he to go? He returned to the Mount of the Ascension and this time paid his way in by giving up his scissors to the guards.

Stripping Down to an Identity (2)

Ignatius was continuing to strip himself of his possessions in an effort to catch on to the total rhythm of the end of Jesus's life. Bethpage was the starting-point of Holy Week, the place from which Jesus began his momentous movement into the city. The Mount of the Ascension was the place of Jesus's final apparition to his disciples after his resurrection, and his final disappearance. Ignatius was moving over this geographical keyboard in an attempt to find his own way through to God's will. It was as if he were storing up energy, by moving back and forth through a magnetic field. He had to strip himself of his possessions in that process. Fortunately for us, before he was stripped down to his nakedness, or taken captive, his search was interrupted.

By this time the Franciscans had missed their independent-minded pilgrim, and had sent out a local Christian to find him. Armed with a great stick and manifestly very angry, the Christian found Ignatius and seized him as he was descending the Mount of Olives; he made a great show of pretending to strike him. Having seized him by the arm, he found that Ignatius let himself be led away without resisting. As Ignatius continued down the road, thus held by the local Christian, he received a great consolation. Indeed, he continually saw Christ above him, and this consolation lasted with great intensity right up to their arrival at the monastery.

In this 'vision' are found the two characteristics already described: his isolation and determination, as well as his passivity in so far as he lets himself be led. The movement down the mountainside reinforced the sense of passivity or 'letting go', after the ascent of the mountain and the intense searching for detail. Not only was he once again isolated, but the 'vision' confirmed him in his resolution. It was not the matter or content of the resolution that was confirmed, for that changed unexpectedly when he learned that Our Lord – and St Peter's successor, as expressed in the papal bulls which thus authorized the sons of St Francis – did not want him to stay in the Holy Land at the present time. But the resolution to search for the will of Christ, and to follow him as closely as possible: this was at the heart of his whole determination. There is something excessive in his looking for footprints, and then, after having gone to Bethphage, to return to ascertain the direction in which the footprints pointed. There is something both ironic and humorous in his willingness to give up the little writing instruments in order to approach the place from which Jesus disappeared. But, like a hunter, or a hunting dog, Ignatius was on the trace of someone: Jesus. And he found him, not on the top of the mountain, but as he descended. For he discovered that he himself was being hunted by a servant of the very authorities who had so limited the time he was to spend in the Holy Land he loved. To his surprise, once he was caught and trapped by the grasp of his hunter, he himself caught what he sought: Christ was with him, 'above' him. The vision of Jesus was as intense as at Manresa; only this time it was at Jerusalem itself. Ignatius once again made a fool of himself for Jesus. But he was fooled into greater intimacy with the one he was resolved to follow.

The episodes in Jerusalem reveal the newly acquired strength and proportion of Ignatius more than in any previous place. His strength and flexibility are matched by his foolishness and weakness. The pattern is most transparent here at the centre of the book. The rest of the story is the recounting of a long effort to return, with even greater presence, and companions.

7. *Return to Venice*

After the confrontation in Jerusalem, and Ignatius's obedience to the authority of the papal bulls, the story returns to the kind of simpler incident already mentioned. Since he had no money, the captain of a wealthy Venetian ship refused to take him aboard, even though many people had recommended him. The captain even mocked his good reputation, saying that if he were a saint, he could walk on water as St James had done. Two other ships were sailing: a Turkish vessel, and a very small one. Ignatius found passage on the small one. The very afternoon of their sailing a tempest separated the three ships. The Turkish ship was completely lost – passengers, crew and cargo. The Venetian ship sank near Cyprus, and only the passengers and crew escaped. The smallest ship was the only one to reach Italy. Ignatius's rejection and humiliation worked unaccountably to his good fortune. But he did not spell out that moral for his listener, any more than he was inclined to spell out the morals of his other stories.

This principle of neither over-telling a story nor spelling out its moral recalls the second Introductory Observation in the *Spiritual Exercises*:

> Someone who gives to another a way and a plan for meditating or contemplating must provide a faithful account of the history to be meditated or contemplated, but in such a way as to run over the salient points with only brief or summary explanations. For if the other begins contemplating with a true historical foundation, and then goes over this history and reflects on it personally, he or she may by themselves come upon things which throw further light on it or which more fully bring home its meaning.
>
> Whether this arises out of the person's own reasoning or from the enlightenment of divine grace, more gratification and spiritual fruit is to be found than if the giver of the Exercises had explained and developed the meaning of the history at length. For it is not much knowledge but the inner feeling and relish of things that fills and satisfies the soul. (par. 2)

Once in Italy Ignatius notes how cold it is; it was indeed snowing. Yet he had only the simplest clothes, including a coat that descended only to his knees, leaving his legs bare. In Venice one of the two hosts who had previously welcomed him in their house happened upon him, and gave him fifteen or sixteen 'Julians' for his journey home, as well as a piece of cloth that he could fold twice to put over his stomach to protect himself from the cold. Here again was the chance reversal of his situation: arriving in the cold with little clothing, no friends and no money, he finds friends who gave him both money and clothing.

8. *The road to Genoa*

Now that he knew that Our Lord did not want him to stay in Jerusalem, he reflected much on what he was to do. He found himself more inclined to study, so that he would be able to help souls. With this intention in mind he resolved to return to Barcelona.

Thus it is along the lines of the second and previously unexpressed part of his Jerusalem project that he now advanced openly. He decided to study in order to equip himself to help others. His years of study will require that he learn to defend his decision to study against two contrary tendencies: distraction from his studies by too much prayer and spiritual illumination (as would be the case in Barcelona), or distraction from his studies by too much 'helping souls' (as would be the case in Paris). In both periods Ignatius was to grow aware of the excess and withdraw from what diminished the time he had decided to give to his studies. What is more, as if to consolidate his resolution, he communicated it to others, as if they were his confessors. This seems to be the result of the lesson he has learned in Jerusalem.

On the first lap of his journey on the road to Genoa, he relates two incidents. The first is clearly concerned with his poverty and with a certain foolishness that poverty then entailed for him; the second is concerned with a complex form of foolishness that was much more dangerous. It was so foolish, in fact, that one man thought that Ignatius had gone mad.

The first incident began as Ignatius was praying in the principal church of Ferrara. A poor man approached him for alms. Ignatius gave him a 'marqueta', worth five or six 'quatrini'. A second beggar came, and Ignatius had nothing but some 'Julians' which he had received in Venice; although it was a silver coin, worth one tenth of a Roman crown, he gave one away. Once the other beggars saw that he was giving alms, they didn't stop coming to him until he had given all of his money away. When still more of the poor began to come, he had to beg them to excuse him, since he no longer had any money at all.

Stripping Down to an Identity (3)

Ignatius is careful to give details of his financial stripping down.

The first mention of finance is at Navarette, where it was a matter of obtaining his salary of a few silver ducats. With this he paid certain debts, and with part of it he paid for the repair of a statue of Our Lady, which he also paid to be handsomely adorned. We should recall that at Onate he had also repaired a statue of Our Lady, but no money was then mentioned.

In Barcelona he begged the money necessary to buy the sea-biscuits, but left his extra change of five or six 'blancas' on the bench in the port.

In Rome he received six or seven ducats for his pilgrimage, but he later decided to give them as alms to beggars, spending the remainder of that sum for his first night's lodging at Venice.

In Jerusalem no money is mentioned, but his knife and scissors are bartered.

On the road from Venice to Genoa, the point now reached, he gives away his only 'marqueta' (worth five or six 'quatrinis') and his silver 'Julians' (each worth one tenth of a Roman crown).

Other instances of financial activities will be noted, but their significance is heightened by the fact that Camara ends his Epilogue with a question of money: he records that Ignatius spoke in particular about how he spent forty days praying over the question of whether a church of the Society could have any income and whether the Society should make use of that. Each day he said Mass on the question, and each day with many tears.

The second incident occurred as he journeyed from Ferrara to Genoa. It is a story of his disregard for the fear of others, as well as for his own fear, even though he was in danger of imprisonment, torture, and death. He was taken prisoner, but his desire to be like Jesus, deliberately exposing himself to mockery, resulted paradoxically in his liberation. The story is told in six episodes.

FIRST EPISODE: Between Ferrara and Genoa lay the battle lines between the Imperial and French armies. As Ignatius approached them, certain Spanish soldiers of the Imperial forces gave him shelter for the night. They were shocked to learn that their guest intended to pass right through the middle of the armies. The wars between Emperor Charles V and King François I for possession of the Duchy of Milan were intensifying and leading toward the Battle of Pavia which would take place the following year.

A review of the precise dates of Ignatius's journey is helpful. He had arrived in Rome for Easter, 1523. He arrived in Jerusalem on September 4 and returned three weeks later to Jaffa on September 23. He reached Venice in January, 1524, and arrived back in Barcelona the following month. As he had crossed the 'No Man's Land' between the Christians and the Turks in the Holy Land, so here he crosses the 'No Man's Land' between European Christian opponents. They are the same opponents who were fighting over the fortress of Pamplona where Ignatius's story began. His limp and scars were the only outward sign of his former participation in this ongoing war. His present fearlessness, however, is rooted in a profoundly different understanding of himself and the times he lives in.

The Spanish soldiers' advice that he should not take the main road through the district but a side road went unheeded.

SECOND EPISODE: By walking straight ahead, Ignatius came to a burned village. He found no one to give him anything to eat. At nightfall he reached a fortified town where the guards arrested him on suspicion of being a spy. These were most likely Imperial soldiers of one of the armies linked to the command of Charles V. They put him in a room and began to interrogate him, but to all their questions Ignatius simply said that he knew nothing. They stripped him of his clothes, examined his shoes and every part of his body to see if he were carrying a letter. He, the Jerusalem letter-writer, had nothing. They bound him to take him to their captain who, they said, knew how to make spies talk. He asked to be permitted to put on his cloak, but they refused, so off they took him in his knee-breeches and waistcoat.

THIRD EPISODE: On his way to the captain's quarters, two things happened to him. First he had an experience or 'representation' of Christ being led away to his trial. He noted that it was not a 'vision' like the others, although the two characteristics previously mentioned are present: he was both alone and deeply decided on his goal and on his means. Yet this was hardly going to be a spiritual conversation. Nevertheless, as he was led through three long streets towards the captain's quarters, he walked along, not sadly, but joyfully and contentedly. It was this consolation which strengthened him to take an initiative: he began preparing himself for the interrogation to come, and he resolved to use the most familiar form of address he could imagine. The lessons of Loyola, Montserrat, Manresa, and Jerusalem have been learned so thoroughly that he managed to go through the following steps of discernment before arriving at the captain's desk:

– He was in the habit of addressing everyone with the second person, 'you', since it was thus that Jesus and his apostles spoke with one another. (This was instead of the the polite form which, in Spanish, is a third person form.)
– As he approached the captain, however, the thought came to him that he should address him as 'your lordship', since he feared possible torture.
– Recognizing this as a temptation due to fear, he resolved not only to refuse to use the more respectful form of speech, but also to omit any bowing or removing of his hat.

He had determined that his inner attitude would be expressed by his speech, bodily gesture, and his clothes.

FOURTH EPISODE: Once at the captain's quarters, he was left for a while in a lower room, but this wait did not affect his resolution, nor his consolation. When the captain finally called for him, Ignatius did as planned: he refused to show any sign of politeness, and responded in a few words which were so spaced out from one another that their oddity could not go unnoticed. The captain took him for an idiot, and told the soldiers that their prisoner had obviously lost his reason, should be given his belongings, and released.

It may be supposed that this came as a surprise to Ignatius. Yet he may have expected to be surprised whenever he imitated Jesus, even in paradoxical ways. The return from Jerusalem is like a honeymoon of foolishness: a discovery of new resources in himself whenever he overcomes and reverses the instinct of his fear.

FIFTH EPISODE: Hardly had Ignatius left the place where he had been kept than he happened upon a Spaniard who lived nearby. This Spaniard took him home, fed him, and offered him lodging for the night. Here, once again, chance or providence comes as a consequence of some incident in which Ignatius has worked out his discernment of the spirits, made his decision and held to it as closely as he can in his desire to follow the pattern of Jesus's example. In this instance, a 'representation' of Jesus being led to his trial had confirmed his resolution, and the chance encounter with the Spaniard confirmed it even further. Whereas Ignatius had subtly and dialectically reasoned out his irrational behaviour, in order to follow Jesus and suffer for him, the captain took him for a man who had lost his reason![11]

SIXTH EPISODE: The next day Ignatius walked until nightfall. Two soldiers spotted him from a tower, seized him, and led him to their captain who was French. Ignatius was once again in the hands of the French, as he had been when he fell wounded at the fortress of Pamplona. This meeting with the French – in this later stage of the same war – was just as unexpectedly positive as the last had been. On learning that Ignatius came from Guipuzcoa, the captain said that he himself came from a nearby country, Bayonne, on the French side of the Basque country, and he ordered his soldiers to release him, give him his supper, and treat him well.

Ignatius is no longer hiding his place of origin, nor does he seem to hide his destination. Too much has happened since those days in Barcelona when he went to beg for his sea-biscuits, and feared to yield to vanity if he revealed his origins and his destination. Just as there was a time for letting his hair grow and a time for cutting it; a time for abstaining from meat and a time for eating it; so there is a time for the greatest discretion in one's speech, and a time for total frankness.

The six episodes in this recounting of his crossing of the battle lines in northern Italy follow a double movement: increasing tension and fear, which is penetrated by both consolation and resolution, followed by the surprise of liberation and subsequent gestures of hospitality. This sort of reversal expresses Ignatius's insight into the practice of 'companionship' with Jesus. If you believe 'in' him, you move 'with' him, and eventually find him 'in' you. The movement is not just an endless circling, but an 'indwelling', a form of remaining together which can withstand and survive separation from one another.

9. *Back to Barcelona*

On arrival in Genoa Ignatius happened to be recognized by a Biscayan named Portundo, whom he had known from his days at the Imperial court from 1517 to 1521. Portundo helped him to find passage on a ship to Barcelona. The ship was pursued by Andrea Doria, the Genoese admiral then working for the French. Although they were in danger of being captured, they got away.

The description of the journey back to Barcelona lists a series of further difficulties overcome: physical difficulties such as storms, cold, hunger, and fatigue; financial difficulties; confrontation with political and military authorities. Each difficulty was resolved by Ignatius's faithfulness to his resolution to imitate Jesus, even though this sometimes increased the possibility of meeting even greater difficulties. His inner presence and dialectical initiatives brought him through these circumstances which lay like so many obstacles on his path back to Barcelona. This city now represented for him the place of study which was necessary if he were to realize his intention of 'helping souls'. It will be revealed to the reader of the *Autobiography* only much later, when Ignatius is studying in Paris, that he intended to return to help souls in Jerusalem. It looks as if he were keeping this secret from the reader until that particular moment. One pilgrimage was over, but another was being prepared.

Ahead of Ignatius lay four further periods of his life, in which he would undertake studies in view of returning to Jerusalem. He would even prepare himself and his companions for the eventuality of not being able to return there. These periods correspond to the four places where he studied: Barcelona, Alcala, Salamanca, and Paris. Throughout these periods he will struggle to integrate his intellectual life into the pattern of the spiritual and physical activities that he has found so helpful. In addition to this, he will be drawn toward the ministry of 'helping souls', and this sometimes comes into sharp conflict with his studies. His various attempts to form a community with other students meet with increasing difficulty and eventual disappointment, before he ultimately finds the basis on which the 'Companions of Jesus' are to be founded.

Chapter 7

BARCELONA: BACK TO SCHOOL

Ignatius spent two years in Barcelona, from Lent 1524 to March 1526. As at Loyola, he worked out the order of his activities in both the physical and spiritual areas, and this order followed the kind of oscillating rhythm previously noted.

– An old friend, a person whom he had met in Barcelona on his way to Jerusalem, offered to support him. This was Isabel Roser, who provided him with food and lodging.

– A local teacher, Master Ardevol, offered to teach him grammar, without recompense.

– Ignatius sought out a Cistercian monk at Manresa, with whom he had hoped to stay while he studied, so as to be better able to give himself up to spiritual exercises and to helping souls, but he learned that the monk had died. So he returned to Barcelona and studied under Ardevol, accepting Isabel Roser's support and spiritually caring for himself.

Thus the order of his life is more or less arranged by interrelating, in a juggling, rather clumsy way, his physical needs, his studies, and his spiritual life.

In this stage of spiritual self-reliance, he found that his memorization of grammatical forms was being interrupted by new spiritual illuminations. The same sort of thing had happened at Manresa, when his sleep had been affected by the illuminations that came at night, until he resolved to ignore them and devote himself to sleep. Ignatius now tried to do likewise, but was unable to chase the 'holy thoughts' away by himself. He reflects on this and notes that the 'illuminations' did not come when he was in prayer or at Mass, but rather when he was memorizing. He gradually understood that these illuminations were temptations, so after praying he sought out his teacher and asked him to accompany him to a nearby church. There, where the solemnity of the place gave weight to the resolution he was about to make, he confessed to his teacher the nature of his weakness and promised never to miss a single lesson during the two years of courses, as long as he was able to find enough bread and water to live. After he had taken this resolution with such firmness, he never again experienced the temptation or yielded to it. Thus he staked out a new area in his life: together with his spiritual life and his physical needs, a life of study now emerged in view of helping others, as well as himself. He staked it out, not just by his personal resolution, but by making the resolution before the relevant public witness, his teacher.

Hardly had he succeeded in balancing his studies with his spiritual life than he began to experiment again in the area of his physical activities. Since he no longer had the stomach pains which led him to wear shoes, he desired and decided to return to some of his old penitential practices. He began by making a hole in the soles of his shoes, which he enlarged little by little, until by the coming of winter nothing remained but the tops. This intensification of his penance on his feet was more than an experiment; it was part of the pattern which kept Ignatius sensitive to the movements of the spirits, so that he could discern what it was better to do, in whatever area a decision had to be made. After having resolved to give less time and energy to 'illuminations' and more to study, he pulled up even further slack, in this triangular sail of prayer-study-penance, by increasing a form of discipline on his feet.

At the end of two years of study, he had made such progress that his teacher told him he was ready to enter the

Faculty of Arts, advising him to enter the University of Alcala. Ignatius, however, did not take his advice immediately, but made doubly sure by asking to be examined in grammar by a doctor of theology. After the examination, the doctor gave him the same advice, to begin his university studies.

The major lesson of Barcelona was that he learned how to reach a balance in his new life, limiting his spiritual illuminations so that they did not interfere with his studies, calling on a witness to reinforce his decision, and yet increasing his physical penance. His insistence on being doubly sure of his ability to begin university studies was less a matter of personal scruples than a way of being certified by others that he was ready. He wanted the witness of both his teacher and of a doctor of theology.

There was a further activity that Ignatius was beginning to learn in Barcelona. Although he does not mention any companions in his story of the Barcelona period, Camara begins the description of the next period at Alcala by saying that Ignatius already had companions when he left for Alcala. This may mean that Calisto, Artiaga, Caceres, and Juanico, the companions who will be specifically named in Alcala, were already with him in Barcelona, or that some other companions preceded them. This failure to mention them may have been due to the fact that Ignatius did not yet really consider them fellow companions, as he will at Alcala. The gradual evolution of a 'company' will undergo the same difficulties as did the other areas of Ignatius's development. In other words, Ignatius will have difficulty in communicating to others the lessons he has learned. He will eventually lose the four companions of Alcala, but after gathering and again losing another group of friends in Paris, he will finally learn – on the third attempt – to live with a group that 'lasts', and their companionship will become so deep that it survives even the failure of their common project to return to Jerusalem.

As the years of study advance, both the formation of a group of companions and the desire to help souls will pass through periods of excess, followed by discernment of that excess and the resolution to contract, reduce or summarize to the essential. The formation of such a group and the work of helping souls will occasionally bring Ignatius and his group into conflict with ecclesial, academic and municipal authorities. These conflicts, however, sometimes tend to propel the group all the more surely toward its goal. As Ignatius is still learning to juggle his spiritual, physical, and intellectual pursuits, he is also learning to juggle three interrelated areas of interpersonal relations: helping souls, living with companions, and answering to authorities who question him about the nature of that help and the nature of his companions.

Chapter 8

ALCALA: THE BEGINNING OF UNIVERSITY STUDIES, AND OF A COMMUNITY

The events at Alcala fall into three stages: first, the establishing of an order in his life in this new place; secondly, the interrogation he undergoes, followed by an acquittal; and lastly, his visit to the Archbishop of Toledo, in search of counsel. The second stage contains four episodes.

1. *Ordering his life*

In a single line at the opening of this period, Camara writes that Ignatius already had companions when he left for Alcala. But then the actual ordering of his life begins with the question of his means of livelihood.

For ten or twelve days he had to live by begging. One day a clergyman and some other persons who were with him laughed at Ignatius and made an injurious remark about his being one of those beggars who nevertheless managed to look rather well off. The director of a nearby hospital happened to be passing by at that moment, overheard the remark, and was so pained that he called Ignatius to his side and brought him to the hospital where he was given a room and all that was necessary. Once again chance played a role in caring for him, but on the condition that he remain poor, indifferent to money, and ready to accept scorn, even from churchmen.

Again and again Ignatius begins his stories with his need for the means of subsistence, which he obtained by begging. Money or riches form the first step of a pattern that is repeated. In the *Spiritual Exercises* 'riches, honours of the world, and overweening pride' are signalled out as the three steps by which the Evil One leads the soul to all other vices. This is outlined in the points of the Meditation on the Two Standards [142]. The three vices are countered by the three steps of poverty, willingness to accept insults or contempt, and humility, as exemplified in the life of Jesus [146].

The *Autobiography* is more than just an illustration of how the *Spiritual Exercises* were lived by Ignatius; it is more than an account of how Ignatius lived before he wrote the *Exercises*, or as he was writing them, or after he had written them. It is a story that overlaps the *Exercises*, that can be occasionally recognized in the meditations or observations of the 'retreat manual' but which extends beyond it in detail, depth and the 'human factor' that escapes conceptualization. Why does it go further than the *Exercises* themselves? Because it is embedded in the story, and so appeals to readers at the level of the heart, and to the stories that they themselves are living, suffering, and trying to survive, by the decisions they are able to make.[12]

At this stage, with a place to live, the description passes to his studies, which will extend over a period of a year and a half.

Next he gives an expanded account of what he means by 'helping souls'. This will get him into trouble, and his companions will be implicated as well. But the supreme irony lies in this: even those who arrest, imprison, and interrogate him about his efforts to help souls are no less 'souls' whom he means to help as he has been helped. Every obstacle is a new challenge to the means and end of this man who had been stripped down to his identity. He had left his castle homestead, his family, his sword and dagger, his fine clothes, his mule, his inheritance, his money, his references to his origins and to his destination, and he had even left that destination of Jerusalem, as well as his knife and scissors in order to approach twice the place from which Jesus disappeared. But he had found something that was worth all that and more. He had found Jesus, in some mysterious way. It was a hard path to follow, but Ignatius's effort to follow it, and his belief that he was close on Christ's trail, is so clear, incomprehensible, touching and ludicrous by turns, that a reader cannot but wonder, increasingly, at the force that drives this man. Sometimes he seems to be itching for confrontation with authority and the consequent humiliation; at other times he switches to a passive attitude of submission and graciousness. At all times there is that electricity in the air that we sense when we are in the presence of people who are fully alive, fully in love, and resolved to live out that love to the end, despite all their fragility and the infidelity of which they know themselves capable.

But what is this apostolate, or ministry, work of 'helping souls'? It began when he was convalescing at Loyola, when he spoke with people about spiritual things, about his discovery, and also wrote it down in his book. During his stay at Alcala he spoke of giving the *Spiritual Exercises* and of teaching catechism. The book had become his way of helping people to discover that they had souls, that they were souls embodied. They had a profound desire and capacity for freedom: for understanding, reflection, imagining, remembering, feeling, discernment, judgement, deliberation, love and decision that would have no satisfaction until they reached and were reached by the Source of everything that is: by God. They had deep possibilities for interior life that were subtly related to each and every area of their physical needs and the world around them. The stages of discernment and decision took place in an area yearned for, reached and established by both the physical and spiritual aspects of oneself. Those aspects were part of one's very human nature, as created in the image of God, and they rose to meet one another in the decision to do God's will, a decision sometimes confirmed by tears, visions, or other assurances. God used every means of His creation in order to enter, dwell within, labour with, and rest in those who loved Him.

This apostolate of giving the *Exercises* and explaining the catechism thus contributed to the glory of God, because God's glory was reflected or radiated there in the human creatures He had created in His image, when they truly, really, met with one another and with Him.

The apostolate or mission had two other effects; it created a sort of cybernetic circle by which it both reinforced itself and also attracted a resistance to itself. First, many people came to have a deeper knowledge and love of God, and a more vital interest in spiritual things. Others experienced diverse temptations. This caused some comment among the local people, above all due to the large crowds who came to the places where he taught catechism. A local printer and his brothers were especially generous in helping him with whatever they had, whenever Ignatius came to them representing some immediate need of the poor. Thus the needs of the apostolate reinforced the group of companions.

The last effect was that his work and life with his companions were spoken of so widely that word of them reached the ears of the Inquisition in Toledo. Thus the apostolate and the group brought about resistance to itself.

2. *Responding to the Inquisition*

The story of Ignatius's interrogation by the Inquisition is told in four episodes, and their sequence is important in order to understand Ignatius's way of dealing with these authorities. It is easier to typecast Ignatius as a strategist than to appreciate him as a human being who is groping through the unknown as carefully as he can. As we follow him through the episodes, we may wonder if he has any strategy at all, and we may come to see that he is operating from a level of the heart which is deeper than all strategies.

FIRST EPISODE: He heard from his host at the hospital that the Inquisitors had come from Toledo and that they suspected him and his companions of being 'enlightened ones' – a term for certain Christians of the period who claimed to be in direct communication with the Holy Spirit. Consequently, it was most likely that they were to be tortured. In fact, the Inquisitors did open an inquiry and a trial of the kind of life and works that Ignatius and his friends were undertaking, but since they hadn't come to Alcala for that purpose, they returned to Toledo without convoking them. They left the inquiry in the hands of Vicar Figueroa.

SECOND EPISODE: Figueroa convoked the companions a few days later to inform them that an inquiry and trial had indeed been planned in their regard. Since no error had been found in their teaching or life, they could continue to act as before without hindrance. Their clothes, however, presented a difficulty. Since they were not religious, Vicar Figueroa thought that it was not right for them all to wear the same habit. Ignatius and Artiaga were to dye their clothes black; Calisto and Caceres, grey; Juanico, the young Frenchman, could remain as he was.

Ignatius said that they would obey, but he added that he wondered what good interrogations on such external vestiary matters really did. More important matters were left unquestioned. Only recently a priest had refused to give communion to a person, because he communicated once a week. The same had happened to himself. So Ignatius wanted to know whether the Inquisitors had found any heresy in their behaviour.

Figueroa, perhaps surprised, answered: 'No, because if they had found a heresy, they would have burned you.'

Ignatius did not hesitate to reply: 'As they would burn you too, if they found you were a heretic.'

Such a reply was surely not expected, although it only reminded the Inquisition that it too was subordinate to the truths it was mandated to defend. The boldness of the remark revealed Ignatius's position on this issue. External capital punishment could deter heresy through fear, but it did not correct the heresy itself. It was the inner attitude toward the truth which was Ignatius's concern. This concern with the inner attitude stands right at the beginning of the *Spiritual Exercises* as their Presupposition:

> So that the giver of the Exercises and the exercitant may the better help and benefit each other, it must be presupposed that every good Christian should be readier to justify than to condemn a neighbour's statement. If no justification can be found, one should ask the other in what sense the statement is to be taken, and if that sense is wrong the other should be corrected with love. Should this not be sufficient, let every appropriate means be sought whereby to have the statement interpreted in a good sense and so to justify it. [22]

After this exchange, the students dyed their clothes as they were told, but fifteen days later Figueroa ordered Ignatius not to go barefoot. Ignatius obeyed as he always did whenever someone in authority gave him an order of this kind, and he put on his shoes. It was in Barcelona that Ignatius had deliberately taken off the soles of shoes to leave only the tops. Now that even the tops of the shoes had disappeared, and Ignatius was walking barefoot in Alcala, he was summarily told to put his shoes back on.

THIRD EPISODE: Four months later Figueroa made a second inquiry about them. It concerned a married woman of quality who used to come to see Ignatius at the hospital (or hospice) by night, in order not to be recognized. She came veiled, as was the custom, but once inside she lifted the veil and went to Ignatius's room. The Inquisitor did nothing; he neither called for a trial, nor did he say anything to Ignatius about it. One may wonder how Ignatius later learned of the inquiry.

FOURTH EPISODE: Four months after the preceding incident, a civil servant one day asked Ignatius to follow him to headquarters. He did so, and was abruptly put into prison. He remained there for seventeen days before he was interrogated. Nonetheless, during that summer the prison was so lightly guarded that he was able to teach catechism and give the *Exercises* to those who came to visit him, just as if he were free. He refused to hire a lawyer, although many offered their services. To one noble lady who offered to get him out of prison, he said: 'He for whose love I have entered here will surely get me out, if it is for His service.'

When Figueroa finally called him for questioning, he raised many points, as if beating around the bush. Then he focused his questions on a certain case: Did Ignatius know a certain woman and her daughter who had set out on a pilgrimage? And did he know about it before they set out?

Yes, Ignatius admitted that he knew them. But due to an oath he had taken, he said that No, he hadn't known they were going to set out on pilgrimage.

The women, both widows, had set out on foot to make a pilgrimage to Jaen in Andalusia where they wanted to venerate Veronica's veil. A certain Doctor Ciruelo in Alcala, a protector of the two women, thought that Ignatius had put them up to it, and that was why he had been arrested.

Ignatius politely offered to tell Figueroa more about the case, and how he had discouraged the two women from going about the world to help the poor, telling them that they could very well serve the poor in Alcala and 'accompany the Most Holy Sacrament'.

This reference to the Mass and the Host is interesting for several reasons. First, Ignatius had referred to the Mass in his first interrogation when he spoke of his being refused communion each week. Secondly, the Mass will take on great meaning for him during the later period at Vicenza, and in the final period in Rome. Thirdly, we have already seen how he asked Nadal, Polanco, and Cogordan to say three Masses on the question of whether he should or should not write his *Autobiography*. To 'say the Mass' is to bring oneself and others into the presence of Jesus at that moment when he offered himself to his Father's will out of love for others, delivering himself deliberately into a trap set by his enemies and false friends. To say the Mass is to enter into the presence of Jesus and his intentions, and thereby to test one's own desires and intentions. Just as the glittering serpent-form at Manresa grew pale beside the cross above the river, so our more superficial or twisted desires and illusions are shed as we faithfully enter into the movement of the Mass. When Ignatius used the expression, to 'accompany the Most Holy Sacrament', he was referring to the Mass itself and the procession of the Blessed Sacrament as a pilgrimage. Jerusalem and all the relics associated with the passion and death of Christ, such as the veil of Veronica, are less important than the Mass itself. Perhaps the round 'vision' of Jesus that Ignatius had seen, a body without distinct members, was a vision of Jesus in the Host.

Figueroa took note of all that Ignatius had told him. Meanwhile Calisto, who had been in Segovia, returned to Alcala as soon as he learned that Ignatius was in prison. Even though he himself had hardly recovered from an illness, he wanted to share Ignatius's prison, but Ignatius told him to present himself first to Vicar Figueroa. The Vicar welcomed him, but told him that he was going to send him to prison too, and he was to stay there until the two women returned to town, to see whether their statements confirmed Ignatius's testimony. Calisto spent a few days in prison but became so sick that Ignatius called on a doctor, one of his good friends in town, to obtain Calisto's liberation, which he did.

The Rhythm of the Episodes

Once again the rhythm of the episodes is evident, as it passes from the apostolate to prison, from one imprisonment to two, from recourse to a friend to liberation. The lives of the friends intertwine like two melodies. Ignatius's imprisonment leads to Calisto's, yet Ignatius's friend, whose assistance he refuses for himself, arranges for Calisto's liberation. We have seen such counterpoint before, as in the episodes on the road from Gaeta to Rome. Ignatius's sense of honour led him to accompany the mother and daughter on the road to Rome. He defended their honour at the inn and left his place in the stable to take to the road with them. After spending the night in a leaky church, and being refused entry into the closed city, the two women went on their way, leaving him alone. But he begged help from a local noblewoman, with whom he entered the closed city, and then continued on his way.

Forty-two days elapsed before Ignatius was freed. The two women had returned from Jaen, and their stories confirmed Ignatius's version. Nonetheless he and his companions were once again told to dress like the other students, but it was added this time that they were no longer to speak of matters of faith for a period of four years – that is, until they had completed their studies. Ignatius knew more on these matters than his companions, but even he always began any response to an interrogation by admitting that his knowledge of matters of faith was rudimentary. This sentence, however, left him hesitant, because it closed the door to his apostolate without giving him any reason other than his lack of instruction. In the first interrogation it had been a matter of the physical aspect of the group of friends, their clothes; but in this second interrogation it is a matter of the 'spiritual exercises' which stem from spiritual conversations in the course of helping souls. Despite his being found blameless in the case of the two women who chose to go on their pilgrimage against his advice, he and his friends were sanctioned. The sanction hit at both his apostolate and his friends; it invaded the pattern itself, and not simply a detail of it. What was he to do? In the past he had resolved his hesitation in various ways, from loosening the reins of his mule on the road to Montserrat, to spending a week without eating or drinking in Manresa. In this instance he decided to go to visit the Archbishop of Toledo and to put everything in his hands. It happened that the Archbishop was then visiting Valladolid, so Ignatius went to meet him there.

Similar gestures of recourse to higher authorities will be made later, as when Ignatius twice takes the initiative to go to question the Inquisition in Paris, and when he and his companions go to Rome to put their case and their hopes in the hands of the Pope.

3. *Visiting the Archbishop of Toledo*

Ignatius went to Valladolid and was granted an audience. He faithfully told the Archbishop everything that had happened; he said that even though he was no longer under the jurisdiction of Alcala and was not obliged to observe elsewhere a sentence passed in Alcala, he would do whatever the Archbishop commanded in that regard. He spoke to the Archbishop using the second person pronoun, as he was accustomed to doing with everyone he met, even with the captain of an Imperial army in northern Italy. The Archbishop received him very well. When Ignatius mentioned his desire to go to Salamanca, the Archbishop said that he had friends there, as well as a college, and that they were both at Ignatius's disposal. In addition he gave him four crowns, and sent him on his way.

Once again Ignatius had insisted on going to the higher authorities. He risked losing more, but he also risked gaining more. He took the issue of his apostolate out of the merely juridical area of the court of the Inquisition, and placed it in the pastoral context of an Archbishop's care. What is more, he showed complete readiness to follow the Archbishop's advice, although he had every intention of continuing his studies in a place where he would also be allowed to work.

When Ignatius said that he would do whatever the Archbishop commanded, he was showing the kind of magnanimous attitude that Nadal expressed toward Ignatius many years later in Rome, when the latter admitted that he had made no progress in dictating his *Autobiography*. This attitude of magnanimity and generosity is recommended to the person who is beginning the *Spiritual Exercises* [5]. Magnanimity is to be great-souled, or great-hearted: to give freely of what one is, and generosity is to give freely what one has. This attitude is formulated as 'indifference' in the opening statement on 'The Principle and Foundation' [23]. Magnanimity and generosity reappear at the end of the Exercises in the final prayer of the exercitant, when he offers himself to the Lord, asking God to take and use all that he is and all that he has.

Later, in Paris, he will increasingly limit his apostolate in order to complete his studies more successfully. His year and a half at Alcala show that his life with his companions, and his apostolate, are integral parts of the new life he intends to live. The conflict between his inner convictions and the outer constraints at Alcala led him to the Archbishop, and the advice of the Archbishop pushed him on to Salamanca.

Chapter 9

SALAMANCA: CONTINUING HIS UNIVERSITY STUDIES AND MAINTAINING A COMMUNITY

The events of the Salamanca period also fall into three stages: again Ignatius begins by describing the physical and spiritual details of the ordering of his life; then he is once again arrested and interrogated, and these interrogations take place in three separate episodes; finally Ignatius decides to leave Salamanca for Barcelona and Paris. As at Alcala, the second stage is articulated into four episodes.

At first the Alcala and Salamanca periods seem to have so much in common that they are indistinguishable. But a closer, deeper reading shows how carefully Ignatius has grasped the periods of his life and related them to Camara. The Alcala and Salamanca periods are not only laying the foundation for the confrontations in Paris and Rome, but they recapitulate the interview with the Franciscan Provincial in Jerusalem. Thus the story is a series of conversations, interviews, interrogations, trials, exchanges that rise toward the final conversation with Camara himself. It is in the early pre-Manresan period at Loyola that Ignatius resolved to go to Jerusalem, and even before that he conversed with the people of the house about the experiences he had been having. Within the simplicity of the series of conversations, there is a rising and recapitulating complexity of responses to the various obstacles that present themselves, period after period, stage after stage, episode after episode. It is the simplicity and flexibility of the design, or pattern, which makes it capable of bearing such weight and intensity and extensiveness.

1. *Ordering his life again*

The ordering of his life involved his prayer, his lodging, his clothes, his sacramental confession, and his accepting an invitation to Sunday dinner. Thus the physical, spiritual, and social aspects of the pattern are evident.

His four companions had preceded him to Salamanca. When he himself arrived in the town and went to pray in a church, a devout woman recognized him as a member of the group, and she took him to where his friends were staying. She may have known them from Alcala.

His friends were now dressed as ordinary students, as the Vicar of Alcala had commanded. Since Ignatius had said that they hadn't enough money for such clothes, the Vicar himself had generously provided them with clothes, hats, and everything that the students required.

In Salamanca Ignatius went for his weekly confession to a Dominican at St Stephen's Convent. Ten or twelve days after his arrival, his confessor told him that the Fathers of the Convent wanted to talk with him, and to that purpose he was invited to Sunday dinner. The confessor warned him that there were indeed many things that they wanted to learn from him. Little did he know that he was about to be arrested for twenty-two days, and that the precision of their objections to his apostolate would oblige him to move on to Paris, thereby losing his companions. He was to lose his companions at least partly out of his loyalty to the apostolate, the desire for which had arisen from so deep within his experience that it was now a vital part of the pattern of his existence.

2. *Responding to another inquisition*

As at Alcala, the inquisition fell into several episodes. But the Salamancan interrogations led into matters deeper than the colour of their clothes, the wearing of shoes, and mere speaking of matters of faith. The interrogation unearthed an experience rooted in the early period of Ignatius's convalescence at Loyola.

FIRST EPISODE: It is ironic that the interrogation by the three Dominicans – the Sub-prior, the confessor, and a third – should have taken place after dinner, for, as Ignatius recounted of himself during the stay in Venice, he had the habit of speaking little at meals, the better to be able to speak of the things of God afterwards. So it was in Salamanca. He and Calisto were taken into a chapel and questioned. The Sub-prior spoke affably of the information the Convent had received about them: their good moral reputation, and their preaching as the Apostles had done. But then the questions began:

QUESTION: What studies had they made?
ANSWER: Ignatius admitted that although he had studied more than the others – and he gave clear details about the studies he had made – those studies as yet had little basis.

Q: What do you preach?

A: We don't preach, answered Ignatius. We content ourselves with speaking familiarly of the things of God, as for example after meals with those who have invited us.

It would be hard to have replied more transparently, for Ignatius situated the interrogation itself within the framework of his apostolate. The inquisitors had before them an example of what he did, at the very moment he was doing it. The Dominicans are an 'Order of Preachers', and thus they were naturally interested in knowing what Ignatius 'preached'. Ignatius, however, spoke of his work as one of 'speaking familiarly'. His work remained within a form of conversation which did not reach for the genre of preaching, for preaching did not suppose an immediate verbal response from those who listened. Ignatius's familiar speech with people depended on an exchange with them that reached their shared appreciation of the presence of Jesus and the great goodness of God.[13]

The Dominican Sub-prior continued his questioning:

Q: But what are the 'things of God' that you speak about?

A: Ignatius replied that they spoke sometimes of one virtue or another, by praising it; at other times, of one vice or another, by blaming it.

Q: You have not studied, concluded one of the Dominicans, and yet you speak of virtues and vices. Now one can speak in only one of two ways: by science or by the Holy Spirit. And it is what you hold from the Holy Spirit that we want to know.

A: Ignatius reflected for an instant, because this way of arguing did not please him. After a moment of silence he said that it was useless to speak further on these questions.

Q: The Dominican insisted; 'At the time when so many errors are circulating, errors of Erasmus and many others which have deceived everybody, you refuse to explain what you teach?'

A: Ignatius simply replied that he would not say any more unless he was before superiors who could oblige him to do so.

At this point in the interrogation, Camara – always careful not to miss a detail, even if it is not quite in chronological order – adds that the friar had already objected to the ill-fitting clothes of Calisto. When Ignatius told him that they had been imprisoned in Alcala and ordered to dress as students, and that Calisto had given his student's clothes (a gift from the Vicar Figueroa) to a needy ecclesiastic, the friar muttered between his teeth that charity began at home. Only after this concern with a physical detail and its spiritual explanation does Camara return to the Dominican's response to Ignatius's refusal. Perhaps Camara saw a parallel between the friar's final remark about Calisto's clothes and his final remark about

Ignatius's refusal to answer further questions unless obliged by higher authorities.

Q: 'Very well then,' said the friar. 'Remain here. We know well how to make you tell everything.'

Thus ended the first episode of the Salamancan interrogations. But there was an interesting interlude between this first interrogation and the second.

INTERLUDE: Ignatius and Calisto stayed in the Convent for three days, behind closed doors. They ate with the friars of the community, and were often visited by some of the friars who came to see them.

The visiting friars were in touch with the judges, but nothing was communicated to the captive guests. Ignatius continued to speak on the usual subjects. From then on there was even a difference of opinion between the friars, for many were favourable to them.

After three days they were put into a prison where they remained for eighteen days. They were chained in such a way that one could not move without disturbing the other. When some townspeople learned of their imprisonment, they sent them bedding and other necessities in abundance. Many came to visit them, and Ignatius continued his spiritual conversations as before.

SECOND EPISODE: This interrogation began when the Vicar of the Bishop of Salamanca, Bachelor Frias, came to question them individually. Ignatius gave him all his papers to examine; we can assume that these 'papers' were the *Spiritual Exercises*, in whatever form they then existed. The Vicar asked them if they had other companions. They answered affirmatively, and gave their addresses. Men were immediately sent to bring Lope de Caceres and Juan de Artiaga to prison, although they did not bring Juanico. These two were imprisoned in a separate cell underneath the cell of Ignatius and Calisto. Once again Ignatius refused the services of a lawyer or sworn witness.

THIRD EPISODE: The third interrogation began four days later, when Ignatius alone was brought before the four judges. All had seen the *Exercises*.
Q: They asked him all kinds of questions, not only on the *Exercises*, but on theology, as, for example, on how he understood the articles of faith on the Trinity and the Blessed Sacrament. These were indeed subjects that he had thought long about, and which were the first and fourth of the five 'lessons' he had learned from his Schoolmaster during the period at Manresa.
A: Ignatius always began his responses by admitting how little basis he had as yet. Nevertheless he spoke in such a way that they had nothing to which they could object.
Q: Bachelor Frias asked him about a case in canon law.
A: He was obliged to answer, although he invariably began by repeating that he did not know the opinion of the doctors on these questions.
Q: They then asked him to speak about the first commandment in the way he usually did.
A: He put himself to the task, and dwelt so long on each point that he raised, saying so many things about this first commandment, that they had no desire to ask him further.
Q: Before that, when they had questioned him on the *Exercises*, they had insisted much on one point which was at the beginning: When was a thought a venial sin, and when was it a mortal sin? They wondered how Ignatius could judge such matters without having studied.
A: He explained his position, and added: 'If it is the truth or not, that is for you to see; and if it is not the truth, condemn it.'

Finally they withdrew without condemning anything.

Two incidents occurred during their prison days as they waited for a sentence. Both reveal how the companions, or at least Ignatius, viewed their imprisonment in a way reminiscent of scenes from the *Acts of the Apostles*.

First, among those who came to speak with Ignatius in prison was Don Francisco de Mendoza, who had become Cardinal of Burgos by the time Ignatius dictated his

Autobiography. Don Francisco came in the company of Bachelor Frias, and asked Ignatius in a gentle way how he was supporting prison life, and whether it did not weigh too much on him to be detained as he was. Ignatius answered this visitor in a way that developed the response he gave to the lady who visited him in prison at Alcala. To her he had said: 'He for whose sake I have been put in prison will surely get me out, if it is for His service.' To Don Francisco he said: 'You show by your compassion over my imprisonment that you yourself do not desire to be a prisoner for the love of God. Is prison such a great evil? As for me, let me tell you that there are not enough bars and chains in all Salamanca that I would not desire to be further detained by them for the love of God.' He said nothing about getting out of prison, but emphasized rather the love that would make him happily stay in. His visitors probably recognized the references to the *Acts of the Apostles*: Paul's words before Festus in Caesarea (26:29) and before the Jews in Rome (28:20).

The second parallel to *Acts* is found in the incident that occurred one night when there was a prison break in the lower cell. All the captives escaped except Caceres and Artiaga, who chose not to flee. When the two men were found the next morning, standing behind the open doors, everybody was impressed and it was much spoken about in the city. They were immediately moved to a nearby palace which was to be their prison until sentence was passed. The parallel is found in *Acts* 16:25–34, when Paul and Silas were held in prison at Philippi. Although an earthquake had shaken the foundations of the prison and unfastened the fetters of all the prisoners and opened the doors, Paul and Silas refused to escape; they believed they had captured their captors in the truth of their cause.

These two incidents took place during the lapse of time between the third interrogation and the delivery of the sentence.

FOURTH EPISODE: Twenty-two days after their arrest, the companions were convoked to hear their sentence.

SENTENCE: No error had been found in their life or teaching, so they could continue living as they had before. They could teach catechism and speak of the things of God, on just one condition: they would never determine whether an act or thought was a mortal or a venial sin until they had finished four more years of study. After reading the sentence the judges expressed much sympathy toward them, as if they hoped that this would help them to accept the judgement.
RESPONSE: Ignatius said that he would do as he was told, but would not be able to accept it interiorly. For, as he saw it, without condemning anything, the judges were muzzling him in such a way that he could no longer help souls with the means that he had.
S: Dr Frias was most affected by this position of Ignatius, and insisted, but in vain.
R: Ignatius limited himself to repeating that he would do what he had been ordered to do as long as he was under the jurisdiction of Salamanca.

He and his companions were freed immediately.

After prayer to God and reflection with himself over what should be done, Ignatius saw great difficulties in his remaining in Salamanca. To forbid him to define a mortal sin or a venial sin was, in his eyes, to close the door to his apostolate. For if he, an ordinary layperson, did not know the difference, how could any other ordinary man or woman know it? That is why he decided to leave Salamanca and to continue his studies in Paris. Thus he had gradually formed the idea of completing the full cycle of ecclesiastical studies, and he conceived his future work as that of a priest. Perhaps he had decided this previously, even as long before as during his pilgrimage to Jerusalem, but he did not tell Camara until he really needed to. Just as at Loyola he had not told his older brother Martin that he intended to go to Jerusalem, but told him rather that he was merely going to Navarrete, so he told Camara only as much as he needed to know, at each period of the story. This withholding of information could be interpreted as secrecy, but also as a form of disciplined economy that is integral to the temperament of Ignatius, and which contrasts neatly with his forceful and outspoken generosity and magnanimity in other circumstances. The sharp extremes of the broad spectrum of his temperament are what attracted so many to the centre of his character, to his values, and to his faith in God's ways which he had learned from his own experience.

3. *Back to Barcelona and off to Paris*

During his convalescence at Loyola, Ignatius had thought of either travelling from place to place in a spirit of penance, or entering a religious order such as the Carthusians. When he thought of a religious order, he felt the desire to enter one that was little reformed, so that he could suffer from that and also pray for God to come to their aid. His entrance into such a religious order would thus be a means of reforming it. He was sure that God would give him all the confidence he would need to support the affronts and injuries of such a life in order to help others.

By the time he had reached Salamanca, he had not lost his desire to help souls. On the contrary, he wanted to help souls by his studies, and to assemble more men animated by the same ideal, while at the same time keeping those companions he already had.

Now, after the restriction placed upon him at Salamanca – a restriction that touched the heart of an issue that was deeply necessary to speak of if one were to help souls – he had decided that he must leave to study in Paris. He arranged with his companions that they would wait in Salamanca, while he went ahead to find the means for them to follow him.

Although many friends in Salamanca tried to keep him from leaving, they were not able to convince him to stay. This is yet another instance of his resistance to the efforts of others to hold him back from a goal that he had set for himself. At the castle of Pamplona, on the operating table at Loyola, during the temptations at Manresa, in the streets of

Barcelona, on the ship from Venice to Cyprus, in the office of the Franciscan Provincial in Jerusalem, on the roads across northern Italy, before the inquisitors at Alcala, in dialogue with the Archbishop of Toledo, Ignatius held on to his basic resolutions. Although remaining open to the positions of others, he yielded only when he was opposed by a cannon ball, by the commission of a sin, or by apostolic authority. Less than fifteen or twenty days after his liberation, Ignatius left Salamanca alone, with a little donkey that carried some books.

Among those books was his own book, the *Spiritual Exercises*, which has just been mentioned in the trial at Salamanca and which played no less important a part in the interrogation at Alcala. This is the second mention of the fact that his notes had taken book form – notes begun on his sickbed in Loyola. He had first referred to these notes as a book when he left Montserrat for Manresa in order to note some things in his 'book'. The whole *Autobiography* is the story of the growth of those notes; for the *Constitutions* also grew out of the *Exercises*, just as the *Exercises* grew out of the notes, and as the notes grew out of his readings and bedside conversations. Beyond the *Constitutions*, at the end of the *Autobiography*, the reader catches a glimpse of the *Diary* that Ignatius kept and used as a help to composing the *Constitutions*.

The *Diary* that Ignatius reveals in the final interview with Camara in Rome is another form of those carefully written bedside notes, originally meant only for himself. His works, including his letters, form a cycle which is vital to him. It is the orally dictated *Autobiography*, which he did not write, that connects his written works in a dynamic way. The bedside notes led to letters, which led to the *Exercises*, which led to the *Constitutions*, which led to the *Autobiography* which referred back to the *Diary* which was part of the notes that helped him to compose the *Constitutions*. The letters, *Exercises*, *Constitutions* and *Autobiography* are like four points of a compass which radiate from the pivot of the notes or diary. All of the other writings are mentioned in the *Autobiography*, for it relates the story of the other works, in both senses of the word 'relation': it tells their story, and it establishes the relationships among them. The written works are more or less the literary traces of his apostolate. His apostolate was a mission that arose from the deepest seams of his experience, and he expressed it in the means he had at hand. Ignatius, once a military accountant, found his pen at hand. He had a mission to write; he had to write of his mission.

On his arrival at Barcelona, everyone who knew Ignatius advised him not to go to France. After the French had lost the battle of Pavia in 1525, while Ignatius had been studying under Master Ardevol, the wars had broken out again. They cited precise examples of atrocities, saying that the French even skewered Spaniards. But although Ignatius had once been very seriously wounded by a French cannon ball, and had once fought hard to overcome his fear in order to cross the Imperial and French battle lines between Ferrara and Genoa, he now felt not the least fear. He packed the donkey with his books and headed off for Paris.

Chapter 10

PARIS: THE COMPLETION OF UNIVERSITY STUDIES, AND OF A COMMUNITY

The story of Ignatius's seven years in Paris is clearly divided into two stages: the years of study of the Humanities at the College of Montaigu, and the years of study of Philosophy and Theology at the College of Ste Barbe. During each cycle of studies he ordered his life as before, according to the physical, spiritual, academic, and apostolic areas of his activities. But this pattern of activities was increasingly determined by his life with his companions. Special difficulties had to be overcome in each area. Each cycle of his studies ended with a rather summary meeting with the Inquisitor of Paris. It was in Paris, however, that his life with his companions reached a new equilibrium, a dynamic yet restrained proportion, which resulted in the commitment by vows to live and work together. When Ignatius left Paris, he left with that same group of companions, unlike the companions who had drifted away after he left Salamanca. The perseverance of this new group of men, who would later call themselves the 'Companions of Jesus', was due to the quality of the experience they had shared during those years in Paris. In view of this, it is important to see how Ignatius grew during this time of his studies, and how he succeeded in communicating to others the rhythmic pattern he had discovered in his own life.

1. *Humanities at Montaigu*

This period of his studies has a subtle unity, due to the fact that Ignatius's financial difficulties were linked to his effort to maintain contact with his former companions in Salamanca. The whole range of his physical controls and spiritual life is exposed. The shy pattern is revealed, discreetly but unmistakably. Articulating the successive episodes helps us to perceive this.

• Ignatius arrived in Paris by foot in February 1528 and found lodging with a group of other Spaniards who were studying Humanities at Montaigu.

• He had been pushed through his studies so rapidly in Spain that he still felt that he had no solid foundation. So he studied with children, following the courses and method of Paris.

• On his arrival a merchant gave him twenty-five crowns for a draft that he had brought from Barcelona. Obviously, his sense of poverty was no longer limited to begging for each day's food; he was planning ahead in view of larger long-term goals. He put the money in the keeping of a Spaniard in his lodging-house, but the student spent it all in a short time and had no way of reimbursing him. By the time Lent was over, Ignatius had no more money and was forced to beg, as well as to leave the house where he had been staying.

• He found lodging at the Hospital of St Jacques, which was inconveniently far from the College. In order to get back to the Hospital at night before the doors were closed, he had to leave the College when the evening Angelus struck, and he could not leave the Hospital until its doors opened at dawn. In addition, he had to beg for food.

• Nevertheless, since he had had no stomach pains for five years, he now began to renew his harsher penances and abstinence. His stomach pains began to recur toward the end of his years of theological studies, and this was one of the reasons why he left for Spain alone, ahead of the others who would meet him in Venice. This intensification of his penance was probably a means he used to see more clearly through the present difficulties toward a better solution. It would have long-ranging effects on the group.

• After a period of begging while living in the Hospital, he became aware that such a life was not helping him to make the requisite progress in his studies. He began to think of getting a job in the service of one of the lecturers, because he saw that such servants also had time to study. He felt considerable consolation at this thought, and even gave himself up to imagining how he would obey the orders of his employer as if the employer were Christ, and the other students were the apostles. This fantasy was not to be realized, however, and Ignatius's recalling of it may be his way of showing how deluded his imagination had been and how false his consolation. It may also be a sign of Ignatius's sense of humour about himself. (This is a point easy to overlook when he tells the story of how he exchanged his knife and then his scissors to see the footprints of Jesus on the Mount of Olives.) Despite many efforts on his part, and his requests for help from Bachelor Castro, a Carthusian monk, and many others, he found no work.

But a Spanish monk did tell him that it would be better for him to go to beg each year in Flanders, then occupied by Imperial Spain, even though he would lose two months of classes, because that region was so rich that he could find there enough funds to last him for a year. Ignatius prayed over this, and the means seemed to be good, so he went off to Flanders each year of his stay in Paris to beg for his livelihood. Once he even went to England and gathered more alms than he had in other years.

• After returning from his first trip to Flanders, however, he had new confidence in his financial situation, so he began to give more time to 'spiritual conversations' and even gave the *Spiritual Exercises* to three persons at about the same time. This led him into his first difficulties with his fellow students and with a university official. The pattern was beginning to expand again. Once the physical and spiritual poles of his own life were well established, and his studies were progressing, his over-expansion into the apostolate got him into trouble. In the past, his arrest was more than once followed by a trial or interrogation and by a liberation. In this first period of his studies in Paris, this pattern was repeated.

• The three persons to whom Ignatius gave the *Spiritual Exercises* were so affected that they changed their lives, and gave all they possessed – even their books – to the poor. When they too began begging in the streets of Paris, and also went to live at St Jacques Hospice, their behaviour created a considerable stir at the University, because two of them were well known: Bachelor Castro and Peralta. The third was a Basque from Pamplona, of all places, whose name was Amador and who studied at the College of Ste Barbe. The Spaniards tried to convince Castro and Peralta to return to the University, but they failed, so a crowd of them came one day to the hospice and forced them to return. They made an arrangement whereby the two men would first finish their studies and only then pursue their new way of life and apostolates.

At this point Ignatius digresses in his story-telling to relate what happened later to Castro and Peralta. Castro became a Carthusian monk at Valencia, and Ignatius visited him on his way from Paris to Venice after he had finished his studies in Paris. Peralta tried to go to Jerusalem by himself, but a captain in the service of his family had him arrested somewhere in Italy and took him to the Pope, who ordered him to return to Spain. Both of these men moved off on vectors that Ignatius himself had once considered.

In Paris, it was especially the Spaniards who murmured against Ignatius, and Master Diego de Gouveia, the regent at Ste Barbe, accused him of driving Amador, one of his own students, almost out of his mind. Gouveia even resolved to give Ignatius a public flogging, but this never took place.

Even though this flogging did not take place, it indicates the system of trial and punishment that surrounded Ignatius's apostolate of helping souls. For to help people discover that they 'have' souls and that they are souls embodied was to awaken them to ever-expanding ranges of freedom and possibilities of commitment. This must necessarily have upset those people who had settled down to lives which were no longer challenging to themselves or to others.

• Thus Ignatius had failed in his second attempt to form a group of companions, animated by the ideal he had discovered for himself. In counterpoint to the story of Castro, Peralta, and Amador, he then tells a longer story involving money, his former companions in Salamanca, a possible new companion aboard a ship in Rouen, a journey which brought him into deep conflict with his own fear, an interrogation by the Inquisition in Paris, and an acquittal. If the previous episode was an effort to make new companions, the present episode was an effort to combine a new companion with his older ones. This led him into a much deeper conflict with himself, and it also led to a deeper conflict with the authorities. But both conflicts were overcome, leaving Ignatius alone, but wiser, at the end. Let the story be called:

The Road to Rouen

The story begins with Ignatius's concern for the Spaniard with whom he had lived at the beginning of his stay in Paris. This was the Spaniard who had spent all of Ignatius's money without reimbursing it. The re-emergence of this Spaniard shows how the final story embraced all the elements of the Montaigu years. The Spaniard left Paris for Rouen where he intended to board a ship for Spain. While waiting there he fell ill. Ignatius learned by letter that the Spaniard was ill in Rouen. He decided to go to visit him, and to help him, thinking that he would be able to win him over to the idea of leaving the world and consecrating himself completely to the service of God.

As a means of reaching that end, he considered undertaking a more intense physical penance: he felt the desire to walk the twenty-eight leagues from Paris to Rouen barefoot, without eating or drinking. As he prayed over this desire, he experienced a first wave of fear. Finally he went to the church of St Dominic and there he resolved to do as he had at first desired. The great fear he had of tempting God by such physical penance disappeared.

In the morning as he rose to dress, he was filled with a second wave of such fear and apprehension that he could barely get into his clothes. Despite his repugnance, he left the house and the city just before dawn, barefoot and without taking anything to eat or drink.

The fear kept a grip on him, but he persisted until he came to Argenteuil, a town only three leagues from Paris on the road to Rouen. It was in Argenteuil that the robe of Jesus was venerated. Although he passed the town in the same state of anguished fearfulness, as he was walking up a ridge the anguish began to dissipate, and in its place came such a great consolation and spiritual exaltation that he began to shout for joy in the middle of the fields, speaking spontaneously with God. That night, after fourteen leagues, he lodged with a poor beggar in a hospice, and the next night he slept in a barn; on the third day he reached Rouen. During all that time he had taken nothing to eat or drink, and he had walked barefoot as he had decided.

At Rouen he comforted the sick Spaniard and helped him to get aboard ship. He also gave him some letters for Calisto, Caceres, and Artiaga, and told him to contact them.

At this point in the story Camara sweeps ahead, as he has done before, to relate what happened to the three former companions. Ignatius helped Calisto to get a scholarship for Paris, but Calisto passed it up and went off to Mexico, whence he returned rich to Salamanca, surprising those who had known him before. Caceres returned to Segovia where he lived such a life that it was clear that he had forgotten his first plan. Artiaga became an army commander and eventually a bishop in Mexico, where he died of accidental poisoning.

There is no mention of whether Ignatius's penitential walk to Rouen had its desired effect. It seems to have failed at least in part. The sick and spendthrift Spaniard, in whom Ignatius had hoped to find a servant of God, and perhaps a companion for the spread of God's kingdom, disappears from the pages of the story as he sails from Rouen, with letters to three men who will also disappear from the story of the project they have begun. But the walk succeeded in helping Ignatius to overcome his own fears, and to discover further potentialities in his relation to Jesus and in his service of others, even if the others did not respond as he himself had hoped.

When Ignatius returned to Paris, he learned that Castro and Peralta's behaviour had created such a stir that the Inquisitor had asked to see him. Ignatius did not waste a minute, but went immediately to find the Inquisitor to tell him that he had learned that he was being looked for, and that he was completely at his disposal. He asked him, however, to get on with it without delay because he intended to begin the course of Arts on the feast of St Remy, and he wanted all other business finished with first, so he could the better apply himself to his studies. But the Inquisitor merely told him that people had in fact mentioned certain aspects of his behaviour, said no more, and never called for him again. And so Ignatius entered the course of Arts on October 1, 1529.

There is a growing momentum in this series of experiences: from his lodging to his loss of money, to his finding money and then finding lodging, from his finding companions to his losing them, from his fear to his calm, from his increased repugnance to his consummate joy: Grace is not just a 'state' but a trend, with a momentum to the end. By the time he came back to Paris, learned of the Inquisitor's request, and then presented himself immediately to the Inquisitor, he was animated by a spirit completely free of fear. Something has happened here, not just in the life of Ignatius, but in the story-telling. At this point Ignatius had no companion at all among the University students, neither in Spain nor in France. And yet on the road to Rouen he had made a new discovery in the conquest of his own repugnance, and he had found a new strength in himself that was centred in Jesus. The period of over-expansion, both in reaching for companions and in apostolic activity, is over. He will now settle down more completely to his studies, as if mastered by a new sense of proportion, discretion, and confidence. Paradoxically, it is now that the permanent group of companions will begin to assemble. One may fancy that the robe of Christ, which Ignatius had passed at Argenteuil, somehow fitted him and made him into a more unified and trusting person. He had 'put on' Christ, by the means he had taken to reach the soul of another man who was sick and in need, and to keep in touch with the old companions through a new one. To do this he had to live from what was best in his own soul, purified by the penance that he thought necessary. But it is only later on the road to Rome, at the village of La Storta, that he will pray to be 'put with Christ'. On that occasion he will pray to overcome his fear of Rome, so that he might fulfill through Rome the mission that was deferred by the failure of a Venetian ship to sail for Cyprus and the Holy Land, that year of 1537.

2. *Philosophy and Theology at Ste Barbe: a new equilibrium*

During the episodes that occur during the period of studies at Ste Barbe, various areas of the pattern combine into more and more comprehensive units. Ignatius begins with a new equilibrium. Two events occur which may explain why Ignatius finally begins to find a stable group of companions.

- Limiting the companions and apostolates

First, he began his studies with the desire of keeping only the companions who had decided to serve God, without recruiting any others, so that he could study more seriously. This limit that he set on his apostolate would not dispose him to study more seriously, but it would give him and his companions the opportunity to deepen their relationships, rather than simply to keep expanding them.

• Limiting pious thoughts

Secondly, once he began studying more seriously, the temptations that he had experienced when studying grammar returned to harass him. During his studies at the Faculty, he couldn't keep his attention centered on the course because of many pious thoughts that came to him. Seeing that he was making little progress, he did as he had done with Master Ardevol in Barcelona; he went to find his teacher, but without taking him into a nearby church, he promised him never to miss attendance at a lecture, as long as he could find bread and water for his livelihood. After he had made this promise in that public and inter-personal way, the temptations to devout thoughts disappeared and he quietly advanced in his studies.

It is after curbing the excesses of both his apostolate and his spiritual life that Ignatius tells of developing his relations with Master Pierre Favre and Master Francis Xavier, whom he later led to the service of God by giving them the *Exercises*. Thus it would seem that these two men are not new acquaintances, since Ignatius has just resolved not to recruit new companions. Indeed, it is by not recruiting new ones that his relations with these two men deepened to the point that they made the *Exercises* and took the decision to serve God with their whole lives, together in a common life.

3. *A fragile equilibrium*

Ignatius had reached a certain tranquillity in his relations with others, in his studies, and in his spiritual life, and as a result he was not troubled by the authorities. It was a fragile tranquillity, however, for an excessive concern with companions, with the apostolate, or with his interior graces, could upset the new equilibrium.

A certain Doctor Frago, his professor in Sacred Scripture, remarked to him one day that he was surprised at the tranquillity he enjoyed, and at the fact that no one was causing him any problems. Ignatius replied by revealing both the real cause of his tranquillity and his intention to risk its loss at a later time:

> The reason is because I do not speak to anyone about the things of God, but once this course is over, we shall recommence our practice. (*Autobiography*, para. 82)

By chance or by providence, it was at that very moment that Ignatius's hard-won tranquillity began to be threatened. As they were speaking, a monk came to ask Dr Frago to help him find lodging because in the room where he then lived there were many deaths; local people attributed them to the plague. In fact, the plague had begun to spread again in Paris.

In order to help the monk, Dr Frago and Ignatius went to the house with a woman who had a good reputation for detecting signs of the plague. After entering the house, she affirmed that the plague indeed was there. Ignatius wanted to enter the house and did so. There he found a sick man whom he comforted by touching his wound with his hand. After he had comforted him somewhat and encouraged him, he went off alone. His hand began to hurt, and he imagined that he had caught the plague. His imagination got such a grip on him that he couldn't control it, until – by a sudden movement – he brought his hand to his mouth and held his fingers there, turning them again and again, and said to himself, 'If you have the plague on your hand, well then you will have it in your mouth as well.' Once he had done this, his fantasies disappeared completely, as well as the pain in his hand.

Ignatius had an uncanny self-knowledge. He knew that his vivid imagination, once out of control, understood only one language, and that was the language of a gesture and a word that went exactly in the opposite direction from that of the imagination. At Manresa it had taken him a long time to finally discern that the voice which discouraged him was linked to the vision of the serpent-form that consoled him. In Paris it took him only a matter of minutes to see the connection between his fearful fantasies and the physical pain in his hand. He countered what he saw as the single source of both fear and pain by a deliberate gesture and an ironic remark, coming from a single decision to trust God. Such behaviour would be excessive if Ignatius were not the kind of person who, at that period of his life, could only be reached by such excess.

When he returned to the College of Ste Barbe where he studied and had his lodging, his fellow boarders fled from him and would not let him enter because they knew he had been in the plague-infected house. So Ignatius was obliged to remain outside for several days, in a sort of quarantine, after which he was readmitted.

This was the only adventurous episode that Ignatius tells of his years of Arts studies from 1529 to 1533. It confirms, by the internal and external difficulties that he experienced and overcame, that the man's self-discipline was no tranquil achievement. It was a constant and unrelenting struggle against fantasies and feelings that could pull him wildly away from the good he intended. He had every reason to believe that the plague was in the house, but his gesture of charity toward the sick man was spontaneous and true, even if ill-advised. After he left the house, he recognized that his fantasies and pain were groundless, but his knowledge was not enough to make him overcome his feelings. Only the gesture of turning his fingers in his mouth, accompanied by the self-mocking remark, was enough to shock him out of the extremity of his groundless fear. We may again suppose that Ignatius was telling this story not merely to show how he had overcome fear, but to show how foolish he had been.

Ignatius tended strongly to complete what he had begun, to hold firmly to the original intention, and to resist forcefully whatever opposed him, by whatever permissible means he knew to be effective. If Dr Frago ever heard of Ignatius's being excluded from his College for a few days, he may have regretted letting Ignatius accompany him to the monk's house. But perhaps he never heard of it, and never reflected on how Ignatius's visit to the house led to a disturbance in that tranquillity that the Doctor had initially remarked upon. Whatever the case, no-one but Ignatius, and finally Camara and his readers, knew of the lengths to which he went to overcome the feelings raised by his imagination.

In the *Spiritual Exercises* this dialectical principle of deliberate opposition to imaginary feelings is formulated more abstractly, and it is found in various contexts as the exercitant advances through the four weeks [13, 16, 97, 157, 167–168, 319, 325–327]. One of the clearest examples is found in the final note concerning scruples [351]:

> A good person of this kind may wish to say or do something in accord with the Church and with the mind of authorities, something which promotes the glory of God; and in these circumstances a thought, or rather a temptation, may come from without not to say or do that thing, a thought proposing specious arguments about vainglory or something similar. In that case, one should raise the understanding to one's Creator and Lord, and if one sees that the proposed action is for God's due service, or at least not against it, act in a way diametrically opposed to the temptation – like St Bernard in his answer to a similar temptation, 'I did not begin because of you, and I am not going to give up because of you.'

4. *Financing the teachers' party*

As the period of his philosophical studies comes to a close, Ignatius relates an incident in which he at first hesitated, and then made another decision that some people criticized.

It was the custom in Paris that graduates of Arts pay a crown in order to receive their Bachelor's degree. Many poor students could not afford this, and Ignatius asked himself whether he should do it. It is not clear what the crown was for: a reception for the teachers, or some other form of tribute to them.

Since he was hesitant and undecided, he resolved to put the matter in the hands of his Master of Studies, and on his advice he offered the crown for the reception. Nevertheless there was no lack of criticism of his decision, and Ignatius recalls that at least one Spaniard took careful note of it.

Three interesting points deserve mention here. First, Ignatius has a new freedom and indifference with regard to the use of money in the area of his studies. We have seen how careful, even scrupulous, he has been in his use of money, as when he bought the sea-biscuits in Barcelona and left his change on the bench in the port; when he paid for his lodging in Venice; when he gave alms to the beggars in Ferrara. In those instances he used money in the areas of his physical needs and of the needs of others. In the present incident, however, Ignatius used his money – presumably the money begged during his annual trip to Flanders – in the more intangible area of traditional customs arising from his studies.

Secondly, he had the presence of mind to put his case in the hands of someone whom he trusted. A more humorous instance of such an act of trust occurred when he loosened the reins of his mule on the road to Montserrat. A more serious instance occurred when he went to visit the Archbishop of Toledo.

Lastly, the incident witnesses to his willingness to make an unpopular decision.

5. *An unsolicited penance*

The last fact that Ignatius recalls from this period of his philosophical studies is that his stomach pains returned. He is switched back to the physical area of the pattern. Every two weeks he experienced cramps that lasted for an hour and brought on a fever. Once the crisis lasted for sixteen or seventeen hours. This recurrent illness continued during his two years of theological studies. He mentions no other incident during those years: no difficulties with companions, with finance or lodging, with excessive spiritual illuminations, with apostolic adventures, with well-nigh uncontrollable fear, with the authorities. In other words, all the poles of the Ignatian pattern were in equilibrium, except for the health of his body. His interior life, his companions, his studies, his apostolate had reached that new, if fragile equilibrium which it had taken him years and pains to reach. It was precisely those 'pains' which were now taking their toll, and pushing him off in an unexpected direction at an unexpected time. Except for those pains, his life had reached such a balance during the last two years in Paris that there was nothing more to say about it. There is no story but that of the pain. As it grew worse, the doctors said that only his native air could cure him. His companions supported this advice and greatly insisted that he follow it. Despite himself, he was sent off to his homeland by the doctors and by his friends. He foresaw how he could combine this journey with other goals, so that he could pass through Spain on his way to Venice, where he would await his companions who would come directly overland from Paris to the Adriatic, as it was from Venice that they were intending to sail to the Holy Land.

6. *The Jerusalem project*

It is in the context of describing how Ignatius's companions insisted that Ignatius return to his homeland for his health, that Camara relates the nature of the project that the fellow students planned to undertake. They had decided to go to Venice and then to Jerusalem to spend their lives there for the good of souls. This was the old intention that Ignatius had left unexpressed in his interviews with the Franciscan authorities over twelve years before in 1523. If the companions did not obtain permission to stay in Jerusalem, they had decided to return to Rome and present themselves to the Pope, the Bishop of Rome and the successor of St Peter, the Vicar of Christ. They were resolved to ask him to use them in whatever way he judged that they could best contribute to the glory of God and the 'good of souls'. They had also decided to wait for one year in Venice, if they had to, for a ship to take them to the Holy Land. If, after a year, no ship had come, they would be free of their vow to go to Jerusalem, and would go to Rome instead to present themselves to the Pope.

Since the *Autobiography* was written for the Companions, it was assumed that they knew how Ignatius and six of his companions had assembled in a chapel on Montmartre in Paris on August 15, 1534. There they had vowed their poverty and their chastity as an active religious apostolic body, and had vowed to go to Jerusalem, or Rome, as described above. By the time they were to leave Paris early in 1536, ten months after Ignatius's departure for Spain, three other companions would have joined them. Behind the specific goals of Jerusalem or Rome, one recognizes the underlying attitude of putting the whole group in the hands of a trusted authority, just as Ignatius, only shortly before in his narrative, relates how he put the decision of spending a crown for the Bachelor's degree in the hands of his Master of Studies. In the same way, the companions have decided into whose hands they will place their 'body', in their desire to spend their lives in the service of God and in the service of helping souls.

Ignatius's trip to Spain for a brief convalescence in his native air – the same air in which he had convalesced after the battle of Pamplona – was also an opportunity for him to settle affairs at the homes of some of his Spanish companions. He was to go from Spain to meet them in Venice. By that time they would have finished their studies in Paris and travelled overland to meet him. There they would wait for passage to the Holy Land. Such was the plan; all seemed to be in order.

At Montaigu he had gone to help a sick friend who was leaving for Spain, and he used that opportunity to bring his new friends into touch with his old friends. After finishing at Ste Barbe he himself is sick, and he is sent to Spain for his health, but he uses the opportunity to keep in touch with old friends and to do favours for his new friends. Ignatius does not spell out these repetitions for his readers, but lets the readers inwardly relish them for themselves.

7. *A final inquiry*

Just as Ignatius was about to leave Paris, he learned that someone had denounced him to the Inquisitor, and that he was to be tried. Seeing that he was not convoked, however, he himself went to find the Inquisitor to tell him what he had heard. He added that since he was on the point of leaving for Spain and had companions, he wanted to have the sentence pronounced as quickly as possible. Ignatius's initiative and directness may have impressed the Inquisitor, because he replied simply that it was true that there had been an accusation, but the matter seemed of little importance. He desired merely to see the book of the *Spiritual Exercises*. Ignatius submitted it. After reading it, the Inquisitor praised it highly and asked Ignatius for a copy. Ignatius made one for him, but nevertheless insisted once again on pursuing the trial to its conclusion. Since it was clear to him that the Inquisitor didn't want to do that, he returned to the office with a notary and witnesses and had their testimony legally recorded, so that his innocence of the charges would be registered. Once this was done, he mounted a little horse that his companions had bought for the journey, and set out for his native land.

Ignatius had arrived in Paris with a donkey, but he left on a horse. His attitude toward his means of transportation, as towards his finance, food, and clothes, had grown increasingly flexible. Whatever inflexibility he showed was a means of disengaging himself from the habits that had confined his freedom. Once that freedom was refound, the actual matter with regard to which he had been inflexible tended to become irrelevant.

Ignatius had not been back in his Basque homeland since

he left it that winter in 1522, resolved on arriving at Montserrat for the feast of the Annunciation. It was now the spring of 1535. The bedside 'notes' started in Loyola had taken the form of a book that he had recently handed to an approving Inquisitor in Paris. His companions were to follow him by another road to their meeting-place in Venice. Jerusalem was once again envisaged as the primary place of their common apostolate. Yet the depth of their realism had prepared them for possible disappointment; their plan had a flexibility that expressed the reverence toward papal authority that Ignatius had shown before the Franciscan Provincial during that memorable interview in Jerusalem in the fall of 1523. The grandeur and radicality of the plan were tempered by the humility he gained from the companionship of the crucified and risen Jesus, who continues to be crucified in the multiple passions of the just and the unjust, in the concrete details of history as it is lived.

Chapter 11

THE ROAD TO JERUSALEM: BACK TO LOYOLA AND VENICE

The next period of Ignatius's story has four stages: the episodes in Spain, the crossing of northern Italy, his residence in Venice while waiting for the arrival of his companions from Paris, and their waiting together during the prescribed year for their passage to the Holy Land.

1. *The road through Spain*

Besides noting that he felt better as he travelled, Ignatius tells of only one incident along the road. He had entered his home province of Guipuzcoa and had left the highway to take a little mountain road that was more solitary, although it also had a bad reputation for the murders committed there. Despite that reputation Ignatius set off on the mountain road. Hardly had he taken it than two armed men rode toward him, passed him, and then turned to follow him in haste. Ignatius was seized with fear, but he overcame it by taking the initiative of speaking to them first. He learned that they were servants whom his brother Martin had sent out in search of him. The news of his coming had been spread by someone who had recognized him in France at Bayonne. The servants went off to announce his coming, and returned to meet him when he was only a short distance from the family castle. They insisted that he come with them to his brother's house, but Ignatius resisted all their efforts. He went to live in the local hospital and shortly afterwards he began to beg in the neighborhood.

The pattern emerges very clearly. Not only did he overcome his inner fear by taking an active initiative to address the horsemen on the road, but once at Loyola he began his apostolate by refusing any but the poorest lodging, and he also insisted on being financially dependent on the alms of the public.

Thus his life in his native air began with his ordering the habitual areas of his pattern of life: lodging, finance, and apostolate. Previous to that, he had overcome his inner fear by taking an active initiative in addressing the horsemen on the road. At the hospital he engaged in conversation about 'the things of God' with those who came to visit him, and he had considerable effect on them. From the time of his arrival he had resolved to teach catechism each day to little children. His brother greatly objected to this and said that no one would come. Ignatius simply answered that one child would be enough. The brothers, Ignatius and Martin, seemed to differ over each issue now, as they had also differed in the past over Ignatius's second operation and over his resolution to leave the family home. Yet, from the very first catechism lesson, not only did many people come, but Martin came as well. Ignatius also preached on Sundays and holidays, and people came from miles around to hear him and to be helped by him. Although he had come back to his native province to regain his health, he did not see that his apostolate might be a hindrance to that. In undertaking it, he started from the bottom – with the children – and then worked his way up to the authorities.

During his stay he corrected certain abuses in the area. First, he convinced the local judges to prohibit gambling and to enforce the prohibition. Secondly, he persuaded the local governor to make a law that would prohibit men's mistresses from publicly and shamelessly wearing veils, as if they were married to these men. The custom in the area was that unmarried girls became the mistresses of priests and other men, and remained faithful to them as if they were married. It was common for them to say quite shamelessly that they wore their veil for this man or that, and everyone recognized them for what they really were. After Ignatius had persuaded the Governor to punish a woman who wore a veil for a man to whom she was not married, the abuse began to disappear. Thirdly, Ignatius arranged that an order be given so that the poor should be provided for officially and regularly. Lastly, he had another order given that the Angelus should ring at the proper hours to call people to prayer, as was the custom at Rome.

Just as Ignatius began his apostolate by working from the bottom – from instructing children to preaching in the church – so he also worked from the top down, by convincing the judges and by persuading the Governor to make laws and issue orders. The pattern is clear: he was not only concerned with the spiritual aspect of prayer, but with the physical and moral aspects of ostentatious concubinage, gambling, and needless poverty.

These efforts of teaching and preaching, together with the energies he expended to convert sinful local habits, tired Ignatius to the point of illness. The return to his 'native air' had not really been the best prescription for the nature of his pains. Although he had felt well at the beginning of his stay, he ended by falling seriously ill. Once he was better, however, he decided to leave so that he could care for the business his companions in Paris had charged him with. He decided to make the trip without any money, and to go on foot. His brother was greatly irritated by his choosing to leave in this way, and by evening Ignatius had condescended to go on horseback with his brother and their relatives as far as the border of the province. But once he had crossed that border, he descended from the saddle, and without accepting anything he set off walking towards Pamplona.

One may wonder if this horse which he now abandoned was the same horse that his companions had offered him when he left Paris. One also wonders whether Ignatius ever re-entered the family castle in Loyola, whether he went back to the room where he had spent so many months convalescing, whether he visited the family chapel where there hung the Flemish painting of the Annunciation, or whether he stood once again at the window from which he had looked up at the stars. Such unmentioned points are left for us to meditate upon.

Ignatius says nothing about his feelings or his memories as he walked by the castle of Pamplona. He went on to Almazan, the homeland of Lainez, one of his Parisian companions. Then he passed through Siguenza, Toledo, and Valencia. In all the regions where he passed to visit the relatives of his companions, he never accepted anything, although they strongly insisted that he accept what were often very important gifts. In Valencia he visited Bachelor Castro, one of his early companions in Paris, who was now a Carthusian monk. During his convalescence at Loyola, Ignatius himself had once considered entering the Charterhouse at Seville, and had even made concrete inquiry through one of the house servants about the Charterhouse at Burgos. But such a vocation had not been his.

As he was about to leave Valencia for Genoa, his friends begged him to give up the thought because Barbarossa the Corsair was sailing off the coast with many ships; he risked falling into the hands of the pirates, of being captured and possibly killed. Although they told him many stories to frighten him, nothing made him hesitate. He boarded a large ship and went through such a fierce storm that this was one of the three times in his life when he thought he was going to die. As when he had been threatened with a deadly illness at Manresa, he experienced neither fear because of his past sins, nor fear of future damnation, but only a confusion and suffering arising from his regret over the little use he had made of the gifts and graces he had received. He arrived in Genoa, which he had not seen since the winter of 1524 on his journey back to Barcelona from Jerusalem, and he headed off across northern Italy toward Venice.

2. *The road through Italy*

On his way from Genoa to Bologna he suffered a great deal, particularly when he followed a high path along a river. The path became narrower and narrower until finally he could neither retreat nor advance. He had to go along on his hands and knees for a certain distance, in the grip of a great fear of falling into the river. He says that this was the greatest physical effort he ever made, and afterwards he experienced the greatest tiredness.

One cannot but notice how Ignatius's stories are often centred on his fearlessness, or on his need to overcome his fear: his fear of armed horsemen, his fearlessness faced with pirates, his fearlessness when threatened with death in the storm, his great fear of falling in the river. Could it have been that Ignatius dwelt on this theme deliberately, in order to show how much he had to struggle at times with his fearfulness? Was he also deliberately describing his fearlessness at times, to show how the grace of God had changed him? The various stories certainly show Ignatius in contrary emotional states, in circumstances where he sometimes makes a fool of himself, and where his story-telling would seem to underline this.

Although he has just barely survived falling from a dangerously high path into a river far below, he recounts how on entering Bologna he fell from a little wooden bridge into a stream. When he arose, covered with mud and water, a good number of people who saw the accident could not keep from laughing. He set about begging in Bologna, but he didn't receive a single 'quatrino'. He fell ill there for a while, but later he continued to Venice, walking and begging in his usual way.

Although he had been advised to go to Spain for his health, his illness had recurred at both Loyola and Bologna. Although these illnesses are sometimes explained as the result of his penitential fasting at Manresa, their recurrence in the various periods is not just incidental; they form one more obstacle that he has to patiently overcome, in the physical pole of the pattern.

3. *The apostolate in Venice and the ordinations*

He arrived in Venice some time before his companions, and the pattern of apostolate and subsequent difficulties with authority repeated itself. He devoted his time to giving the *Exercises* and entering into spiritual conversations. He gave the *Exercises* to Master Peter Contarini, an administrator at the hospital for the incurables, to Master Gaspar de Doctis, vicar of the Papal Legate in Venice, and to a Spaniard named Rosas. Bachelor Hoces, a Spaniard from Malaga, and the Bishop of Chieti also came to see him frequently. Hoces had a certain desire to make the *Exercises*, but he hesitated for a while before finally deciding to do so. Three or four days after he had begun, he admitted to Ignatius that certain people had made him so fearful of being exposed to some false doctrine that he had brought with him some reference books to consult. This man drew such great profit from the *Exercises* that he even decided later to join the group of the companions. He was the first of the companions to die, and his death formed an integral part of the final period of Ignatius in Rome.

As Hoces's fears indicated, Ignatius was already suffering from the misconceptions of others in Venice, and some people gossiped that he had been burned in effigy in Spain and Paris. The rumours got so out of hand that a trial was held, and the sentence was favourable to Ignatius. The first time that such rumours began to follow Ignatius was in Manresa, where word of his passage through Montserrat and of his dispossession of his fine clothes and arms grew out of all proportion and caused him some painful misunderstanding. Rumours had indeed followed him across Spain and France. But the image of being burned in effigy, though less painful than the burning threatened by Vicar Figueroa in Alcala, was typical of the way false rumours tended to reach for the most highly dramatic capital punishments. Thus false rumours were yet another obstacle that Ignatius had to overcome – in Manresa by means of patience, in Venice by means of a trial.

The nine companions arrived in Venice from Paris at the end of 1536, some six months after Ignatius arrived there. They separated from one another in order to work and lodge in different hospitals in the city. After two or three months they went to Rome to get the papal benediction for their pilgrimage to Jerusalem. Ignatius did not go with them, not only because he already had the benediction from his previous pilgrimage to Jerusalem, but because there were two men in Rome who might cause his companions some difficulties if they were seen with him. These two men were Doctor Ortiz and Cardinal Carafa. Doctor Ortiz had been a lecturer at the College of Montaigu in Paris, and he had made life difficult for Ignatius during the first stage of his studies, when Castro, Peralta, and Amador had made the *Exercises*. Cardinal Carafa was the Bishop of Chieti (Theate) who, with Bachelor Hoces, had come into contact with Ignatius before the arrival of the companions in Venice. Together with Cajetan of Thiene he had founded the first order of clerks regular, the Theatines, in 1524, and he showed interest in the manner of life of the 'companions' whom he had heard about from Ignatius. Ignatius later addressed a letter to him with his specific criticisms of the rule and manner of life of the Theatines, but it may never have been sent. Bishop Carafa was called to Rome in September 1536 and in late December was elevated to the Cardinalate. Thus one can understand Ignatius's reasons for not wishing to be seen with his companions in Rome at that time. Carafa was later elected Bishop of Rome in 1555, shortly before Ignatius's death, and orally blessed the 'Society of Jesus' in 1558.

When the companions returned from Rome, they came not only with the papal benediction, but with drafts for two to three hundred crowns, which they had received as alms for their pilgrimage! They did not want to take the money, but only the drafts. When they were later hindered from going to Jerusalem, they returned the drafts to those from whom they had received them. The companions had returned to Venice on foot, begging as they walked in three distinct groups, making sure that each group contained different nationalities. It was after their return that those who were not priests were ordained. The Papal Legate in Venice, whose vicar had made the *Exercises* with Ignatius, authorized their ordination. They were ordained under the canonical titles of 'poverty and sufficient instruction in letters'. They also pronounced vows of chastity and poverty.

The Shy Pattern (4)
In this story there is a combination of the physical and spiritual poles of the pattern, for when the companions returned from Rome, they brought with them both the papal blessing and *the drafts. The detachment and freedom with which they took and kept the drafts was proved by their returning them when their passage to Jerusalem became impossible at that time. Their freedom of choice walks the path between the physical and spiritual poles. The path continues between a further set of poles: expansion into the area of apostolic service of others, and into the area of studies. Only gradually, and after several failures, does it become possible for Ignatius to share this path with others. It is in this company with others that Ignatius continues his apostolate for others, even when they are opposed by others. In instance after instance, oppositions are overcome, but never definitively. The whole process is alive; although it is fragile, it has its momentum, and it is in this very momentum that the companions experience the 'companionship' of Jesus, in his witness to the Kingdom of God, and in his opposition to the Kingdom of Satan. Travelling, momentum, companionship, and the 'mission' are at the heart of the experience of this new group that aims to work in the Holy Land.*

4. *The year's wait in Venice and environs*

Since the Venetians had entered into an alliance with the Papal States, their relations with the Turks deteriorated. Consequently, no ships left Venice for the Holy Land at the traditional time of the feast of Corpus Christi that spring of 1537. So the companions followed the plan they had agreed upon in Paris. They separated into groups, and spread across the countryside around Venice, with the intention of waiting through the period of the year they had determined for themselves. If no ship sailed during that time, they were to set off for Rome. Seeing that Ignatius did not want to go to Rome with his companions when they went to ask for the papal blessing, this second alternative was not an easy one for him to face. It was his supreme fear – which he would learn to overcome – as it would also be the occasion for the highest grace he was to obtain at La Storta. For the time being, however, there was still hope that a pilgrim ship would sail.

It was Ignatius's lot to be in a group with Pierre Favre and Diego Lainez. The order of their life followed the pattern that had emerged as Ignatius moved from place to place. As for their lodging, they lived outside the town of Vicenza, in a house without doors or windows. They slept on straw. Twice a day, every day, two of them went to town to beg for food, but they received so little that they had barely enough to eat. They usually ate a little bread, and one of them stayed at home to prepare it. They spent forty days in this way, intent on nothing but prayer. At the end of this 'retreat', their fellow companion, John Codure, came to live with them, and they all resolved to begin their apostolate of preaching. On the same day and at the same hour they would go to four different places in the town, and begin their preaching by calling out to people in a loud voice while waving their hats. These sermons created some response from the town. Many people were brought to live a more Christian life, and the necessary material help that the companions needed began to be more abundant.

Here too the pattern shifts from pole to pole: from the physical pole of begging to the spiritual pole of the forty-day 'retreat'. Only then is the apostolate undertaken, and this has both a spiritual effect on the people the companions minister to, and a physical result in easing their own problem of making a living. The apostolate affects both the physical and spiritual bases. The circularity of this pattern is not just the experience of an individual, but the experience of a group. Ignatius's personal discovery had been communicated to others, and had resulted in the formation of a community.

During this sojourn in Vicenza, Ignatius began to experience many spiritual 'visions' and almost continual consolation. This was the opposite of what he had known in Paris, where he had disciplined his life in view of his studies, the better to prepare himself for the apostolate after his studies. He knew that an apostolate led to the usual difficulties, as he had assured Dr. Frago during his years of philosophical studies. During his travels through Spain and Italy, and especially in Venice as he was preparing to be ordained a priest and to say his first Mass, he experienced what he called 'great spiritual visitations', like those he used to have at Manresa. An example of such a grace is given in the story he tells of the walk to Bassano.

While he was at Vicenza, word came that one of his companions, Simao Rodriguez, was sick to the point of death at Bassano. Although Ignatius himself had a fever, he set out to visit him, and walked so fast that his companion, Pierre Favre, could not keep up with him. This was the opposite of the situation ten years before, when he himself could not keep up with his companions who had hurried ahead to get their health certificates at Padua. But what is common to both experiences is that during the journey Ignatius received God's assurance. He was so certain that he even told Favre: their sick companion would not die of this illness now. On their arrival at Bassano the sick man was consoled and grew rapidly better.

The Shy Pattern (5)
The 'visions' or visitations of Ignatius do not occupy a pole of the Ignatian pattern. They appear or occur gratuitously at its centre – there where Ignatius's freedom is committed to the path that combines both the spiritual and the physical poles, both the apostolic and the academic poles, as the best means to reach the more perfect goal. Like an arrow that is propelled by the bow-string strung from each tip of the bow, Ignatius's choices are propelled by the tension he has gathered through the proper adjustment of both the physical and spiritual poles of his existence. He has discovered that, in a sense, he is all weapon, all arrow.
This recalls the verse of the prophet Isaiah (49:2):

> *'He made my mouth like a sharp sword, in the shadow of his hand he hid me; he made me a polished arrow, in his quiver he hid me away.'*[14]

The walk to Bassano not only repeats and recapitulates the walk to Padua, when Ignatius was temporarily abandoned by his chance companions on the road to Venice during his pilgrimage to Jerusalem, but it also recalls that walk from Paris to Rouen, when Ignatius went to visit the sick Spaniard who might also have become a companion in God's service. This time, however, on the road to Bassano, Ignatius was in the company of one companion, walking toward a third, and he was confident that all would be well. He also shared this confidence with his companion. The 'companion' pole of the inter-personal pattern is temporarily complete. Such completion is always, and can never be other than, temporary, in that it is temporal.

Finally, all ten companions came to live together in Vicenza for a while, and some went to beg alms in neighbouring villages. When the year came to an end, ships were still not allowed to sail for the Holy Land. The second plan had now to be followed; they had decided to go to Rome, and this time Ignatius was to go with them. The two persons in Rome whom Ignatius had most feared had proved to be most welcoming to the companions who had gone there for the papal benediction. This reversal of expectations recalls how courteous the French army proved to be, *after* they had entered the surrendered castle of Pamplona. The attitudes of those two former adversaries in Rome may have partially lessened Ignatius's fears, as he and his companions, in three or four separate groups, set off along the road to Rome. It is hard to estimate the depth of disappointment in Ignatius and the other companions over their failure to find a ship embarking for the Holy Land. Although they had an alternate plan, their primary plan had been to go to live and work among the Turks in Jerusalem as 'companions of Jesus'. Ignatius had succeeded in communicating his own love for the holy places and his deep belief in the need of 'helping souls' there. Yet that love had been tempered with time and experience. Fourteen years had passed since that September in 1523, when he had climbed the Mount of Olives to visit the site of Jesus's ascension into heaven. During each of the years of his studies, he had intended to return there to continue the mission that Jesus had begun. But Jesus's community, his Church, was not only in the Holy Land; it was in various places around the world. And the Bishop of Rome, Peter's successor, was there to be consulted. It was toward that Bishop that Ignatius now walked, not alone, as he once walked to visit the Archbishop of Toledo, but together with nine companions who had vowed to spend their lives together in the service of the Kingdom of God, in communion with the church that Jesus had founded.

Chapter 12

THE ROAD TO ROME, AND BEYOND

The stories of the Roman period follow three discernible stages: first, the story of the entrance into the city; then, a description of the various works undertaken; and finally, an account of certain problems that arose and how Ignatius dealt with them. Only then does the drama of the telling of the *Autobiography* itself take on its full meaning and offer that meaning to those readers who have the patience to discern it.

1. *The entrance into Rome*

Ignatius walked in a group with the two other men who had been with him at Vicenza; Pierre Favre, the first of his permanent companions who was his room-mate in Paris, and Diego Lainez, the companion who was to succeed him after his death as the second Superior General of the companions in Rome.

He told Camara that during that journey he was 'very specially visited by God'. When Ignatius was confronted by difficulties, he always went to the root of the situation, and then went to the top, in order to go *through* the difficulties, beyond them. At Pamplona he went to the commanding officer and convinced him that the castle could be defended.

In Jerusalem he had sought out the Franciscan Custodian and the Provincial Superior. In Barcelona and in Paris he had made personal resolutions before his teachers. At the end of the period in Alcala he went to seek counsel from the Archbishop of Toledo. In Paris, on two different occasions, he went straight to the Inquisitor when he heard that he was being informed against. As recently as at Loyola, he put an end to the abuses he found, by teaching the children and preaching in the church, but also by contacting the Governor and judges so that laws and ordinances could be put in place to ensure the spiritual and material good of the public. Now, due to a political situation out of his control – the deterioration of relations between Venice and the Turks – he and his companions were headed towards the top: towards Rome, and specifically towards the Pope. This led Ignatius to go even higher, to the One who was Most High. It was to God the Father Himself that he was to pray a new prayer, a more radical prayer than he had ever prayed before. He prayed, through the mediation of the Mother of Jesus, to be 'put with the Son'. This request was linked with the decision he had made after his ordination, to wait a year before saying his first Mass. Had he put off the Mass for a year in the hope that he would be able to say it in the Holy Land? The fact that he chose to say his first Mass on Christmas Day at the altar before the manger in St Mary Major's Basilica in Rome may indicate the place where he had hoped to say his first Mass, had he reached the Holy Land in time. It may also indicate the place where the thought first came to him to become a priest.

Ignatius may have first heard the call to become a priest during his pilgrimage to Bethlehem on September 8 and 9, 1523, when he prayed in the cave where Jesus was born. The *Exercises* give us a clue. It is in the Second Week, in the meditation on the birth of Jesus, that Ignatius proposes to the exercitant:

> Making myself into a poor and unworthy little servant, I watch them [Mary, Joseph and Jesus], and contemplate

> them, and as if I were present serve them in their needs with all possible respect and reverence ... [114]

This is the second time he does this in the *Exercises*. The first time is in the very first exercise of the First Week, where Ignatius recommends that the exercitant place himself before the crucified Jesus and ask himself: 'What have I done for Christ? What am I doing for Christ? What ought I to do for Christ?' [53]. Since Ignatius would always have the exercitant situate himself inside the scene of the meditation, not only at the death of Jesus, but even at his birth, it is clear that Ignatius saw the self-offering of Jesus in the Eucharist and on the cross as beginning at his very birth. It is logical that it would have been there, at the place of his birth, that Ignatius first felt the desire to be a priest, as he understood a priest, as one present at the offering of Jesus to his Father, out of love for his Father and for the others around him, his disciples, those to whom he sent his apostles, as well as those who were trying to get rid of him. When Ignatius came to say his first Mass before the manger in St Mary Major in Rome, he not only said that Mass before the revered relic, but he said it in the heart of a city which had once been the capital of a pagan empire. His Mass was said at one of the key places in the spread of the Kingdom of God. It was not in the original place of the birth, but in an advance post of Jesus's mission, where the birth was still celebrated and still pointing toward the mission to be accomplished.

The point here is that the self-discipline Ignatius asked of himself was linked with his strong desire to be 'put with the Son'. It was in a little chapel only a few miles outside Rome that he prayed this prayer again, and there he experienced such a change in his soul, and saw so clearly that the Father had put him with Jesus, His son, that he would never doubt that the Father had indeed done so.

Within the context of a long sequence of roads, and of so many difficulties overcome, so many fears vanquished, so many events that occurred by chance or by providence, so many illusions and temptations resisted, this 'change in his soul' was the final goal toward which he had so long aspired. It was not just that Jesus was with him, but that he was put with Christ. This is the experience that Jesus prayed for in his final prayer at the Passover Mass, as described in John's Gospel. There Jesus prayed: 'Father, I desire that those that you have given me might be with me where I am so that they might see the glory which you have given me in your love for me before the foundation of the world' (17:24).

This was a prayer in which he asked (actively) 'to be put (passively) with Christ'. On the physical road to Rome, he prayed the spiritual prayer for a higher degree of union with Christ for the good of the apostolate, or mission, that lay before him, and the opposition that it would entail for him and his companions as a body. This episode, in this period, combined every pole of the personal and interpersonal pattern. He prayed to God not just for himself but for the group of companions; he prayed for their apostolate; he prayed for deliverance from the resistance he expected toward their apostolate.

Through this ultimate spiritual experience, he entered into the greatest intimacy in the relation between the Father and the Son, through the mediation of Jesus's mother. This is followed immediately, in the story-telling, by Ignatius's warning to his companions to be ready to meet numerous forms of resistance and obstacles in Rome.

As the prayer had to do with the most spiritual relationship, so the warning had to do with the most physical. As so often, the extremes of interior and exterior, highest and lowest came together. In particular, Ignatius told his companions to be on their guard in sexual matters, and not to engage in spiritual conversations with women who were not of noble birth. This advice proved to be necessary and helpful.

Later in Rome, Master Francis Xavier was confessor to a woman whom he sometimes visited to speak of spiritual things. She was found to be pregnant, but 'the Lord permitted the discovery of the man responsible.' The same thing happened to John Codure, when one of his spiritual daughters was accidentally discovered with a man. The interest of this warning that Ignatius gave to his companions is two-fold. First, in so far as it came right after the change in his own soul, it was as if the new intimacy he had with God gave him a strong sense of the resistance they were going to face, and of their need to be especially on their guard in the area of their chastity. Secondly, he was concerned not just with each individual, but with their group as a body. It was as if a corporate body's chastity, as well as its other virtues, was as important on the larger corporate and institutional level of relations as an individual's chastity and virtues were important on an interpersonal level.

Thus the spiritual experience in the chapel of La Storta, and the warning to resist the temptations that could arise in spiritual conversations, were the final appearance in this period of the spiritual and physical poles of the pattern. It is also true that 'the change of soul' was a vision, confirming the decision of the companions to go to Rome. Ignatius could not have received such a grace in Jerusalem. He had to lose Jerusalem and their long-conceived plan to spend their lives there, and to walk faithfully and blindly towards Rome, before his broken and literally disappointed heart could be ready to grasp the grace that he received. Just as he had to lose Jerusalem the first time in order to 'see' Christ 'above him', so he had to lose Jerusalem a second time in order to be 'put with Christ' beside him.

Just as the hands have to separate from one another in order to catch such flying objects as beach balls, falling timbers, or leaping children, so the heart has to be broken in order to learn and teach and – with its many-severed sides – embrace and endure some of the rending experiences which it is created to bring into existence. Leon Bloy wrote that there are parts of our hearts that never exist until certain sufferings bring them into existence. By 'suffering' he meant both passive and active experiences where we reach beyond ourselves toward one another, out of a self-forgetful, self-negating, other-concerned love for another. 'Nada'. 'Todo'. Nothing. Everything. Yet in that act, in risking all, in losing all, out of love for all, or some, or one other person, one receives all. Yet one must really *not* care, but give all, even if one receives nothing in return.

After relating these two incidents on the road to Rome – the answered prayer at La Storta, and the warning addressed to his companions – Ignatius has only two other stages to describe: the continuation of the apostolates in Rome, and then the problems that arose from the accusations made against him and his companions. He met the accusations by going to the top: first, by going to see the Governor of Rome, and then by going to see the Pope himself. These stages recapitulate and confirm two other basic areas of the pattern: the apostolate, and opposition to that apostolate.

The prayer of Ignatius at La Storta and the consequent warning given to his companions recall the exaltation of the three disciples after the transfiguration of Jesus on the mountain, followed by the severe warning that he gave them afterwards (Mark 9: 2–13). There is another parallel of this structure in the *Spiritual Exercises*, in the 'Rules for Discernment of Spirits, proper to the Second Week', where Ignatius warns the exercitant to beware of the secondary kind of thoughts that come to a person who has been graced with 'consolation without cause'. After defining this form of consolation [330] he goes on to warn the exercitant of a possible deception [336]:

> When consolation is without cause, even though there is no deception in it (since as has been said, it comes solely from God our Lord), nevertheless the spiritual person to whom God gives this consolation must scrutinize the experience carefully and attentively, so as to distinguish the precise time of the actual consolation from the period following it, during which the soul is still aglow and favoured with the benefits and after-effects of the consolation now passed. For during this second period, it often happens that owing either

> to thinking based on conclusions drawn from the relations between our own concepts and judgements, or to the agency of the good or bad spirits, we form various plans and opinions which are not directly given by God our Lord. These require, therefore, to be examined with very great care before being given complete credence and put into practice.

2. *The work in Rome*

Ignatius does not mention the usual details of their lodging and finance. He moves right into the subject of the apostolate, beginning with giving the *Spiritual Exercises*.

First, he tells in detail how he went to Monte Cassino to give the *Exercises* to none other than Dr Ortiz. The details show how this story overlaps many previous periods. For Ignatius to go to the great Benedictine monastery near Rome was a repetition of his previous pilgrimage to the Benedictine monastery of Montserrat. At Montserrat his written spiritual exercises were still in a rudimentary form, yet they were promising enough for him to have decided at Montserrat to go off to Manresa for a few months to work on 'his book'. Now the book was not only complete, but it had been read and approved by Inquisitors in Spain and France. It would also be approved in Rome. It had been carried with him across land and sea, across battlefields, by mule and donkey, on horseback and on foot. It had been used to 'help souls' in Spain, France, and Italy. Now he gave those *Exercises* to Dr Ortiz, the very man whom he had so feared only a little more than a year before that he had thought it best for him not to go to Rome lest he create unnecessary difficulties for his companions. In brief, Ignatius was now giving the *Exercises*, which he had conceived in Spain, in a Benedictine monastery in Italy, to a man who had opposed him in France, because of the trouble that Ignatius's apostolate of giving the *Exercises* was causing there. In this incident there is a recapitulation of places and a reversal of roles, in so far as the man who was once opposed to the *Exercises* was now benefitting from them, under the direction of the author himself.

Yet the story includes a further resolution. While at Monte Cassino for the forty days of retreat, Ignatius had a vision, similar to the one he had when he was walking with Pierre Favre to Bassano. Only this time, instead of having the certainty that a companion was not going to die, Ignatius now saw his companion, Bachelor Hoces, 'entering heaven'. From another source than the *Autobiography* we know that Ignatius experienced this as he was saying Mass; many tears began to flow from his eyes as he received great spiritual consolation over this death and passage into heaven. Hoces, who had been so hesitant about making the *Exercises* in Venice, and who had so candidly revealed how he had brought books along on his retreat to make sure that he was not taught false doctrine – this Hoces was the first of the companions to die. The mention of his death completes the area of the pattern which was concerned with the formation of a permanent group of companions. Hoces lived this life of companionship until his death. It was while giving the *Exercises* that Ignatius experienced, at the visionary centre of the pattern, this 'entry' of Hoces into heaven. Ignatius's experience of Hoces's death and salvation, while giving the *Exercises* to Dr Ortiz, was a confirmation of the reality of the 'body' of the Companions of Jesus. As in his warning to them about the dangers to be found in Rome, so here too, in his experience of Hoces's death, Ignatius had a spiritual or sixth sense of what was happening or could happen to the members of their 'body'. Ignatius even added to his description of this incident the little phrase that has appeared occasionally at a few important points of his story-telling: he saw it so clearly that if he said the opposite, he would have the impression that he was lying.

Not only did Ignatius give the *Exercises* to one of his old opponents; not only did he experience at Mass the passage of his companion Hoces into heaven; but Ignatius brought down from Monte Cassino a Spaniard he met there, Francis Estrada, who was to be the first new companion at

Rome. As Hoces entered heaven, Estrada took his place on earth.

The brevity and density of those days of retreat at Monte Cassino are proof of the degree to which Ignatius examined his experience, meditated on his graces and sins, and sought out their fullest dimensions until he could offer himself to God. Similarly, although he tells Camara relatively few episodes concerning the final period in Rome, he is careful to choose a set of incidents which not only refer to several of the periods and places of the past, but which tie together the three interpersonal areas of the apostolate, a former opponent, and the group of companions, into a single baroque knot.

After returning to Rome, Ignatius simply employed himself in 'helping souls', as he had intended to do in Jerusalem. He even gave the *Exercises* to two persons at the same time, one of whom lived at St Mary Major's (the shrine of the manger) and the other at the Ponte-Sixto. Ignatius's mastery at giving these *Exercises* to different people in different places at the same time recalls Johann Sebastian Bach working at his *Art of Fugue* on his very deathbed. As mentioned previously, in that work he created a sequence of fugues that begins with the most simple and advances to the increasingly complex. The final unfinished fugue has four distinct subjects or melodies, one of which is the musical transposition of his own name. Ignatius's signature, too, is within his work, something like the face of Velasquez peering around the corner of his canvas, as he paints the King and Queen of Spain in *Las Meninas*. It is as unmistakable as the literal signature he inscribed on his letters regarding current affairs.

In Ignatius's description of the retreat with Dr Ortiz at Monte Cassino, and of his several retreats in Rome, as well as in the description of his opposition to his accusers in the stage that follows, we are presented with the most intense instance of the pattern that has yet emerged. The pattern has been forming gradually, as the wounded soldier was transformed into a pilgrim, a writer, a student, a graduate, a leader of companions, a priest. He has moved along the roads and across the seas, from house to house, from period to period, from physical penances to spiritual graces, from personal vocation to apostolates, from solitude to companionship, from studies to ordination. He has gradually learned to master the relationships between the various poles of the pattern, to juggle the various areas of his activities, and to juggle them with others. The final episode that he relates is concerned with certain accusations that were brought against him and the Companions of Jesus. These pushed Ignatius to the furthest limits of his resistance. Just as his return from Rouen and initiative in going straight to the Inquisitor in Paris flowed from the exaltation that followed the breaking of the bonds of his fear on passing Argenteuil and its relic of the Holy Robe, so his return from Monte Cassino and his insistence on going to the Pope himself for a sentence in his favour flowed from the experience at La Storta of 'being put with the Son', and from the experience of seeing and feeling what was happening to the 'body' of his companions.

3. *Accusations and response*

The last stage that Ignatius narrates comprises two related episodes. In these he responds to accusations, and his responses are not only examples of his active initiative and resistance, in his going right to the top, but also of his passive waiting for the opportunity to go even higher, and to obtain a sentence in writing. The episode is a good example of the story-teller's art, for it ends with both recapitulation and surprise. It is not just a story however. It is the result of a man's long meditation on his lifetime, as proposed in the *Exercises*: a meditation on his sins, the disorder from which they arise, the 'world' to which they contribute and in which they are implicated, and the hell towards which they are headed and carried forward by their own selfish and destructive momentum. This meditation is counter-balanced by reflections on one's graces, the tranquillity in which they have been given, the 'kingdom' to which they contribute and in which they are implicated, and the heaven toward which they move, into which they enter, by laws more subtle than gravity or radiation. There is also a meditation more radical than either of these: the Meditation on the Two Standards, in which the exercitant prays to be given the grace to see and respond to the fact that deep beneath the layers of sin, disorder, the world, and hell, there lurks Satan – the 'prince of this world' and the inhabitant of hell. The exercitant also prays to be given the grace to see and respond to another fact: deep beneath the layers of grace, order, the kingdom, and heaven, there reigns Jesus Christ – the 'prince' (Apoc. 1:5), who has ascended into heaven. To move down through the four layers, in opposing directions, is to move from the outside to the inside, from the active to the passive, until – at the most opposite poles – one realizes that the opposition of Satan and Christ is a transcendent opposition, beyond all our capacity to describe it in terms of exteriority and interiority, activity and passivity. It is the opposition of NO and YES, of 'I will not serve' and 'Behold the handmaid of the Lord'. There is no middle ground there.

Although the accusations made against Ignatius and his companions in Rome were not made directly by the Accuser himself, they were repelled by Ignatius with all the energy he could muster, because they were lies. If one has no sense of the transcendent context of Ignatius's vision, and of his perception of the role that lies and calumny play in the compounding of disorder, the strengthening of the 'world', the momentum of the movement toward hell, and the 'wiles' of Satan [142], one will never understand why Ignatius behaved as he did in the final episode. His response to the two accusations gives proof of his self-confidence before both the highest civil authority in the city and the highest religious authority in the Church, and in both instances it was a question of faithfulness to the truth of the lives they had lived together up to that time.

THE FIRST EPISODE was triggered by a personal accusation against Ignatius, made by a certain 'Michael' who was a former servant of Francis Xavier in Paris, and who had now come to live in Rome. He spoke evil of Ignatius, and Ignatius had him called before the city Governor, and showed him a letter that Michael had once written in which he had much praised him. The Governor interrogated Michael and the case was concluded by Michael's banishment from Rome. This incident was limited to Ignatius's personal reputation, but the next touched on the companions as well, and it was this which made Ignatius decide to go to the top – to the Pope himself.

THE SECOND EPISODE relates an incident begun by two priests, Mudara and Barreda, who spread the word that Ignatius and his companions had been expelled from Spain, Paris, and Venice. From other sources we know that these two priests were intent on destroying the good name of the companions because the latter had criticized the preaching of an Augustinian monk whose doctrine was suspected of dangerous heresy; the priests in question were supporters of this monk. Once they had been interrogated by the city Governor, as well as by the Papal Legate, the two priests admitted that they had nothing for which to reprove the companions, in either their behaviour or their teaching. The Legate ordered that all keep silence on the matter, but Ignatius did not think it wise to do so. He wanted a final sentence. No one was pleased with his position of wanting a final sentence despite the Legate's order for silence – neither the Legate, the Governor, nor those who had shown themselves most favourable to Ignatius. Ignatius, however, waited patiently until the Pope finally returned to Rome, for he had been absent for several months in an effort to reconcile the Emperor, Charles V and King Francis I of France, the sovereigns whose forces had been at war at Pamplona, in northern Italy when Ignatius was returning from Jerusalem, and on the Spanish–French border when he was determined to go to Paris. On hearing that the Pope had returned, he went out to see him at the papal residence at Frascati. He presented to the Pope the reasons why he and his companions needed a final sentence regarding this false accusation. The Pope took the matter in hand, and ordered that a favourable sentence be passed.

This was not the first time that Ignatius refused to remain silent about a matter that he thought to be important. He had responded frankly to the Franciscan Provincial in Jerusalem. He had responded similarly to Vicar Figueroa in Alcala, and he found it impossible to remain quiet under the jurisdiction of the court in Salamanca. In Paris he had twice taken the initiative of going to see the Inquisitor to put an end to circulating rumors. In this Roman incident, faced with the disapproval of the very authorities who had exonerated him, he called upon deeper reserves of his patience and determination. Patiently, with active passivity, he waited for the Pope to return to Rome before continuing his resistance to the slander right to the very end. We have seen in the course of his story that Ignatius has had to defend his group of companions a number of times before different authorities. The difference this time is that he has to defend a truth of Christian doctrine, and not just a style of life or the companions' inadequate theological formation.

This is the final example of Ignatius's struggle for the good name of the group of companions. For the good of their apostolate, he defended the reputation of the group against the groundless charges of the two priests. All three of the areas of interpersonal relations in the pattern are here revealed.

The *Autobiography* ends with the simple statement that the companions initiated several good works in Rome, such as a work for catechumens, a work for prostitutes and abandoned women; another for orphans, etc. The works were basically positive, such as instruction, and works which involved caring for those hurt and handicapped by their own fault or those of others. After the story of the incidents that led Ignatius to go to the highest authorities, he ends by bringing the story of his work right down to teaching the basic lessons of the faith and caring for abandoned women and children. Here in Rome the pattern of apostolates resembled closely the pattern established during his brief stay in Loyola on his way to join his companions in Venice. The same pattern was found in the works undertaken in Venice and Vicenza. The same pattern of works would have been initiated in Jerusalem. Ignatius was still defending the castle, only this time he was not alone, and the castle was the Kingdom of God.

At this point Ignatius tells Camara that Master Nadal can relate the rest of the story. In other words, Nadal and Camara – who had each heard different parts of Ignatius's story – were now referred to each other. Nadal could tell the rest of the story, because the rest of the story was known to the companions. Ignatius's story about them disappears into their stories about him, as a member of their company. Ignatius's story disappears here, as Jesus's story disappears in the story of the ascension from the Mount of Olives. From that point on, we have only the *Acts of the Apostles*, the *Letters*, and the *Apocalypse*, which continue his story in the lives of his disciples, right to the end of the old creation, and to the beginning of the new one: symbolized in the holy city of Jerusalem, the Bride of the Lamb. The man who has dictated his *Autobiography* has passed his story on to the two members of the group who requested it. The conclusion is self-effacing.

And yet Camara wanted more information. His desire, mixed with his curiosity, led to the final interview that took place in Ignatius's rooms in Rome that October in 1555.

Chapter 13

THE EPILOGUE: THE FINAL INTERVIEW

On October 20, 1555, the morning before Camara's departure for Spain, Ignatius finished the dictation of his story. The narrative was complete. Camara then relates the two final episodes, touching on his own requests.

1. *The first request: two final questions*

Camara asked Ignatius two further questions: Now that he had finished telling the story of his life, could he say how he had written the *Exercises*, and how he had written the *Constitutions*? Perhaps Nadal had asked Camara to pose those last two questions, since he had the task of promulgating the *Constitutions* among the companions, and such information could be helpful to them.

Ignatius answered the first question immediately. The *Exercises* were not composed all at once, but whenever he observed something in his own soul that he thought might be useful to someone else, he wrote it down. He told Camara that the paragraphs on the 'elections' (resolutions, decisions) had been drawn from his experience of the diversity of spirits and thoughts he had known at Loyola, when he was still convalescing from the operations on his leg. Then, characteristically, Ignatius put off speaking further about how he had composed the *Constitutions*. He said that he would speak of that in the evening.

Let it be noted that his answer to the first question referred back to the first period of his life story. The answer to the second would refer to the very last period of his life, the period in which he and his fellow companion were holding their conversation.

2. *The final interview: Ignatius's response in six steps*

That same day before supper, Ignatius called Camara to his rooms. Camara came promptly. He had learned his lesson that day, the previous March, when he thought that he could be late for an appointment with Ignatius, because he had not expected Ignatius to be on time. Ignatius welcomed him 'with the air of someone more recollected than usual'. Then he went straight to the subject. He began his answer, which was unexpectedly long and circuitous, but it ended with a direct and simple statement. Ignatius's answer advanced through six steps.

FIRST STEP: He began by protesting that his true intention, in all that he had related, was to narrate the simple facts. This was as he had written in the *Spiritual Exercises* [2]. He was sure that he had not exaggerated. He had offended Our Lord many times since he had begun to serve Him, but he had never consented to a single mortal sin. On the contrary, his devotion had increased, and he could easily find God – now more than ever before. At any hour that he wanted to find God, he found Him.

Before continuing, it is important to note the introductory nature of this protestation. Ignatius was indeed circling in to answer Camara's question about the composition of the *Constitutions*, but the steps of his circling reveal subjects raised in some of the periods of his past:

- In his answers to the Inquisitors in Alcala and Salamanca, did he not always begin by admitting how little basis he had?

• In the interrogation at Salamanca, did the Inquisitors not notice the teaching of Ignatius on the difference between a mortal and a venial sin? In his present answer to Camara, this confession of Ignatius's past sinfulness comes as a prologue to his revelation of the extraordinary graces and insights he is now receiving.
• He admits that since he began to serve God, he has never committed a mortal sin. This 'service' would therefore seem to date from the period at Loyola, when he saw Our Lady and the Holy Child so clearly and so deeply that afterwards he never again consented to a sin against his sexuality.
• Moreover, his growth in finding God has reached this degree of intimacy only after the vision at La Storta on the road to Rome, when he was 'put with the Son'. This is the closeness of which he speaks to Camara.

Thus the first step of Ignatius's answer is a prologue that contains in simplified form a summary of the itinerary of his life from Loyola to Rome. From this 'general confession' he will go on to describe his experience in increasingly specific steps.

SECOND STEP: Ignatius then began to specify his 'visions' in detail: how often Christ had appeared to him as the 'sun', especially when he was engrossed in important matters, and even when he was talking with certain people about important affairs. He took these visions as a confirmation of the grace that was present in the matter at hand. As an example of an 'important matter', he related that he had many visions when he was saying Mass, and when he was writing the *Constitutions*.

Ignatius moves from the subject of his visions of Jesus to the Mass and the Constitutions, but he does not yet link these last two subjects, as he will do later when he reaches the fifth step of his answer.

That very morning he has said that the *Exercises* were written over a long period of time, as he moved from place to place. He now distinguishes the *Constitutions* as being written in Rome, within a more stable context, although it is taking him several years to work them out. The *Autobiography* ends with this description of how the other two written works came into being.

THIRD STEP: After the introductory words protesting his veracity, and after telling Camara of the visions he had while writing the *Constitutions*, Ignatius went on to prove it: he told Camara that he kept a *Diary* of what happened in his soul each day.

This is similar to the short diary that Ignatius recommends the exercitant to keep during the four weeks of the *Spiritual Exercises*, as a way of eliminating particular sins or faults [24–31]. One might also keep a daily record of the insights or graces received over the course of the *Exercises*, as a help toward better discerning the spirits in one's soul [77]. It is from such a record of insights and discernment that Ignatius developed his 'notes' taken at Loyola into the shape of the retreat manual of the *Spiritual Exercises*. It is not surprising that he also kept such a record of his interior life during his composition of the *Constitutions*.

FOURTH STEP: He then took a further step: he confirmed the words he had just spoken by showing Camara a large pile of 'notes'. Camara might have said that he had no need to see them, as Ignatius had protested in Jerusalem, when the Franciscan Provincial made ready to show him the papal bull which gave him authority to excommunicate disobedient pilgrims. But Camara did not make that gesture.

FIFTH STEP: Ignatius read some of these notes to Camara. They referred to visions he had had in confirmation of a certain point in the *Constitutions*. He specified the content of the visions, their duration, and even one of the subjects which occasioned them. In the process he also mentioned the Mass, as a part of the method of his composition.

As for the content, sometimes he had 'seen' God the Father, sometimes the three persons of the Trinity, as at

Manresa, sometimes the Mother and Child, as at Loyola, interceding for him or confirming him in his resolutions.

The durations of these visions had varied. But on certain points of his deliberations, he had spent as many as forty days, which was more or less the duration of the retreat of the *Spiritual Exercises*.

The method followed on each day of the deliberation was the same. He said Mass for that intention, and at each Mass he shed many tears. He here linked the *Constitutions* to the Mass, as a necessary stage in their composition.

Tears were first mentioned at Montserrat, when he realized how his desire to be poor had caused the harassment of the beggar to whom he had given his clothes. The Mass or act of thanksgiving has been mentioned twice in the course of the two Prefaces; it also figures strongly as an invariable part of the framework of his months at Manresa. It was during the elevation of the Host at Mass that he had a 'vision' of how Jesus was in the Host.

The subject raised in the 'notes' that Ignatius had chosen to show Camara was that of poverty. The visions occurred as he deliberated on the matter of whether the churches of the companions should have any revenue, and if so, should they themselves be able to benefit from it.

At a larger corporate level, Ignatius was taking decisions in his writing which he would later propose to the group of his companions for approval. This was the kind of decision that he once used to take by himself, as when he left his extra coins on the bench in the port at Barcelona, when he distributed all his alms at Ferrara, and when he decided to go to Flanders each year to beg for alms to continue his studies in Paris.

Now, as he was praying his way through the writing of the *Constitutions*, the writing itself was his penance, his prayer, and his vision. And it was coming within an integrated timespan, within a sort of compositional 'once and for all', in a determined period over forty days. He was writing it for his companions and their apostolate, in order to forestall any resistance in the future. Thus the composition of the *Constitutions* refers to the whole shy pattern that we have discovered in his story. It is the recapitulation both of his personal discoveries (the first three stages), and of his more interpersonal discoveries (the last three stages):

1. It was at Loyola and on the road to Montserrat that Ignatius, the man, was transformed into the convert, by his discovery of the movements of his own interiority.
2. It was at Manresa that the mystic combined his earlier discovery with a profound liberation from his past and a more realistic sense of his future.
3. On the road to and from the Holy Land, the pilgrim integrated his two previous discoveries with a new grasp of the importance of passivity and patience, in their relation to initiative and action.
4. This set of three personal discoveries was now brought to his studies, as the student began to lay the foundation of his academic life during the years in Barcelona, Alcala, and Salamanca.
5. It was at Paris that Ignatius became the master, for it was there that he learned how to juggle his personal spiritual life with his studies, and his life with close companions with his very limited apostolate.
6. Finally, in Spain, Venice, and Rome, the apostolates of Ignatius and his companions took root and expanded. It was as a companion with them and as a priest that he experienced a further grace, and overcame certain radical obstacles.

The writing of the *Constitutions* was a further development of those bedside 'notes' that Ignatius had begun to take at Loyola. His telling the story of how he wrote those *Constitutions* was the final up-dating of the entire story.

SIXTH STEP: Then, after he had told Camara about the visions and the notes that witnessed to them – notes which he showed him and even read to him – Ignatius answered

Camara's question about how he wrote the *Constitutions* with a simple, direct statement: he proceeded by presenting the problematic point to God at Mass each day. In this way, he would pray over the point in the presence of Jesus in the Eucharist and on the Cross and in the Manger. As he prayed over such points at Mass, he found that he always wept.

In his composition of the *Constitutions*, Ignatius was once again involved in that searching movement that we noticed on the Mount of the Ascension. He passed from thinking and writing about a point, to praying over that point during the Mass. Only then did he bring the point back into his writing. His passage from thinking and writing to prayer, and then once again to writing, was accompanied by tears. His tears confirmed that he was on the true path.

It was a strange scene for Ignatius to relate as the conclusion to his story. The man, the convert, the mystic, the pilgrim, the student, the master, the companion – they were all one and the same man, whose story began in Pamplona, as he charged about the fortress in a defiant effort to defend it. His story ended here in Rome, as he wept over the altar at Mass, and over a point of composition in the *Constitutions* that he was writing for his companions. Ignatius had followed a road that finally led to Rome, and through Rome to the various lands where the 'Companions of Jesus' were sent to live and work – in Europe and Asia, in Africa and the Americas – around the world which had so recently been circumnavigated by Magellan. This world was just becoming conscious of its global shape, of its being a planet, with the challenges, dangers, and opportunities for good and evil that the discovery entailed. Ignatius and his companions had hoped to establish themselves in the Holy Land, to work among the Turks. At the end of his life, Ignatius was trying to compose *Constitutions* which would hold the dispersed companions together, whether they were out at the edges of the world, or working among the Turks in the Holy Land or among the Jewish converts in Rome.

3. *Camara's last request and Ignatius's refusal*

It was then that Camara made his third and last mistake: his curiosity was whetted by seeing the pages of the 'notes' and by hearing that part of them which Ignatius had chosen to read. He was no longer curious to see Ignatius's face and eyes, but rather to see his 'large pile of notes' for a longer time. He asked Ignatius if he might have more time to look through them.

Ignatius refused. He had spoken of them, shown them, and even read something from them. That was enough. The refusal did not hide the essential, but rather affirmed that the essential had already been revealed, for him who had eyes to see.

Camara's desire for 'more', in this case, was a disordered desire – an act of concupiscence, a desire to have that was confused with a desire to be. He should have been satisfied with what he had already seen and heard from the 'notes' on the desk. It was in his relation to Ignatius that the 'more' really lay. The 'special recollectedness' which he had noticed in Ignatius that evening before supper pointed to the fact that Ignatius had gone as far as he had decided to go – at least, with words. Not only that, but he had invited Camara to his rooms just before supper, as if to let the call to supper set a limit to the time of their interview: a limit, in addition to the coming night and Camara's departure the following day, and in addition to his own approaching death, which would fix the limits in which the essential might be said, or at least shown.

Such terms as concupiscence and disordered desires may at first seem unfamiliar to us, but today's readers are no less aware, at times, of their own obsessions, their selfishness, their excessive or defective behaviour in certain social situations, driven by a false conception of themselves or others. Life is a loose self-correcting process – sometimes too loose, and sometimes deadly swift. And if we don't correct ourselves, others do it for us, or take advantage of us, until chance or grace wakes us up to the situation, which might still be saved. The point here is that Camara's desire for more was about to meet a limit, and more than a limit.

Camara was now confronted with those limits that Ignatius placed before him and shared with him: limits to his place and time, to his seeing and listening, to his curiosity to know further particulars, to his desire for more time. It is this curiosity and vain desire which constituted the concupiscence underlying the vanity that Camara had once confessed to in the garden in 1553. Ignatius says at the very beginning of his story that vanity was the source of his own disorder right up to the battle at Pamplona and the early stages of his recovery. For vanity is a disordered desire for oneself, a concupiscence aimed at oneself, a desire to have oneself, to own oneself in a merely self-referential, self-interested, self-enamoured mirror-like way. It is hard to know more about this scene; like Camara, we ourselves may be pushing into more particulars than we need to know, because we too may have missed the essential.

Ignatius's life was a long series of refusals. He began his story with his refusal to surrender the castle of Pamplona to the French, and he ended it with the refusal to take the advice of political and ecclesiastical authorities in Rome who requested that he forget all about the accusations of the two Spanish priests against the Companions of Jesus. He had patiently waited until he could go right to the Pope for a final sentence on the case. Just as he had refused to yield to his fear, so he had refused to accept a false limitation to his apostolate. Yet all these refusals were pointing to something that became clearer to Ignatius with time, and that became clearer through the progressively more precise imagery he used to describe his 'visions'. This 'something' was someone. It was Jesus. Each refusal was necessary to Ignatius in his search for what was better. But as he came to follow Christ more closely, and especially after he was 'put with the Son' at La Storta, he had a familiarity with Jesus that was disconcerting – disconcerting, unless we the readers catch on, and dare to enter into it with him, dare to concert.

Not only does his own story begin with a NO and end with a NO, but at the beginning and end of the stories of his two companions, Nadal and Camara, as related in their Prefaces, we also find Ignatius's refusals. This final interview in 1555 is a sort of 'spiritual conversation' between Ignatius and Camara, and it ends with a NO, just as Nadal's first request for Ignatius's story back in 1551 had also been met with a NO. These were refusals that ultimately led to consent, to affirmation, to revelations, and to tears. But there was a point where enough was enough: where either one had got the point, or one had passed the moment when the point could have been got. Both Ignatius's *Autobiography* and the stories of how it came to be told end with his affirmation that he had reached the point where it was 'enough'. But nothing would stop him until he had reached that point ... of 'colloquy', as he calls it in the *Exercises*, at the end of each meditation.

The *Spiritual Exercises* end with a parallel statement, addressed to God; 'Give me only the love of you, together with your grace for that is enough for me' [234]. According to John's Gospel, Jesus died after saying his final word: 'It is accomplished' (Jn.19:30).

Again and again in the episodes of the various periods of his life, Ignatius switched from one means to another to reach his goals. Although he counselled only permissible means, to achieve ends that were only to God's glory and for the salvation of souls [23], his special insight lay in the moving switching rhythm that his story describes again and again. And visible, 'envisioned', behind and through that movement lies the shy pattern. It is this rhythm which knows or feels when it is time to stop: when it has had 'enough'. It is this refusal to say or show more which ends Ignatius's story. It seems that Camara had not expected it to end in such a way.

4. *Camara's acquiescence, or response?*

Camara's last interview with Ignatius was a mixed success. He had been warned. Ignatius's more than ordinary recollectedness, and his admission that he saw Jesus when he spoke of important things, should have made Camara aware that something was up. Ignatius was recollected in Jesus. Whether he was having a 'vision' is impossible to determine; but it is reasonable to suppose that, since Ignatius was considering an important matter at the present time with one of his companions, he would hope that this companion would also share his 'recollection', and the subject of it. Whatever state Ignatius was in, it seems that Camara was not equal to it. He didn't rise to it.

Camara had not caught on to the mood that Ignatius was in. He was not able to respond to it. Ignatius's mood was one in which he was trying to share something. This was the sharing, the 'accompaniment' that he found in his relationship with God, and which he brought into his relationships with people. This was why he could tell Camara that he sometimes had visions of Jesus while he was speaking with people. Such shared visions or shared graces may be likened to the one that Augustine describes in his *Confessions* (Book IX), when he and his mother conversed at the open window in Ostia, shortly before her death.

Yet who can be sure that Camara was insensitive to the challenge raised by the limits of the situation within which he and Ignatius found themselves? Ignatius had refused to give Camara more time to read the notes. He had said that Camara had already seen enough. 'Enough'. What is enough? The full text of the prayer that Ignatius placed at the end of the *Spiritual Exercises* in the final 'Contemplation for Obtaining Divine Love', is as follows:

> Take Lord and receive all my liberty, my memory, my understanding and my entire will, all that I have and possess. You gave it all to me; to you I return it. All is yours, dispose of it entirely according your will. Give me only the

love of you, together with your grace for that is enough for me [234].

Could it be that Camara had got the point? And that when he heard Ignatius's refusal, he realized that Ignatius had given all he could? And that it was up to the others, his readers, to see that in the limited episodes of the stages of his life, and in the limited time of that final interview, Ignatius had given all that he had received, because he had given, or offered, the One from whom he had received it?

In the medium that Ignatius had chosen – the oral word, written down by Camara for future readers – he could go no farther. Camara does not tell us whether he then dared to lift his eyes to meet those of Ignatius. He had been warned, once, not to stare at Ignatius as he spoke. But now the dictation of the story had ended; the interview was over. Words had gone as far as they could go. There remained the union of their hearts. The fact that Camara ends his account of the final interview with Ignatius's simple refusal of his request shows more eloquently than any commentary that Camara had indeed caught on to the reason for the economy of the narrator. No more needed to be said. Supper was ready; Camara was to leave the following day with the mail for Spain; Ignatius was to die within nine months. The story that emerges from their collaboration, and the Prefaces and Epilogue which frame that story, are proof that there existed among them – in the very dovetailing of their contrasting gifts and limitations – that union of hearts, in obedience, which is described in the *Constitutions* (Part VIII, Ch. 1). The book is a witness to a YES that comes through that collaboration. The Epilogue may end with a NO to the request for more information, but the book ends with a YES that underlies the whole composition, that has gathered momentum and spills over the NO of the Epilogue like water over a dam, generating a power that only the imposed limits could bring about.

5. *The reader's acquiescence, or response?*

We may now see why the future companions needed the *Autobiography*. Without it, the *Constitutions* remained too abstract – like legislation without the story which reveals where it comes from, like laws and regulations devoid of the narration of the events that found them. Nadal had been right when he told Camara that it was imperative to have the story of Ignatius's conversion, since it 'founded' the Society of Jesus. This story 'founds' the Society in the same way that any original or seminal document founds an organization: it narrates the story of its birth. It is not sufficient, however, for a group or institution to have its 'founding story', even in the most beautiful, most economical, and most critical editions. It needs to believe in it. Some founding stories may become more and more incredible with time; others may become irrelevant when faced with challenges coming from changes within society and within the Church itself that were never previously experienced. Religious congregations can die, or at least wither in some cultures and thrive in others, until those others also have to come to terms with the same social forces that led to the earlier withering of their companions, and that may well lead to their own extinction in another generation. This study is an effort to unearth the shy pattern found in the *Autobiography*, in the belief – I repeat 'belief' – that the book contains resources that have not been fully called upon, and that all 'companions of Jesus' need to discover in order to find their way through some of the perils of the post-modern age. For that age also contains its opportunities and graces. And the discernment of graces and dangers, inspirations and temptations, is more imperative than ever before. This is the kind of situation that Ignatius thrived upon, and which is described again and again in his story.

His 'story': the framework of the story, formed by its Prefaces and Epilogue, makes the story of a pilgrim into a story that is a pilgrim – a pilgrim story, as yet unread. As the story of a life, the *Autobiography* relativizes both the

Exercises and the *Constitutions*. It places both those works within the fragile context of human communication, as well as within the larger context of Ignatius's complete writings, from his 'notes' and *Diary* to his letters. Moreover, those writings are only part of his apostolate. But that whole apostolate stems from a personal and interpersonal spiritual life, which the *Autobiography* describes in the most continuous way.

There is something baroque about the bi-polarity of the two Prefaces, their two authors, and the two needs that they represent. They form an archway into the text of the *Autobiography* itself, into the heart of Ignatius, and into Jesus, whose life so attracted and animated and saved Ignatius's life. For Jesus was also a pilgrim, going to Jerusalem again and again for the feasts, until he finally broke through the cycle, was broken by it, and literally rose and ascended beyond it. Ignatius's discovery of a new way of entering into the life of Jesus is at the heart of his life, and of his story.

Together with Ignatius's story, the two Prefaces form a tri-polar field. As the *Autobiography* advances to its term, it focuses on two other works – the *Exercises* and the *Constitutions* – and this reveals a further writing: the *Diary*. There is here some kind of disciplined, yet rhythmic expansion, which nonetheless contracts when the time comes to put an end to the *Autobiography* and to the research into the 'notes' which are part of the method of composing the *Constitutions*. The two Prefaces, together with the *Autobiography*, form a whole, just as Nadal, Camara, and Ignatius form a body, in which we can see something, or someone, that is at their origin and at their end: someone who is holding them together. It is Jesus, present in their faith and working through them, as he accompanies them.

Again and again Ignatius experienced this presence of Jesus as he juggled the various facets and relationships which made up his daily life. Those who collaborated with him in writing his story were no less caught up in that experience of Jesus. His readers, even today, may come to feel that presence as they follow Ignatius's story. Indeed, they may find that this reading has helped them to move forward on their journeys with more joyful confidence in the shy pattern of their own lives.

AFTERWORD

Some endings write themselves. Like hanging a coat on a hook, or turning off a computer, some acts are ways of winding down.

Two final things need to be said: a NO to resignation, and a YES to acknowledgment.

As polar ice caps melt and our atmosphere warms, as drug abuse and crime rates rise, as national debts soar and multinationals increase their grips on world markets and production, as the weapons race continues, as satellite systems of communication and weapons' delivery are put in place, as the Internet globalizes us, as the unemployed awaken to their diminishing opportunities to work, as parliaments and legislatures tend to protect their powerful minorities, as so many children, if they are allowed to be born, barely learn to read or are led through the canal-like locks or shifting sands of educational systems, as we eat our chemically treated and genetically produced foodstuffs, as old diseases re-emerge and new diseases decimate populations, cattle, plant life, earth, air and water, as civilizations are said to decline and cultures are said to war with one another, as media barons reign, as religious figures pose and pontificate, as nuclear waste is hidden under the earth or in the sea, what can possibly be the value of a study of the autobiography of a sixteenth-century war casualty?

One might hope, very generally, that such a study of one man's sensitivity to the voice of the creator and redeemer would contribute in a small way to the raising of conscious concern about all the above problems, and to the finding of solutions. One might also despair of its having any such effects. One might oscillate between such a hope and such a despair. In fact, one might begin to wonder just who is this 'I' who oscillates, who desires to do something about it, who desires to live differently, and yet who despairs of the ability to achieve anything. It is this wonder, which can swing across a wide variety of human experiences until it reaches the pole of outrage, that animates this study. We would offer our readers this opportunity to get some 'fix' on their own lives, and on others' lives, so that we may find our way out and onward together. The heart of this study has been the affirmation of the truth that in our deepest relations we reach and are reached by something other than ourselves, something better than ourselves, that we desire with all our hearts. It is this experience which is our hope, if only we can be faithful to it, and forgiving of ourselves and of one another when we are faithless and despairing and hateful. It is this experience which underlies our options, and it is in saying NO to the temptation to opt out, if only partially, that one faces the option of saying YES to those who have been more than helpful on this road.

Thus I have the joy of acknowledging the help of my editor and friend, Paul Haddon, of Campion House, Osterley, and also of his friends, Fr Billy Hewett and Fr Michael Ivens, both Jesuits and of Jo Ashworth at Gracewing Publishing. Without their encouragement this study of the Pilgrim Story would have remained unpublished. A more secret and yet public joy is to recognize and acknowledge here that by their helping me and helping one another, the shy pattern is revealed once again, ever again, at work, at rest. Unknowingly, we have brought about a variation of the pattern once formed by Camara, Ignatius and Nadal. And the reader, too, may come to feel some affinity between his or her own story with its variety of patterns and the story of Ignatius the pilgrim and his companions. The shy pattern of the Pilgrim Story may continue to surprise its readers with the revelation of what lies at the very centre of our lives.[15]

NOTES

1. *The Story Man* (see p. 2). For an interesting treatment of this theme, see Tzetan Todorov, *The Poetics of Prose*, Cornell University Press 1977.

2. *The Baroque Knot* (see p. 16). Frequently in the course of this study we will use the word 'baroque' in referring to certain movements in the Pilgrim Story. By such a word, which is used and abused in the history of art, we mean a movement that can be as deep as it is broad, as interior and shadowed as Vermeer and Rembrandt, as exterior and luminous as Rubens and Hals. The baroque we refer to is the movement itself, capable of both great sweeping and surprising circulations, as well as of stunning pauses. Its inclusion of the viewer or listener or reader into the subject and its revelation of depths and horizons hitherto unreached are of the essence of the baroque, as is the very question whether all this movement is an illusion or a reality. We will expand on the importance of using this word for Ignatius in his sixteenth-century world when we reach the trial in Salamanca.

3. *Lasting and Remaining* (see p. 28). Sometime during the years of his association with Camille Pissarro in the early 1870s, the young Paul Cézanne learned from the older

painter to paint entirely in the open air and to remain on the 'motif', or subject, until the painting was finished. In other words, he was not to take the painting home after a day's work outside, and continue to work on it in the studio at night. He was to trust the night, the passage of time, nature: to rest from work, and to continue the painting, back in the open air, on the following day. There was in this advice a respect for a certain rhythm of creation like that found in the first chapter of Genesis. This may be why Cézanne was fond of calling the venerably white-bearded Pissarro, 'Dieu le Père'.

This lesson of learning to remain on the 'motif', or subject, was a lesson that the artist had to learn about himself, about his time. But there was another lesson he had to learn and which he is still teaching us; it is the lesson that the 'motif' itself teaches: the time inherent in the 'motif', in the subject of the painting itself. Two examples: Cézanne was not the only artist to paint a portrait of the art-dealer, Ambroise Vollard. Even after many hours of work at it, Cézanne was finally satisfied with his realization of only one part of the painting: the art-dealer's shirt-front! Many other artists had painted Mont Sainte-Victoire, but Cézanne kept coming back to paint it again and again and again. What was it about certain 'motifs' – as he called them – that held him spell-bound, and gave him no peace until he had found some new way of expressing them? When Cézanne spoke of his 'motifs', he sometimes brought his hands together so that the fingers would interlock. In that interlocking he saw some image of what he found in nature, and of what he sought to 'realize' – even if only in part – on his canvas. There was always something further in the 'motif' that remained to be 'realized'. Pissarro had taught Cézanne how to take his time; but some interlocking in nature itself kept teaching Cézanne how to take its time.

Similarly, this book is yet another portrait of Ignatius of Loyola. It is a portrait based on Ignatius's own self-portrait that he dictated to Camara. There can be as many retellings of Ignatius's story, as there can be various portraits of the same person, painted by various artists, or by the same artist over and over again, as long as the subject calls for further 'realization'. Our 'motif' is this shy pattern that moves through the autobiography. It is a structure that is only revealed in the movements of its variations. It remains despite all the movement, and yet is only revealed in the movement: a dynamic stasis. Ignatius himself was coming to discover it during his convalescence.

4. *Acceptance of Oneself* (see p. 30). There is a profound illustration of this in D. H. Lawrence's novel, *Sons and Lovers*, chapter XIII. But first let me clarify what I am talking about: it is the experience of a deepening acceptance of oneself and others, as well as the experience of a deepening ability to give oneself to others. In the novel this subject is raised by Clara, who is coming to the end of her affair with Paul, as she readies herself to return to her husband, Baxter.

As they walk along the road together, Clara criticizes Paul: she speaks of 'the cruelty of men in their brute force. They simply don't know that the woman exists.' When he protests that he knows she exists, she replies: 'About me you know nothing.' He feels naturally 'puzzled, and helpless and angry.' When he suggests that *she* knows *him*, the reply is equally hard: 'It's what men won't let you do. They won't let you get really near to them.'

As the conversation continues, Clara goes over their relationship: 'It has been fine .... But is it *me* you want, or is it *It*?' Paul feels guilty and wonders if he does leave Clara out of account, simply wanting a woman. Later, comparing Paul with Baxter, Clara conceeds: 'I don't say you haven't given me more than he ever gave me.' However, the final word seems to be said when she adds: 'But you've never given me yourself.'

This painful struggle to give oneself more completely to another and to accept another more completely is not only relevant to interpersonal relations, and to our relationship with God, but to our relationship with ourselves. Ignatius is caught up within these criss-crossed relationships, and he –

like Paul – is discerning his way through them, through his feelings, towards the light.

5. *Dialectic* (see p. 47). For a clear presentation of the movement from dialectic to conversion to foundations, see Bernard J. F. Lonergan, *Method in Theology*, Herder and Herder, New York, 1972, pp. 235–293. On the general and special categories of religious expression, see pp. 281–293. On the various types of conversion, see pp. 237–-244. As best I can see, Lonergan's sense of dialectic is not to be confused with Fessard's (see note 13), but it can be articulated with it. Lonergan's dialectic can be situated at various levels, be they intellectual, moral, or religious. Fessard's dialectic is not only intellectual, but more precisely and abstractly metaphysical. Both Fessard and Lonergan, however, respect and operate from their respect for Aquinas's distinction between essence and existence. Yet both leave much to be desired in reflection on the complexity and liberation of feelings, the unconscious, and the charismatic component of interpersonal relations.

6. *Complicity with One's Demons* (see p. 75). In his historical study of the case of the Ursuline community in Loudun and their supposed possession by devils in the 1630s, Fr Michel de Certeau notes that Fr Jean Joseph Surin, one of the Jesuit exorcists, explained to the Prioress, Soeur Jeanne des Anges, that she was an accomplice of the demons of which she claimed to be the victim. See Michel de Certeau, *La Possession de Loudun*, Paris 1990, Gallimard/Julliard, p. 47. Surin recognized this in the Prioress, as – like Ignatius – he had recognized it in himself. These recognitions depend upon the truth of one's relations with others, and upon the grace of God, but there is no substitute for one's own responsibility in wishing and working to awaken to the truth, and to where it leads: to a greater truth, especially when it reveals one's own complicity.

7. *Dante and the Long Way Round* (see p. 77). Ignatius's

first failure to stay in Jerusalem in 1522, and his second failure to return with his companions in 1538, and their determination to go to Rome, might be seen as a repetition of the efforts of Dante at the beginning of the *Inferno*, Canto I. There, lost in the dark wood of the middle of his life, he had sought to climb the Hill of Joy by a direct way, but he was turned back again and again, first by a leopard, then by a lion, finally by a wolf. Once again alone in the dark wood he chanced upon a guide who had been especially sent to him – Virgil, as it turned out. The only way up the Hill of Joy, he learned, was the long way round, first down through the terraces of Hell, then up the winding stairs of Purgatory, and finally up through the implicate orbits of Paradise. So the Companions of Jesus might still be considered, or might even consider themselves, on the long way round to Jerusalem, passing through Rome and through more than four hundred and fifty years of history. Is not, however, all humankind on that roundabout road? Or is the Book of Revelation mistaken?

8. *Laughter* (see p. 80). Ignatius of Loyola, *The Constitutions of the Society of Jesus*, trans. Geoge E. Ganss, St Louis, 1970, The Institute of Jesuit Sources, p. 27

9. *Leaving Things* (see p. 81). A story somewhat similar was told to me by an English friend. On a long train trip from the north of England to London, he happened upon a book left on the seat in his compartment. It was Thomas Pynchon's *The Crying of Lot 49*. Intrigued by the first paragraph, he avidly read the short book, increasingly captivated by the intense and chaotic adventures of Oedipa Maas, as she sought for the meaning of her inheritance, 'Lot 49'. As the threads of the story came together in the stunning ending, my friend was no less intrigued by how accidentally this book had come across his path. Definitely planning to keep the book, he began to leave the compartment when it came to him that there could be no finer tribute to what the book was all about than to leave it

where he had found it. Somewhere, perhaps, by however fine a thread of hope, that book may still be knocking about on some seat of a British train.

10. *Currents and Counter-currents* (see p. 82). Robert Bresson, the French film director, wrote:

> Proust says that Dostoievsky is original in composition above all. It is an extraordinarily complex and close-meshed whole, purely inward, with currents and counter-currents like those of the sea, a thing that is found also in Proust (in other ways so different) and whose equivalent would go well with a film. (See Robert Bresson, *Notes on Cinematography*, New York, Urizen Books, 1977, p. 63.)

Bresson himself had once conceived the idea of a film on Ignatius of Loyola, and Julian Green had begun to work on a script, but the plan came to nothing. Bresson went on to do *The Diary of a Country Priest*, *A Man Escaped*, *Pickpocket* (an adaptation of Dostoievsky's *Crime and Punishment*), and other adaptations of Bernanos, Dostoievsky, and Tolstoy, as well as *The Trial of Joan of Arc*, *Au hasard, Balthasar* (the life of a donkey, as it weaves in and out of a young girl's life), and *Lancelot*. One is tempted to find the film on Ignatius subtly informing the whole Bressonian work. Even more informing was another project he long nourished but never managed to undertake: his film of *The Book of Genesis*.

We find such a complex inner movement here in the sequence of events of Ignatius's story, as his resolution to trust totally in God brings him into conflict with different unforeseen difficulties: foreign languages, passage by ship, the requisite sea-biscuits, the scruples, the recourse to a confessor, the reticence in naming his destination as he begs for money to buy the biscuits, the ironic remark of the woman who learns that he is going to Rome, his laying aside of his extra money, his failure to find spiritual direction. There is a sweeping rhythm to these events, as Ignatius rebounds from the physical to the spiritual, from the desire for solitude to the desire for guidance, from the family and the career behind him to the Holy Cities ahead of him. There is a single movement that leads from his armed resistance and fall at Pamplona right down to the ship which now moves away from the shore of Catalonia on its way to Italy.

11. *Madness and Interrogation* (see p. 102). Two of the finest examples of such reversals are found in scenes involving Prince Myshkin in Dostoievsky's *The Idiot*, as well as in the scenes where Inspector Porfiry interrogates Rashkolnikov in *Crime and Punishment*. In another genre, Cervantes also uses Don Quixote's madness to reveal the even greater foolishness of the 'reasonable' people around him.

12. *Story and its Access to the Heart* (see p. 110). The reader is recommended to read Donald Nicholl, *The Beatitude of Truth*, London, Darton, Longman and Todd, 1997, 'Scientia Cordis' pp. 149–191.

13. *The Baroque Dialectic* (see p. 123) This episode in the Autobiography can be compared with the play of mirrors, canvasses, and spectators in Velasquez's painting, *Las Meninas*. Ignatius was doing something new in spirituality, something that Velasquez did in painting about one hundred years later, that Cervantes did in literature with *The Adventures of Don Quixote*, and that Bach did in *The Art of Fugue*. They put the spectator, the reader, the listener, the exercitant explicitly into their works in view of a conversion or transformation, an intensification and progression of life-giving. The spectator/reader/listener/exercitant in gazing, reading, listening, meditating on such works meets others, the Other, and him and herself in new and startling and empowering ways.

Gaston Fessard, the French Jesuit philosopher, maintained that Ignatius, Hegel, Marx, and Kierkegaard all discovered the same dialectic, but in their respective fields, and they expressed it in their different epistemologies. Hegel discovered it in the history of philosophy, but expressed it in his idealistic epistemology. Marx discovered it in political economy, and expressed it in his empiricist materialist epistemology. Kierkegaard discovered it in his philosophy of existential situations, and expressed it in an existential epistemology. Ignatius discovered it in spirituality, and expressed it in the realist epistemology he had learned in his courses of scholastic Thomism at the University of Paris. All of them affirmed that the multiple poles of the many and the one, the past and the future, affirmation and negation, could only be united dialectically. Such a dialectical unification made new demands on the subject and his or her social group, requiring nothing more than a conversion on one or another level of one's self, moving through a correct dialectical position to new foundations. This position can be found in the books referred to here, but especially in the pages indicated below in vol. III. See Gaston Fessard, *La Dialectique des Exercices de Saint Ignace de Loyola*, vol. I; *Liberté, Temps, Grace*, 1956, vol. II; *Fondement, Péché, Orthodoxie*, Paris, Aubier, 1966, vol. III; *Symbolisme et Historicité*, Paris, Editions Lethielleux, 1984, pp. 449–475.

Although, to my knowledge, Fessard does not link Ignatius's dialectic to the baroque movement, this hypothesis seems to arise most logically from the aspects of counterpoint and chiaroscuro that are present in baroque music and painting, and that delight us in Shakespeare and Cervantes, not to speak of Milton. Writings on the baroque movement that have helped me are the following:

– Germain Bazin, *The Baroque*: Principles, Styles, Themes, Modes, New York, W.W. Norton, 1968. Especially recommended for its rich and thoughtful illustrations, and for its sense of an 'interior baroque', as found in Vermeer. His juxtaposition of illustrations is particularly helpful, as when he juxtaposes Titian's *Presentation of Mary in the Temple* with the same subject as painted by Tintoretto. The classic

Titian paints Mary from the side, walking up the staircase from her parents to the High Priest, with pyramid-like stairs leading across the painting from left to right. The baroque Tintoretto pictures Mary walking up the winding staircase as it leads from the lower foreground high into the rear, where the High-priest awaits her.

– Victor Tapié, *Baroque et Classicisme*, Paris, Plon, 1957.

– Eugenio d'Ors, *Du Baroque*, Paris, Gallimard, 1935. A mere collection of articles and essays, but very suggestive of the metaphysical possibilities of the category of the baroque. More poetic than analytical, d'Ors sweeps from Dionysos and Pan to Ibn Tufail, the Jesuits, Defoe, Kipling and Gauguin. His opposition between the classic and the baroque, forms that are weighted down and forms that lift, is never pedantic. His sense of a baroque 'type' or 'eon' leads deeper than he ever really explores. D'Ors therefore might be considered more rococo than baroque, but he knows where he came from

– Heinrich Wölfflin, *Renaissance and Baroque*, London, Fontana, 1964.

– Gilles Deleuze, *The Fold: Leibnitz and the Baroque*, Minneapolis, University of Minnesota Press, 1992. Deleuze defines the basic trait of the baroque as a folding and unfolding that goes on infinitely. His book makes for breathtaking reading, as he concerns himself with the folds of the body and the soul, with the aspects of interiority and exteriority, ascent and descent, activity and passivity, attribution and predication, sufficient reason and freedom. He notes this development in painting, sculpture, architecture, literature, music and philosophy. His concern extends from Leibnitz's philosophical articulation of this new movement to contemporary neo-baroque movements in art, literature, and in his own philosophy. Unfortunately for us, he does not venture into the domain or wilderness of spirituality. Thus the worlds of Surin and Fenelon, Charles de Foucauld and Kiko Arguello remain to be explored, and they could all gain light from the passionate yet humble insights of Deleuze.

As for linking the baroque and modern periods, see Raymond Court, 'Baroque et Modernité' in *Etudes*, juillet–aout 1989 (371/1–2).

On the link between the baroque and the post-modern styles or periods, see David Harvey, *The Condition of Post-modernity*, Oxford: Blackwell, 1989, Ch. 15, 'The time and space of the Enlightenment project'.

On changing conceptions of the baroque, in the history of criticism, see the *Encyclopedia of World Art*, London. McGraw-Hill, 1959, vol. II, 'Baroque Art', pp. 257–263.

I would maintain that the dialectical discovery referred to above by Fessard was also made by Velasquez and Cervantes and to greater or lesser degrees by the whole baroque movement, which now comes down to include what some mean by post-modernity.

This is not the place to define the differences between idealism, materialism, existentialism, and realism; nor is it the time to define those moments when a medium of discursive or symbolic literary writing or painting takes a dialectical leap. But this interrogation in Salamanca is the place and time to note the historical horizons and contemporary relevance of these dialectical and yet progressive inclusions. They form patterns of repetition that guide toward centres revealed in decisive relationships. In a real sense, the interrogation or trial of Ignatius will go on as long as the trial of Jesus continues to raise the question: By what authority did he do what he did? Ignatius, like any one of us, can only answer from the authenticity that we have acquired in the best relationships with others that we have been able to find and maintain.

14. *All Face* (see p. 158). It also recalls an incident which Bresson quotes from the *Essays* of Montaigne. Bresson quotes it to illustrate what he means by wanting his 'models' (not 'actors') to be all face:

> A certain man demanded of one of our loitering rogues, who in the deep of frosty winter he saw wandering up and down

with nothing but his shirt about him, and yet as blithe and lusty as another who keeps himself muffled and wrapt in warm furs up to the ears, how he could have patience to go so ... 'And have not you, good Sir, (answered he), your face all bare? Imagine I am all face.' (See Bresson, *Notes on Cinematography* , p. 16).

15. *Sharing a Singularity* (see p. 191). In the 1930s an American novelist, William Faulkner, wrote a series of novels which changed the very level required of the reader. A literary critic and biographer, Frederick R. Karl, wrote the following paragraph in his book, *William Faulkner: American Writer*, (New York, Weidenfeld & Nicolson, 1989), p. 584:

> 'What the reviewers could not possibly understand was Faulkner had reached so deeply within himself for this novel [*Absalom, Absalom*] they had to accept it completely on his terms, or not at all. In his comments on Cezanne, Rainer Maria Rilke, the German poet, speaks of art resulting from the artist being in danger, "of having gone through an experience all the way to the end, where no one can go any further." The further in the artist goes, the more private and personal the experience, "... and the thing one is making is finally the necessary, irrepressible, and, as nearly as possible, definitive utterance of this singularity," which no one "would or even should understand, and which must enter into the work as such, as our personal madness, so to speak ... like an inborn drawing that is invisible until it emerges." Once the artist accomplishes this, there is no middle ground. To follow Faulkner into the work means picking up the thread which went into the making of the novel. The artistic process has so transformed the material that it cannot be "read" in the usual way; it needs, like all great art, a different set of faculties. It can be understood, but not summarized; it can be experienced, but not re-related. The reviewers, and even more serious readers were confronted by a phenomenon relatively new in American fiction; they failed to see it as such.'

It is this paragraph that I would carefully adapt to Ignatius of Loyola and his fellow Jesuits in the domain, or wilderness, of spirituality. To move carefully through the paraphrase I would say that Ignatius, as a man, was indeed in danger, for he had gone through an experience all the way to the end, where no one can go any further. The further he went in, the more private and personal the experience became, until the thing he made finally came free, irrepressible, a definitive utterance of his singularity, which no one else could or should understand, and which entered into the work as his form of personal madness or folly, like an inborn drawing ... This 'inborn drawing that is invisible until it emerges', that cannot be summarized or re-related, this phenomenon relatively new in spirituality, is the 'shy pattern'. It can only be reached when one has stripped down to an identity that is covered only by the identity of another that one loves more than oneself. The difference is implicit in Rilke's own description, only he did not take thematically, indirectly, the very step he was taking directly in his very utterance: It *can* be re-related to another, assuming that another is as sensitive, as intelligent, as poetic, as *faithful*, as oneself, and even more so (a come-down for the hypocritical relator).

To follow Ignatius into the work means picking up the thread which went into the making of his life and of his story of his life. Yes, it requires a different set of faculties; it requires the 'spirit', the 'heart', where body and soul unite. The further in one goes, the more private and personal it becomes; and yet, dialectically, dialogically, depending on whom one is in dialogue with, the private becomes public, the personal becomes communal, and the mutual recognition is one of fidelity, discretion, and care for others, whom the truth may heal or wound, depending on the love with which it is given, offered, and sacrificed. The domains of poetry and spirituality are close to one another but are not to be confused. What Faulkner presumably did, what Cezanne presumably did, is – we affirm – what Ignatius presumably did, because he believed that

Jesus actually did it. The works of Faulkner, Cezanne, and Rilke himself are of another order than what Ignatius was reaching for, what he was reached by, and what he believed Jesus actually did. For Jesus had his 'madness': he was madly in love with his Father and with all his Father's children. And anyone who gets closer to him, as did Paul of Tarsus, John the 'beloved disciple', and Peter at the lakeside (John 21), discovers this love, this holy and uncompromising compassion, at the heart of Jesus. It is this meeting with Jesus, this reciprocal presence and act of meeting, that the *Autobiography* hides and reveals for those who want to read it, from levels of themselves that are not always so challenged, so touched.

We are invited to strip off the level of ourselves as reviewers, so that we can see, and assume the level of viewers or of actors who will lay down the book, hear the evening news, notice the noise in the streets, feel the blood in our veins, the stirrings in our heart, and ask ourselves: What have I done, what am I doing, what shall I do?

When such questions are asked, (and we can trust that they will be asked until the last man and woman close their eyes on our planet), there is every hope that the subject of this book, and its readers, may still have a considerable impact on the century opening so violently, so simplistically, so cunningly before us.

INDEX OF NAMES

The names cited below are those found outside the text of the Prefaces, Autobiography, and Epilogue. They refer to artists, dramatists, musicians, novelists, poets, theologians, philosophers, explorers, whose works and paths cross our reading of the Pilgrim Story. I have a friend who always looks through the Name Index before reading a book, probably to see how many of her friends are already at that party. Only after she is assured that she will find good company there does she enter the book by the front door: the Contents, Introduction, that first telling paragraph. This brief Index of Names might assure such readers of the company they will find at this party.